T0259663

Pro CDI 2 in Java EE 8

An In-Depth Guide to Context and Dependency Injection

Jan Beernink
Arjan Tijms

Apress®

Pro CDI 2 in Java EE 8: An In-Depth Guide to Context and Dependency Injection

Jan Beernink
Dublin, Ireland

Arjan Tijms
Amsterdam, Noord-Holland,
The Netherlands

ISBN-13 (pbk): 978-1-4842-4362-6
ISBN-13 (electronic): 978-1-4842-4363-3
https://doi.org/10.1007/978-1-4842-4363-3

Managing Director, Apress Media LLC: Welmoed Spahr
Acquisitions Editor: Steve Anglin
Development Editor: Matthew Moodie
Coordinating Editor: Mark Powers

Cover designed by eStudioCalamar

Distributed to the book trade worldwide by Springer Science+Business Media New York, 233 Spring Street, 6th Floor, New York, NY 10013. Phone 1-800-SPRINGER, fax (201) 348-4505, e-mail orders-ny@springer-sbm.com, or visit www.springeronline.com. Apress Media, LLC is a California LLC and the sole member (owner) is Springer Science + Business Media Finance Inc (SSBM Finance Inc). SSBM Finance Inc is a **Delaware** corporation.

For information on translations, please e-mail editorial@apress.com; for reprint, paperback, or audio rights, please email bookpermissions@springernature.com.

Apress titles may be purchased in bulk for academic, corporate, or promotional use. eBook versions and licenses are also available for most titles. For more information, reference our Print and eBook Bulk Sales web page at www.apress.com/bulk-sales.

Any source code or other supplementary material referenced by the author in this book is available to readers on GitHub via the book's product page, located at www.apress.com/978-1-4842-4362-6. For more detailed information, please visit www.apress.com/source-code.

Printed on acid-free paper

For Dominika, who encouraged me to write this book, and for my mum, dad and sister who supported me throughout.

—Jan Beernink

To my mother

—Arjan Tijms

Table of Contents

About the Authors

Jan Beernink works for Google and is a contributor to several projects related to OmniFaces. Jan holds an MSc degree in computer science from the Vrije Universiteit of Amsterdam, the Netherlands.

Arjan Tijms works for Payara Services Ltd. and is a JSF (JSR 372) and Security API (JSR 375) EG member. He is the co-creator of the popular OmniFaces library for JSF that was a 2015 Duke's Choice Award winner and is the main creator of a set of tests for the Java EE authentication SPI (JASPIC) that has been used by various Java EE vendors. Arjan holds an MSc degree in computer science from the University of Leiden, the Netherlands.

About the Technical Reviewer

Chád ("Shod") Darby is an author, instructor, and speaker in the Java development world. As a recognized authority on Java applications and architectures, he has presented technical sessions at software development conferences worldwide. In his 15 years as a professional software architect, he's had the opportunity to work for Blue Cross/Blue Shield, Merck, Boeing, Red Hat, and a handful of startup companies.

Chád is a contributing author to several Java books, including *Professional Java E-Commerce* (Wrox Press), *Beginning Java Networking* (Wrox Press), and *XML and Web Services Unleashed* (Sams Publishing). Chád has Java certifications from Sun Microsystems and IBM. He holds a BS in computer science from Carnegie Mellon University. You can visit Chád's blog at `www.luv2code.com` to view his free video tutorials on Java. You can also follow him on Twitter (`@darbyluvs2code`).

CHAPTER 1

History of CDI

This chapter describes the history of contexts and dependency injection (hereafter referred to by its acronym CDI), starting with precursor technologies to which it's undeniable related and ending with the current state of affairs. We'll cover technologies such as JSF and EJB and key people such as Gavin King. We'll also cover some of the most defining moments in the history of CDI, and you'll learn how something like CDI evolved from a variety of ideas that may seem to be very different on the surface.

You should take note that such a long and complex evolution is hard to describe in full detail, and even if possible, such a full description would take an entire book. This chapter therefore is not a complete history of CDI but merely discusses the most important events.

A Time of Legends

Every journey has a first step, and CDI's long journey is certainly no exception. For the purpose of our book, that first step starts with EJB 1.0. Of course, EJB itself has an origin story, involving persistence technologies such as TopLink, Microsoft's ODBC, and before that X/Open SQL CLI, as well as the origin story of the object broker CORBA and the history of transaction servers such as the early AT&T Tuxedo, which itself was one of the inspirations for the X/OPEN XA standard. Those stories, however, are outside the scope of this book.

EJB 1.0 started as a cooperation between mainly Sun, Oracle, and IBM in late 1997, not long after Java 1.1 was released in the beginning of that same year. Java 1.1 had introduced a number of fundamental technologies that would set the stage for EJB, specifically, JavaBeans, JDBC, RMI, and to a lesser degree at the time reflection (although reflection would later become arguably the most fundamental technology of all "managed bean" models). Not only were these technologies fundamental in a technical sense, they also changed the mind-set of where Java could be used. Java 1.0

J. Beernink and A. Tijms, *Pro CDI 2 in Java EE 8*, https://doi.org/10.1007/978-1-4842-4363-3_1

was strongly focused on applets, *small* applications that executed within their own little box inside a web browser. With the previously mentioned new technologies in Java 1.1 and specifically with EJB 1.0 on the horizon, the idea of using Java for server-side and business computing started to take root.

The promises for EJB were big. Specifically relevant for its place in CDI's history was the promise of a *(portable) component model* and with that a marketplace where developers would be able to buy individual components that could be plugged into any EJB container.

Not entirely unlike the microservices hype of 2017 and 2018, in 1997 and 1998 *distributed objects* were all the rage. It's no surprise then that in EJB 1.0 the components (called EJBs) were designed to be remote only. In a way, you could think of them as a kind of servlet for the IIOP and RMI protocols. A stateful variant theoretically corresponded to a servlet using an HTTP session, and a stateless variant theoretically corresponded to a servlet not using an HTTP session.

On March 24, 1998, during JavaOne of that year, Sun released the initial 1.0 version of EJB. Market reception was initially quite enthusiastic, and EJB was called a "new and promising technology." Despite all the promises, the implementation of the EJB 1.0 specification left a lot to be desired. Specifically troublesome were the many moving parts for what should be relatively simple things and the high cognitive load this put on developers. Simply said, the specification required developers to carry a lot of tasks that the container/runtime should have been able to do automatically. Of course, we have to take the zeitgeist and the state of technology into account. Java, for instance, didn't have a JIT yet, XML 1.0 had just been released a month ago, and the time the EJB 1.0 spec had been in development wasn't that long (late 1997 to early 1998).

The moving parts mentioned consisted of the actual bean, followed by a "remote interface" containing the bean's business methods and a method to remove that specific bean, a "home interface" via which clients could look up and remove beans of various types, a deployment descriptor for each bean being a serialized instance (!) of `javax.ejb.deployment.SessionDescriptor` and `javax.ejb.deployment.DeploymentDescriptor` and various related classes of those, a manifest file, and as the final insult potentially vendor-specific configuration files. On top of that, often vendor-specific tooling had to be used to generate configuration files and/or to compile the files listed. As part of that process, some additional files would be created, such as so-called skeletons and stubs that were needed for the remote communication. Doing all of this for an entire application was already troublesome, but doing this for each and every bean was, well, not so nice to put it gently.

The following shows an example of what such an early EJB looked like:

```
public class MyServiceBean implements SessionBean {

     SessionContext sessionContext;

    public void setSessionContext(SessionContext sc) throws EJBException,
    RemoteException {
        sessionContext = sc;
    }
    public void ejbCreate() throws EJBException, RemoteException {
    }
    void ejbActivate() throws EJBException, RemoteException {
    }
    void ejbPassivate() throws EJBException, RemoteException {
    }
    void ejbRemove() throws EJBException, RemoteException {
    }

     // Business method
    public String sayHello(String name) {
        return "Hello, " + name;
    }
}
```

The `setSessionContext` context method essentially functioned as a primitive dependency injection mechanism (though you wouldn't really call it that), with the `activate/passivate/remove` methods being the lifecycle methods.

The next part to be implemented was the remote interface.

```
public interface MyServiceRemote extends EJBObject {
   String sayHello(String name) throws RemoteException;
}
```

The remote interface was essentially the proxy via which you communicated with the real bean and was what allowed the EJB runtime to add its magic.

You also needed to add a method in the home interface (which could contain methods for other beans as well).

```
public interface MyServiceHome extends EJBHome {
    MyServiceRemote create() throws CreateException, RemoteException;
}
```

The home interface was basically a primitive version of a "bean manager" as used by various later technologies.

The next thing was to add an entry in the manifest file to mark the bean as an EJB.

```
Name: test/MyServiceBean.ser Enterprise-Bean: True
```

Subsequently, a deployment descriptor had to be provided representing the following partially defined classes (shown are only the SessionDescriptor and its superclass and the AccessControlEntry, which takes care of security). These classes would typically not be implemented directly but generated by tools.

```
public class DeploymentDescriptor  implements Serializable {
    protected int versionNumber;
    public DeploymentDescriptor();
    public AccessControlEntry[] getAccessControlEntries();
    public AccessControlEntry getAccessControlEntries(int index);
    public Name getBeanHomeName();
    public ControlDescriptor[] getControlDescriptors();
    public ControlDescriptor getControlDescriptors(int index);
    public String getEnterpriseBeanClassName();
    public Properties getEnvironmentProperties();
    public String getHomeInterfaceClassName();
    public boolean getReentrant();
    public String getRemoteInterfaceClassName();
    public boolean isReentrant();
    public void setAccessControlEntries(AccessControlEntry values[]);
    public void setAccessControlEntries(int i, AccessControlEntry v);
    public void setBeanHomeName(Name value);
    public void setControlDescriptors(ControlDescriptor value[]);
    public void setControlDescriptors(int index, ControlDescriptor value);
```

```
    public void setEnterpriseBeanClassName(String value);
    public void setEnvironmentProperties(Properties value);
    public void setHomeInterfaceClassName(String value);
    public void setReentrant(boolean value);
    public void setRemoteInterfaceClassName(String value);
}

public class SessionDescriptor extends DeploymentDescriptor {
    public final static int STATEFUL_SESSION;
    public final static int STATELESS_SESSION;

    public SessionDescriptor();
    public int getSessionTimeout();
    public int getStateManagementType();
    public void setSessionTimeout(int value);
    public void setStateManagementType(int value);
}

public class AccessControlEntry  implements Serializable {
    public AccessControlEntry();
    public AccessControlEntry(Method method);
    public AccessControlEntry(Method method, Identity identities[]);
    public Identity[] getAllowedIdentities();
    public Identity getAllowedIdentities(int index);
    public Method getMethod();
    public void setAllowedIdentities(Identity values[]);
    public void setAllowedIdentities(int index, Identity value);
    public void setMethod(Method value);
}
```

Note that EJB 1.0 also included a controversial concept called the Entity Bean. Within Sun this concept was already controversial, with some people internally putting up heavy resistance against the idea, but outside Sun it was even more controversial. Even Oracle, which hadn't acquired Sun at that point and was a separate company then, plainly refused to implement it. Entity Beans were massively over-engineered while at the same time missing the most basic features. For that reason, Entity Beans were optional in EJB 1.0.

Despite some of the unacceptable burdens that the EJB session beans put on the developer, at their core they contained the very ideas that we still value and use today: declarative-based services. In the early EJB 1.0 days, these consisted of fixed services for transaction demarcation and security. For instance, using `AccessControlEntry` shown earlier you could declare that the `String sayHello(String name)` method of a bean was accessible only to an `Identity` (which was a precursor type of `Principal`) with, say, the name `foo`.

On December 17, 1999, mere days before the turn of the millennium, Sun introduced the EJB 1.1 specification. The most important difference was that the Java-based deployment descriptors had been replaced by newfangled XML-based ones, and to the detriment of developers everywhere, the deeply flawed Entity Beans were now made a mandatory part of the EJB spec.

On June 7, 2001, during the JavaOne conference of that year, Sun senior engineers and architects Linda DeMichiel and Ümit Yaçinalp presented the draft for EJB 2. Included was a new SQL-based query language (EJB QL) created by Yaçinalp, two new concepts for the security system called *unchecked* and *uncallable* (later called *excluded*) methods, and, most importantly for CDI's history, the concept of a *local* interface as opposed to the existing *remote* interface. The local interface was seemingly a simple concept but at the time represented a major shift in thinking. It moved away from the thinking of an EJB bean being something like a servlet or web service and instead allowed EJB beans to be used locally (within a single JVM), without the overhead of serializing methods parameters and method return values and without the overhead of going through a networking stack. With local interfaces, EJB beans could, more or less, be used as regular classes but still with all the declarative services that EJB beans supported.

On August 22, 2001, Sun officially released the EJB 2.0 specification, a mere five days after another specification that plays an important role in CDI's history had practically started: JSF.

JSF is a component-based UI/Web MVC framework. Initially it may seem strange that JSF would play an important role in a contextual dependency injection framework, but in December 2001, the JSF team led by Sun engineer Amy Fowler started looking at its very own managed bean model (aka component model). The managed bean (originally called Object Manager) that the JSF team was working on was intended to be used for the so-called backing bean. Backing beans are small Java classes that sit between the view and the model. They should not be mistaken with *UIComponents*, which are a different type of class altogether and are used by JSF for the visual components (aka widgets).

The managed bean work that started in 2001 extended into 2002, and concepts such as scopes, names, and dependency injection were added. Specifically, scopes were a rather novel feature of the JSF managed bean system and made these beans contextual. *Contextual* here means that a "session-scoped" bean of class Foo resulted in all clients that found themselves to be within the same HTTP session (but possibly in different requests) getting access to the same bean instance. Clients that were in another session got a different bean instance of Foo. Likewise, a request scope bean Bar resulted in all clients within the same request getting the same instance of Bar, but clients in other requests (even if, say, within the same session) getting a different instance.

The JSF team approached their component model from almost the complete opposite direction as the EJB team did. JSF managed beans were Plain Old Java Objects (POJOs), meaning there was no required interface that the bean had to implement and no base class to extend from. There were also no separate interfaces to generate proxies from, and hence there was no proxy being used whatsoever. JSF managed beans did have to conform to the JavaBeans conventions, and like basically every other managed bean system out there, they did have be bootstrapped by the runtime (i.e., you didn't create them via the new() operator but requested or got them from JSF).

Here's an example. First you create the bean class.

```
public class MyServiceBean {
    public String sayHello(String name) {
        return "Hello, " + name;
    }
}
```

Second, you make it a managed bean by declaring it into the faces-config.xml deployment descriptor.

```
<!DOCTYPE faces-config PUBLIC "-//Sun Microsystems, Inc.//DTD JavaServer
Faces Config 1.0//EN"
"http://java.sun.com/dtd/web-facesconfig_1_0.dtd">
<faces-config>
  <managed-bean>
      <managed-bean-name>myServiceBean</managed-bean-name>
      <managed-bean-scope>session</managed-bean-scope>
      <managed-bean-class>test.MyServiceBean</managed-bean-class>
  </managed-bean>
</faces-config>
```

The previous code fully defines a managed bean in JSF 1.0. Dependency injection is also supported via another technology in JSF: expression language. (The concept of expression language originated from an Apache tag library, which became JSTL in JSP and then was further enhanced by JSF.) In JSF, dependency injection primarily happened via this expression language. The managed-bean-name shown in the previous code example defines the root name that can be used in (sub)expressions.

Here is another example of injecting the previous bean into another bean. First you define the bean that gets injected.

```
public class MyBackingBean {

  MyServiceBean myServiceBean;

  // ... other properties and logic here

  public void setService(MyServiceBean myServiceBean) {
     this.myServiceBean = myServiceBean;
  }
}
```

Then you declare the actual injection to be done.

```
<managed-bean>
   <managed-bean-name>myServiceBean</managed-bean-name>
   <managed-bean-scope>request</managed-bean-scope>
   <managed-bean-class>test.MyBackingBean</managed-bean-class>
   <managed-property>
      <property-name>service</property-name>
      <value>#{myServiceBean}</value>
   </managed-property>
</managed-bean>
```

One thing to note is that the JSF managed bean system supported only method injection. Field injection was never supported.

Enter Gavin King

In 2001 one of the many developers getting frustrated by the aforementioned flawed Entity Beans in EJB was a developer working for an Australian company called Cirrus Technologies. This developer, Gavin King, quickly realized his lack of productivity when working with EJB Entity Beans and his inability to use common object-oriented patterns. Unlike most other developers, though, King decided to confront the problem head-on by creating his own persistence framework. The interesting bit here is that Gavin at the time wasn't even close to being a persistence or SQL expert.

Enter Rod Johnson

Also in 2001, on April 13, 2001, to be precise, a lone developer sitting in his study in London wrote the following lines of code:

```
package org.springframework.beans.factory;
/**
*
* @author Rod Johnson
* @author Juergen Hoeller
* @since 13 April 2001
*/
public interface BeanFactory {
```

The name of this developer is Rod Johnson. Unbeknownst to him at the time, he had just written what would eventually be the start of a revolution unlike one the Java community had ever seen before.

On July 6, 2002, King announced the release of Hibernate 1.0 as an "open source (LGPL) object/relational persistence and query service" and stressed that "Hibernate rejects the use of code generation or bytecode processing. Instead runtime reflection is used." Hibernate would grow to be one of the most popular Java frameworks ever.

On October 23, 2002, a year and a half after he wrote the quintessential lines of code for the BeanFactory, Johnson published what may arguably be the most influential book in the history of Java EE: *Expert One-on-One J2EE Design and Development*. In his book Johnson explains with crystal-clear clarity what had been brewing in the community for more than a year: the deeply flawed nature of the Entity Bean concept.

The conclusion basically boils down to the advice of not using Entity Beans, ever. Johnson did acknowledge the power of the declarative transactions and declarative services offered by EJB session beans. In an interview with TheServerSide in early 2003, Johnson compared these services with a limited form of AOP but suggested these should actually be composable interceptors (à la carte) instead of the EJB approach, which was a "degustation menu where you get everything the chef prepared whether you want it or not." Like King, Johnson argued the case against code generation and favored dynamic proxies and (fast) reflection but acknowledged these things weren't available when EJB was initially designed. Johnson also made a strong case for using unchecked exceptions in most cases and resorting to checked only when absolutely needed. King would later admit to Johnson that using checked exceptions everywhere in Hibernate was a mistake and that he would change it if he could.

On May 27, 2003, the work for EJB 3.0 started. The spec leads were Linda Demichiel and Mike Keith. The goal of this new body of work was to radically simplify EJB by "reducing its complexity from the EJB developer's point of view." The plan was to use the recently introduced annotations in Java SE 5 to make the overly verbose deployment descriptors fully optional and to strongly embrace the "configuration-by-exception" approach. Session beans became POJOs (like in JSF and Spring), without interface requirements and, unlike JSF and Spring, with only an annotation to mark them as a session bean. Entity Beans, on the other hand, were found to be so deeply flawed at such a fundamental level that there was no point in trying to improve them. Instead, a new type of bean was introduced based on the simple model objects used by Hibernate and TopLink. Spec co-lead Keith would later mention the great irony of this in his book *Pro JPA 2*: "...one of the first implementations of entity beans was actually demonstrated by adding an additional entity bean layer over TopLink mapped objects."

AOP, as explained by Johnson, is perhaps the strongest aspect (no pun) of EJB. The quintessential implementation of AOP at that time had always been AspectJ (and at the time of writing still is). AspectJ, introduced in 2001, is a programming extension for Java developed by the legendary Xerox PARC, which introduced the term *aspect-oriented programming* (AOP). While arguably the most pure and powerful AOP framework out there, AspectJ is its own language, and the very nature of it has always had a certain academic and research feel to it. This means a level of complexity is involved with it that makes it less suitable for enterprise developers who often don't need the more powerful features. Like the old EJB2, AspectJ at the time required a separate compilation step and special IDE support.

It's thus no surprise that around 2002/2003 several frameworks were being developed that tried to simplify the experience at the expense of losing some power.

At JBoss engineer Bill Burke was busy working on an AOP framework called JBoss AOP. JBoss AOP was a continuation of JBoss allowing custom interceptors for EJB in its earlier JBoss 3 server. JBoss AOP, like AspectJ, used bytecode manipulation (weaving) albeit done at runtime. JBoss AOP's early contribution to the field, though, was the concept of having the delivery of enterprise services, such as the transactional and security services in EJB, as its main goal. AspectJ and other frameworks were more (academically) focused on AOP itself.

Johnson (and others) were busy in 2003 as well, building the Spring framework that grew out of the lessons and code examples used in *J2EE Design and Development*. In the early milestones of this new framework, AOP already played an important role. Spring didn't use bytecode manipulation but instead used dynamic proxies. These were dynamically generated classes that were of the same type of the class they proxied and allowed the framework to run its AOP logic before the actual class was called. The actual class remained a plain, unmodified Java class. The advantage here was that this method was less invasive and didn't need access to the class loader, although the disadvantage was being less powerful (couldn't intercept fields or private methods), and the programmer sometimes had to be aware of the difference between calling a method via the proxy and calling a method without that proxy (for instance if inside the actual class a method calling another method of that same class).

Enter Bob Lee

A technical architect working at AT&T at the time, Bob Lee (aka "Crazy Bob" as he calls himself and who previously contributed to the *Bitter EJB* book from June 15, 2003), also wasn't happy with the existing or in-development AOP frameworks. He therefore started his own framework: dynaop. An important goal of dynaop was to have an elegant design. It used proxies, just like Spring, but instead of dynamic proxies (which require an interface), it used class proxies (which don't require an interface). Dynaop also introduced a then-revolutionary idea of not intercepting all instances of a given type but allowing to intercept only certain specific instances, e.g., those returned from a specific business method. The initial beta version of dynaop was released on February 11, 2004. Lee would soon after start experimenting with DI/IoC as well, combining yet another

DI engine from that era called *picocontainer* with the still-in-development dynaop. Lee used dynaop primarily himself within his AT&T project (a Struts-based web application).

JSF 1.0, with its included lightweight managed bean facility, was eventually released on March 11, 2004. By chance this happened only two weeks before the final release of Spring 1.0. With both frameworks featuring a somewhat similar POJO-based lightweight "bean container," there was one major difference between the two: Spring's core bean container was a separate container that could be used everywhere, including by parts of Spring itself. The JSF core bean container, however, was embedded within JSF and not shipped separately. It was also targeted exclusively at JSF application developers. Neither JSF, other specs in Java EE, nor application developers primarily using those other specs made use of it. There were plans, though, to separate this core bean container from JSF, but those plans never materialized.

On June 30, 2004, the first draft spec for EJB 3.0 was released. It was immediately clear that this was not a simple evolution of EJB 2.1 but essentially a completely new spec.

The EJB 2 example that we showed earlier is in the EJB 3.0 draft nothing more than this:

```
@Stateless
public class MyServiceBean {
    public String sayHello(String name) {
        return "Hello, " + name;
    }
}
```

Annotations can be used to request in a declarative way the services that the container offers. For example, a method is secured via the `@RolesAllowed` annotation like so:

```
@Stateless
public class MyServiceBean {
@RolesAllowd("foo")
    public String sayHello(String name) {
        return "Hello, " + name;
    }
}
```

Transactional services, however, are applied by default (with the so-called REQUIRES semantics). They can, however, be switched off if not needed.

Interestingly, injection in the early draft was proposed to be done via an annotation called @Inject.

```
@Stateless
public class MyServiceBean {
    @Inject
    EntityManager entityManager;
    public String sayHello(String name) {
        return "Hello, " + name;
    }
}
```

Furthermore, the EJB specification indeed offered an AOP-lite solution called *interceptors*. However, EJB does not eat its own dogfood here. The existing AOP services, specifically the security and transactional ones, were not specified to be based on these new interceptors.

The other major standout feature in EJB 3.0 was a completely new type of persistence, based on Hibernate and TopLink. This new persistence approach was specified in a new subspec of EJB: JPA. Gavin King was a major contributor to this subspec, and Hibernate would become one of the main implementations of JPA. With JPA, King was also finally able to correct his earlier mistake of using checked exceptions in Hibernate. The JPA API heavily emphasized unchecked exceptions.

JSF developer Jacob Hookom, after seeing Bob Lee's dynaop on September 20, 2004, wondered if AOP would not be really useful for JSF, where it could easily validate input before invoking an action method. Many, many years later, this was indeed what CDI and the Bean Validation spec would allow JSF to do. In that same month, James Holmes, a committer on the Struts web framework, also took notice of dynaop and wrote about it in an article for Oracle Magazine.

Around October 15, 2004, Bob Lee accepted a job offer from Google and left AT&T. Despite Lee mentioning this move wouldn't affect the work on dynaop, in the following month commits to the dynaop project dropped dramatically. The last commit was done on April 15, 2005.

On September 19, 2005, Gavin King, now at JBoss, announced working on a new project called Seam. Seam is "an application framework for Java EE 5" which at its heart had a new component model. This component model was inspired by the JSF managed bean model (using stateful components and scopes) but was going to be annotation based, just like EJB 3. A core aspect of Seam was the fact that beans could be injected via a proxy (like EJB) that resolves a call to the bean at invocation time. This allowed a smaller scope (like request) to be injected into a larger scope (like application), something that JSF didn't allow. Seam also emphasized bijection (in- and outjection), which allowed beans to replace objects in their scope, without knowing what that scope actually was (this is somewhat similar to call-by-reference semantics, where the code being called can assign a new instance to a variable).

```
@Stateful
@Scope(APPLICATION)
public class MyServiceBean {

    @In
    EntityManager entityManager;

    @In @Out
    PriceList priceList;

    public void updatePrices() {
        priceList = entityManager.merge(priceList);
    }
}
```

In the previous code, `priceList` can be request scoped, session scoped, or anything else. The code assigns it a new value, which will replace it in its scope (Seam talks about "context"). The next bean invoking a method on its injected `PriceList` proxy will see that call going to the new instance. Next to the request/session/application scopes from JSF, Seam had several additional scopes/contexts among which the so-called conversation context.

Bob Lee published on January 29, 2006, a critical article about Spring titled "I Don't Get Spring." In it Lee criticized the Spring culture of "snubbing their noses at J2EE" and having a large API surface. Lee argued that J2EE's surface was not as large, since in J2EE the API and implementation are strictly separated. Lee also made a point about the Spring practice of externalizing large amounts of "configuration" into XML files. According to Lee, that "configuration" is actually "code," just code written as XML, and therefore the selling point of Spring not touching any code is not quite the case. Lee furthermore criticized the usage of string-based IDs to identify (managed) beans and the need to keep those in sync between code and XML. Lee wondered why just (Java) types weren't enough. Finally, Lee wondered why Spring hadn't adopted generics by now (Java SE 5, which introduced generics, was released on September 30, 2004). Just as with Johnson's book from late 2002, the observations in Lee's article would prove to have a profound impact on the Java enterprise scene.

On May 11, 2006, the EJB 3.0 specification was released. Unfortunately, one of the former tendencies of the EJB team had sneaked back into the spec: the reliance on tools. The no-interface requirement for session beans had been removed again, delegated to "tools can be used for this." Of course, nobody ever really used such tools. Additionally, the `@Inject` annotation had been removed and in its place had come, among others, `@EJB` to inject other EJB beans and `@PersistenceContext` to inject the entity manager.

Despite the setback of having to use (application-defined) interfaces, EJB 3.0 was one of the first, if not the first, component framework to fully embrace annotations at a time where for JSF (which had arrived at version 1.2 by 2006) annotations were curiously nowhere in sight yet.

The Conception of CDI

Even before Seam 1.0 went final, on May 17, 2006, Gavin King announced the JBoss-initiated Web Beans JSR (JSR 299), which took some of the ideas from both Seam and Guice and standardized them. The Web Beans spec was supported by Sun, Oracle, Borland, and others and specifically targeted the unification of the JSF and EJB component models. The idea was that EJB3 session beans could act like a JSF managed bean (by being named and scoped). Web Beans were intended to be used stand-alone as well but would not duplicate the features that EJB provided (specifically the declarative transactions and security).

On June 13, 2006, a month after EJB 3.0 was released, Seam 1.0 was released. Seam's adoption started slowly, but in its second year it did surpasses the number of downloads and users that Hibernate had in its second year.

Just less than eight months after his article where Bob Lee criticizes Spring, Lee did the initial commit of a new DI framework called Guice on August 25, 2006. This commit was done on `google-guice.googlecode.com` and consisted of 26 Java files (excluding tests) in the `com.google.inject` package, which among others contained the very first version of the now famous and very well-known `@Inject` annotation.

```
/**
* <p>Annotates members and parameters which should have their value[s]
* injected.
*
* @author crazybob@google.com (Bob Lee)
*/
@Target({METHOD, CONSTRUCTOR, FIELD, PARAMETER})
@Retention(RUNTIME)
public @interface Inject {

  /**
   * Dependency name. Defaults to {@link Container#DEFAULT_NAME}.
   */
  String value() default DEFAULT_NAME;

 /**
  * Whether or not injection is required. Applicable only to methods and
  * fields (not constructors or parameters).
  */
  boolean required() default true;
}
```

The package documentation describes this very early, not yet public, version of Guice as follows:

```
/**
* <i>Guice</i> (pronounced "juice"). A lightweight dependency injection
* container. Features include:
*
* <ul>
*   <li>constructor, method, and field injection</li>
*   <li>static method and field injection</li>
*   <li>circular reference support (including constructors if you depend upon
*     interfaces)</li>
*   <li>high performance</li>
*   <li>externalize what needs to be and no more</li>
* </ul>
*/
```

Despite Guice not being public yet, a tech lead at Atlassian, Don Brown, added on November 13, 2006, an early version of the Guice DI container to the XWork project, rebasing the classes to now live in the `com.opensymphony.xwork2.inject` package. The stated reason was "to wire together key pieces and constants." XWork itself was a "generic command framework" that became somewhat known for using interceptors, IoC, and the command pattern. It was split off from WebWork, which was an early "pull hierarchical MVC framework" (started on November 18, 2000). WebWork (and thus XWork) at that point was about to merge into Struts.

With all the activity around DI frameworks in full swing, Sun Microsystems, the intellectual owner of Java EE, was not sitting still. On March 2, 2007, a new project was created on Java.net, with the first project setup commit saying, "A module system kernel in 100K." Almost two months later, on April 23, 2007, 84 files were committed by the already legendary Sun developer Kohsuke Kawaguchi (who started the Hudson project, which was later forked off into the now widely known Jenkins project) with the following comment:

> *"brought over the workspace from `https://www.dev.java.net/svn/modsys/tags/move-to-hk2` revision 168".*

The files were copyrighted 2006, so likely Kawaguchi and another Sun developer called Jerome Dochez had been working on it for some time. The `org.jvnet.hk2.annotations` package contained, among others, an `@Inject` annotation again.

```
/**
* Annotation to define a required resource for a componnent.
* Runtime will inject all instance variable annotated with
* @Requires as well as setter methods.
*
* @author Jerome Dochez
*/
@Retention(RUNTIME)
@Target({METHOD,FIELD})
public @interface Inject {
  /**
   * Returns name of the required resource
   * @return name of the required resource
   */
  public String name() default "";
```

```
    /**
     * Indicates that it's not an error even if a component
     * to be injected doesn't exist.
     */
    public boolean optional() default false;
}
```

The initial code commit interestingly enough also contained the interfaces PostConstruct and PreDestroy, which would later become key annotations for CDI beans (though CDI itself would not define them).

```
/**
* Classes implementing this interface register an interest in
* being notified when the instance has been created and the
* component is about to be place into commission.
*
* @author Jerome Dochez
*/
public interface PostConstruct {
    /**
     * The component has been injected with any dependency and
     * will be placed into commission by the subsystem.
     *
     */
    public void postConstruct();
}
```

The initial commit furthermore contains an @Contract/@Service pair of annotations for declaring and respectively implementing a component and also a number of classes related to OSGi-like "modules." While several aspects of HK2 bore a resemblance to Guice, Kawaguchi and Dochez developed HK2 primarily to power the internals of an application server called GlassFish, whereas Guice targeted application developers.

Back in the Seam camp, senior Java engineer and OSS advocate Dan Allen, working at CodeRyte, published on April 12, 2007, the influential series of articles "Seamless JSF" on IBM's DeveloperWorks. This article series presented a clear explanation of what Seam was and how it helped in building more elegant JSF (Java EE) applications. While the Seam-derived Web Beans was still in development, Seam itself slowly started to become more and more popular.

With Seam and Web Beans both in various stages of their development, Bob Lee was not sitting still either. His dependency injection framework Guice 1.0 was officially released and made public on March 8, 2007. At that point, Google had been running it in production for many months, meaning the technical (internal) release would have been somewhere late 2006, possibly around November 13, when XWork/WebWork/Struts incorporated Guice.

During the JSR review ballot for Java EE 6, IBM remarked on July 16, 2007, that it was concerned about Web Beans introducing a new component model.

> *"We are becoming concerned with the direction that JSR-299 seems likely to take in going beyond its stated charter of integrating JSF and EJB components and believe that continued efforts in this direction could warrant its removal from Java EE 6. We do not believe that our customers would find it easy to adopt a Java EE 6 platform that adds yet another component model definition."*

On September 22, 2007, Gavin King presented an initial sneak-peak into Web Beans. A common theme when creating new Java EE specs is that someone proposes that the spec should not be just for Java EE. JSR 299 was no exception. Specifically, Lee argued that JSR 299 should be usable outside Java EE. However, King as the spec lead set the target for JSR 299 clearly at Java EE but did keep the door open for support outside Java EE to be added in a future revision.

The initial sneak-peak used syntax such as shown here:

```
@Component
@ApplicationScoped
public class MyServiceBean {

    @In @UserDatabase
    EntityManager entityManager;

    @In @Available
    PriceList priceList;

    PriceList lastSaved;
```

```
    public void savePrices() {
        entityManager.persist(priceList);
        lastUpdated = lastSaved;
    }

    @Resolves @LastSaved
    PriceList getLastSavedPriceList() {
        return lastSaved;
    }

}
```

In this example, the influence of Seam with the `@In` annotation is clearly visible. Where Seam, however, wanted to distinguish itself from JSF using another annotation to indicate the scope, Web Beans went back to the JSF original using `@ApplicationScoped` (but in a different package). The annotations after `@In` were called *binding types/binding annotations* and were used to indicate a specific kind of type. For example, the previous code distinguishes between the available price list and the price list that was last saved. Both have the same Java type but different binding types.

Finally, the sneak-peak talked about component types. The default one was `@Component` as shown earlier, but additional ones could be created (e.g., `@MockComponent`). Component types had a precedence, and these component types could be globally enabled/disabled. Web Beans would only scan classes that had this component type annotation.

Later drafts would remove the `@In` annotation and would require only a binding annotation, using `@Current` as the default. This would effectively make `@Current` *the* injection annotation, assuming most beans would not need a binding type. Component types would be renamed to deployment types, which when omitted defaulted to `@Production`. `@Resolves` would be renamed to `@Produces`, etc.

Meanwhile, in California, someone was following these drafts quite closely. Scott Ferguson, cofounder of a company called Caucho, had created the Resin server. Resin started as a servlet container (like Tomcat) and was later incorporated into several other Java EE technologies. Ferguson did an initial commit for an independent implementation of Web Beans on November 5, 2007, in the `com.caucho.webbeans` package for Resin 3.1. The implementation was unnamed at that moment. Ferguson would track the Web Beans drafts while they were being developed and update the Web Beans implementation in Resin accordingly.

When Resin 3.1.5 was eventually released on February 27, 2008, its Web Beans implementation had fully implemented the then-current Web Beans draft.

Ferguson, however, was not the only one working on his own independent JSR 299 implementation. The developer Gurkan Erdogdu had been doing the same for some time on SourceForge, and on October 3, 2008, he proposed the OpenWebBeans project as an incubator to the Apache organization.

Later that month, on October 30, 2008, Johson joined the JCP as an exec member, foreshadowing some kind of impactful event.

Though Erdogdu had blogged about starting the OpenWebBeans project, people in the Web Beans community didn't really learned about the existence of this project until a month later when the public review draft was discussed at TheServerSide.

Erdogdu immediately recognized the potential of Web Beans and said that "Web Beans defines the 'Component Model' of the future Java EE," but at the time Java EE advocate Reza Rahman saw this as a problem as it undermined the work being done by the EJB EG to make EJB something people enjoy working with. Rahman argued to put more work in making Web Beans a complementary technology, not a replacement of EJB. Gavin King then mentioned that Web Beans was now mostly a set of services, not primarily a component model. It provided services for scoping/contexts that could be applied to a stateful session bean, and it provided injection services to session beans that go beyond the simple *@EJB* injection annotation, and furthermore there were services to throw and observe events, which again could be used by session beans. These services were basically universal and could be used à la carte by all other component types.

Specifically interesting is that the new REST spec (called JAX-RS) that was in development for Java EE 6 had been developing its own component model and dependency injection system, but at the end of 2008 the belief was it would soon use the Web Beans–provided services for injection.

While during 2008 and early 2009 the EJB EG put up a lot of resistance against even the faintest of hints of potentially being replaced by Web Beans, now or in the future, the JSF EG was far less worried about this idea. In fact, Pete Muir, the JBoss representative in the JSF 2 EG, who formerly contributed to Seam before working for JBoss at a UK-based company called Splendid.co.uk, announced in that time frame that JSF managed beans were to be deprecated in favor of Web Beans.

In the first month of 2009 (January 26, 2009), the name of JSR 299 changed from Web Beans to "Contexts and Dependency Injection for Java," or CDI for short. This name change had been hanging in the air for quite some time, as multiple people and parties had indicated not being happy with the Web Beans name, specifically since it didn't fully cover the problem space (anymore). It would take a little bit of time for the name CDI to catch on, and especially in the early months, people would often refer to it as JCDI instead of CDI.

Meanwhile, the EJB EG remained skeptical about the spec that would ultimately be destined to replace it. Specifically, IBM came to the defense of EJB and, on February 9, 2009, reiterated the concern it raised one and a half years ago by leaving the following comment at the Public Review Ballot for JSR 299:

> *"IBM has serious reservations about introducing another competing component model into the EE platform when this JSR was supposed to be focused on integrating technologies into the platform. Aside from the duplication and confusion caused by this, the specification has expanded to cover a large spectrum of technology that is somewhat ambitious to fully define within a single specification. However, we acknowledge that the spec lead has made substantial progress in addressing feedback and therefore, we are willing to vote yes to allow the specification to move forward on the assumption that the spec lead will continue to address feedback and concerns."*

But IBM and the EJB EG weren't the only ones pushing back at Web Beans. On May 26, 2009, Bob Lee, who previously contributed to Web Beans/JSR 299, and Rod Johnson suddenly started their own competing JSR 330, officially called "Dependency Injection for Java." Unsurprisingly, this caused quite a bit of controversy, but the JSR was accepted nevertheless. The potential for conflict was immediately recognized, though, and Sun commented the following:

> *"We are glad to see the Spring and Guice communities get together to standardize dependency injection for the Java platform, and we are supportive of this effort.*
>
> *Dependency injection is unusual in having a pervasive nature and entailing some powerful network effects that, in the absence of a comprehensive standard, naturally lead to harmful fragmentation.*
>
> *In this respect, we request that this JSR and JSR-299 coordinate their efforts so that they can jointly deliver a single, consistent and comprehensive dependency injection standard for the SE and EE platforms. Such coordination must take place before the Public Review of this JSR."*

Red Hat, leading JSR 299 via Gavin King, was more concerned and commented with the following:

> *"Red Hat is deeply skeptical of the value of this JSR, since it envisages the existence of a separate container that is not part of the SE or EE platforms, and whose semantics and programming model are sufficiently ill-defined that portability of applications between different containers would be impossible for all but the most trivial of applications. This is a break from the Java tradition of "write once, run anywhere".*
>
> *However, we recognize that there is some community support for this proposal, and we,re therefore holding back on forming a final opinion until the Expert Group produces a public draft. If some level of alignment could be reached between this JSR and JSR-299, which does define a truly portable model for dependency injection, we would be more likely to vote to approve the JSR. Red Hat hereby commit to doing our part to help achieve this outcome."*

Gavin King mentioned that a second set of annotations that would do essentially the same thing as those offered by JSR 299 would be a huge mistake. On his blog, Gavin drew the following comparison:

- `@Qualifier` is equivalent to `@BindingType`.
- `@Scope` is equivalent to `@ScopeType`.
- `@Singleton` is equivalent to `@ApplicationScoped`.
- `@Named` is just a built-in binding type.
- The `Provider<X>` interface is equivalent to `Instance<X>`.

Bob Lee defended the new JSR and accused King that for the Java EE 6 targeted Web Beans he only thought about Java EE. Lee specifically mentioned that with Web Beans people would be forced to use EJB Lite, implying that this is a very bad thing to depend on. At this point, Web Beans thus found itself in the middle: IBM said Web Beans didn't depend enough on EJB, while for Lee a potential EJB dependency was seemingly a deal-breaker.

After much debate, the conflict was eventually resolved, and on August 5, 2009, it was announced that CDI would use the annotations and terms defined by JSR 330. The most central annotation of JSR 330 was `@Inject`, from which JSR 330 lent its nickname `AtInject`. Ironically, `@Inject`, was also the very annotation that EJB 3 early drafts were originally using.

At this point, Lee had already greatly reduced his commits to the Guice project, which was largely being evolved by other people now. Lee did his second-to-last commit to Guice on September 30, 2009. The commit was about JSR 330 compatibility. Lee would do one more one-off final commit more than a year later on December 15, 2010, before leaving the Guice scene for good.

On October 14, 2009, the final version of JSR 330 was released. From creation to release the JSR took only five months, which is an absolute record. The JSR remained somewhat controversial, though, and was accused of rubber-stamping what Lee and Johnson had already agreed on and of having too little substance to be of any practical use. The latter meant that while all of CDI, Guice, Spring, and the latter HK2 (Jersey) used the `@Inject` annotation, the code was absolutely not portable between those and the only practical result was clashes between different pieces of code that both use `@Inject` but were intended to be handled by different injection providers.

Only days after this final release of JSR 330, on October 18, 2009, Gurkan Erdogdu managed after some struggle with "weird errors" to pass the JSR 330 TCK with his OpenWebBeans project.

Meanwhile, Scott Ferguson and Reza Rahman, who was now working for Ferguson at Caucho, published on November 3, 2009, the first part of another of those highly influential series of articles, "Dependency Injection in Java EE 6." In it Ferguson and Rahman not only explain CDI in much detail but also introduce the world to the CanDI implementation and how it forms the core of the Resin server. Ferguson and Rahman also mentioned thinking about introducing an `@Transactional` annotation based on CDI.

On November 30, 2009, IBM not entirely unsurprisingly voted against CDI in the final approval ballot, citing the following reason:

> *"The current lack of portability between JSR 330 and JSR 299 applications will create significant difficulties for the community. Application developers who use patterns based on JSR 330 injection annotations and proprietary injection mechanisms will experience integration issues when taking advantage of JSR 299 contexts associated with JSF. Insufficient attention has been paid to these details in the development of these specifications and this will reflect poorly on the Java EE platform as a whole. Although IBM previously voted in support of both JSR 299 and 330 with the clear expectation that the "SE/EE injection programming model must be aligned into a single extensible programming model that defines a core set of functionality for SE and extends that with EE functionality", this has not yet been achieved. IBM will continue to support both expert groups in the development of a single integrated and extensible injection programming model."*

Luckily, though, IBM was the only EC member voting against CDI, so less than two weeks later on December 10, 2009, the final version of CDI 1.0 was released, together with the final release of the full Java EE 6 platform.

Java EE 6 was overall very well received. As the second version of Java EE that focused on developer friendliness, it was clear that Sun was able to maintain this course, and with the introduction of JAX-RS, CDI, Bean Validation, JASPIC, and the `@DataSourceDefinition` annotation big steps for the platform were taken.

Unfortunately, not all was well. Perhaps because of CDI 1.0 going final so late, no other specs had really taken advantage of it.

The JSF 2.0 EG, which seemed to be in favor of deprecating its own managed bean system, has only added a notice that CDI may replace it in the future, not a formal deprecation. Worse yet, JSF 2.0 has introduced annotations like `@ManagedBean` giving it the appearance of having updated its old managed bean system quite a lot (in reality those new annotations are only a thin layer over the existing XML). Nevertheless, the simultaneous introduction of CDI beans and the `@ManagedBean` annotation was seen as one of the absolute low points in the otherwise very well received JSF 2.0.

Likewise, the JAX-RS EG did even worse and (in hindsight) quite needlessly introduced its very own DI (using `@Context`) and bean model. Because JAX-RS 1.0 went final very early, there was enough time for a maintenance release that said the so-called JAX-RS resources could be "CDI-style managed beans" as well, but at that point the cat was largely out of the bag already.

So, while Java EE 6 had as a goal to unite the various bean models and DI systems with CDI, it ended up with a bunch of extra ones instead. Perhaps unsurprisingly, this would cause quite a bit of confusion later with developers, but for some reason this wasn't seen as a very big issue at the time.

Having founded both the Hibernate and Seam projects, which both strongly influenced the Java EE specs JPA and CDI, Gavin King apparently saw his work in Java (EE) completed, and a mere two months later effectively left the Java scene and started working on his own programming language called Ceylon (`https://ceylon-lang.org`). (At the moment of writing, and Gavin is still working on this after nine years, although he started dabbling somewhat in JPA again.) Perhaps thinking the same thing as King, Bob Lee left Google at the same time and moved to Square in January 2010, largely leaving the (open source) Java scene as well. And as if there had been some secret agreement between them, our third DI pioneer, Rod Johnson, had for a time walked away from the community and the business as well after having sold his SpringSource company in August 2009 to VMware (Johnson would eventually leave VMware in 2012). The DI exodus wouldn't be complete with Kohsuke Kawaguchi leaving as well, and lo and behold he indeed did. On April 5, 2010, Kawaguchi announced it was his last day at Sun/Oracle. He moved on to start his own company supporting Hudson (later Jenkins).

The Next Generation

In the third installment of *Dependency Injection in Java EE 6*, published on March 8, 2010, Scott Ferguson and Reza Rahman explained their vision of EJB being redefined as [CDI] managed beans with additional services. The EJB 3.1 Lite container, on which mainly Rahman was working as the lead, would be used as an initial implementation of that idea.

With CDI 1.0 just out of the door, Ferguson's hands were clearly itching to introduce new innovations on top of this, and on March 10, 2010, he indeed introduced the earlier mentioned `@TransactionScoped` scope/context in CanDI. This was a scope based on the current (JTA/XA) transaction. Ferguson didn't stop there, and on May 29, 2010, he also introduced an `@ThreadScoped` scope/context.

Pete Muir announced on December 14, 2010, that Red Hat would soon propose CDI 1.1 with Muir taking over the spec lead role from Gavin King. It was felt that CDI was basically complete, and so CDI 1.1 would only be a small release.

On March 1, 2011, the review ballot for Java EE 7 started. The plan was to update Lee's AtInject spec to 1.1 with an API to configure an injector. But with Lee having left the scene, this never stood a real chance, and so indeed this didn't happen.

For this release, the various EE APIs had their first chance to be based on CDI or build new functionality on top of it. This is expressed in the Java EE 7 JSR:

> *"We also expect the managed bean model to be further refined and expanded so as to remove as many inconsistencies as possible across Managed Beans, EJB, Servlets, JSF, CDI and JAX-RS."*

Richard (aka Rick) Hightower, a developer working at Mammatus who had previously worked on the JCache JSR and had co-authored a book about Caucho's Resin, saw a lot of potential in CDI. However, the early examples weren't quite to his liking, so on March 7, 2011, he founded the CDI Advocate initiative, followed later that month (on March 28) by an announcement of the CDI Source organization (the new name of CDI Advocate). The goal of this organization was an attempt to fill gaps in CDI by providing tutorials and a supporting open source project, for which commits had started earlier that month on March 19 and had seen a high level of activity up till the day of the announcement. Two days later, Hightower announced that his project was getting support from Caucho, meaning covering hosting costs and providing some engineering resources. The next month, Hightower published a popular two-part CDI tutorial on DZone.

At the end of that month, on April 30, 2011, Hightower created an issue on the official CDI tracker for a transactional scope, inspired by Ferguson's scope from the previous year. A few months earlier, on January 10, 2011, Pete Muir created a somewhat similar issue on that CDI tracker to support an annotation to make methods or beans transactional.

This was potentially worrying, though, since it represented a split in thinking about what CDI should be: a facade for most other technologies in Java EE (like EJB was once planned to be) or a core technology on which other specs should be based. Having an `@Transactional` in CDI would mean CDI would be a facade for JTA and would be well on its way to become the next EJB.

Apache's Mark Struberg was quick to respond to this and suggested in the issue that CDI should focus only on the basics and therefore should not include things that could also be done in portable extensions (possibly by other specs).

There was a related discussion among the CDI 1.1 EG members, particularly Adam Bien and Mark Struberg, about reusing existing annotations for existing functionality re-implemented for CDI versus introducing new annotations. Adam Bien argued for reusing the existing annotations, but Struberg disagreed.

On June 17, 2011, Reza Rahman created a number of issues on the new official EJB tracker regarding the decoupling of services from the EJB component model, which represented Rahman's vision as outlined in his earlier articles. In his words:

> *"[...] decoupling EJB services such as @schedule from the [EJB] component model moves towards removing one-off component models in Java EE in favor of unifying around managed beans/CDI"*

Without much fanfare, Rahman left Caucho in August 2011. With him the vision for CanDI seemed to leave as well, as it got eerily silent for CanDI after that. In fact, no new announcements for Caucho's own CDI implementation would be made afterward, and CanDI would not implement CDI 1.1 and later, although occasionally some bugs in the 1.0 implementation would be fixed (such as a bug with generic producer methods, as reported by the authors of this book in September 2013). By then the much-talked-about, Caucho-supported, CDI Source project had stopped as well. In fact, no commits had been done to the CDI Source project after the official announcements in March.

At around the same time, the Seam developers met at a JBoss meeting in Toronto, Canada, to discuss the future of Seam. A problem had arisen, and that was that nobody really knew what Seam was about anymore. Seam 3 was already quite different from

Seam 1 and 2; instead of a fully integrated framework stack, it had been refactored into a set of mainly CDI extensions of varying quality. At the Toronto meeting, it was decided to further unravel Seam by not only having it refactored into those CDI extensions but also scattering those CDI extensions out into the world (away from the Seam project and into other projects).

On September 27, 2011, Red Hat developer and Seam project lead Shane Bryzak announced this decision to the world in an article named "So what's happening with Seam?" with a follow-up on September 30 named "Seam.Next Update." Another Red Hat and Seam developer, Lincoln Baxter III, was quick to mention that "Seam is not going away."

Naturally the community was not happy with this. Among those was Antoine Sabot-Durand, a French developer, who was the lead of the Seam social module. On September 30, 2011, he wrote an open letter to Red Hat, urging them not to let CDI become a "Betamax" by destroying Seam 3.

On October 4, 2011, Pete Muir presented several planned items for CDI 1.1. Among those plans is a general concept of a "ServiceHandler," which would allow one to express something like the following, where the actual definition of the service would come from a rather abstract and general handler class:

```
@QueryService
interface Users {
  @Query("select u from User u")
  public List<User> getAllUsers();
}
```

With CDI 1.1 marching steadily ahead, Shane Bryzak announced on November 30, 2011, that Seam 3 would be effectively disbanded, and the Seam team would together with the Apache CODI team and Rick Hightower's short-lived CDI Source create a new project at Apache called DeltaSpike. Mark Struberg was a big supporter of this new project and heralded it as being a much more open project as compared to Seam, which always had the JBoss ties.

Both Pete Muir and Lincoln Baxter III mentioned that the true Seam.next (an integrated end-to-end full stack framework) would be announced soon. This announcement, however, never came, and in March 2013 the Seam main website was updated with the text "Active development of Seam 3 has been halted by Red Hat."

The development of DeltaSpike would start soon after Bryzak's announcement, and on December 22, 2011, Apache's Gerhard Petracek did the initial commit, followed by Mark Struberg.

A few days later, on December 28, 2011, Petracek added the `org.apache.deltaspike.core.api.config` package with a single marker interface. Later that day Struberg added the `ConfigSource` interface and implementation logic with the following comments:

> *"This new logic will allow a pluggable, ordinal sorted implementation of configurable values."*

Over the next year, however, a pattern emerged. The bulk of the commits to DeltaSpike were being done by either Struberg or Petracek. Former Seam lead Bryzak only did the occasional commit, and from Red Hat only Jason Porter (of Seam Catch) did any significant number of commits, although still far fewer than either Struberg or Petracek. The significance of this is that while DeltaSpike was announced as a multivendor project representing the merging of Seam, CODI, and CDI Source, and specifically as the continuation of Seam (in an InfoQ interview about DeltaSpike with Pete Muir the term "Seam 4" was even used), in practice it was mostly being worked on by the existing Apache (CODI) members and to a far lesser extend by Red Hat people.

In May 2013, Antoine Sabot-Durand, who had been part of the DeltaSpike project since its inception, joined Red Hat, therefore giving Red Hat even more opportunity to contribute to DeltaSpike. Eventually, though, Sabot-Durand would do only a single small code commit to DeltaSpike.

Back in the Java EE camp, people had not been sitting still, and despite some issues regarding ill-thought-out "cloud support," Java EE 7, which included CDI 1.1, was eventually released on May 28, 2013.

The EJB EG, which previously had been so resistant to the idea of being replaced by CDI, took the plunge and together with the JTA EG produced a CDI/interceptor version of EJB's crown jewels: the declarative transaction services. Instead of being a default aspect of EJB beans, these services could now be applied à la carte to CDI beans using the `@Transactional` annotation and went even beyond that by introducing the transactional scope `@TransactionScoped` as proposed by Richard Hightower before. The earlier conflict has been resolved by stating that other specs should build on CDI (instead of CDI including everything) and that existing annotations should not be reused (instead, new ones should be introduced).

Bean Validation 1.1 was also quick to embrace CDI. Its signature new feature, method validation, was based on interceptors, and in Java EE these interceptors were automatically applied to CDI beans. (Method validation is the validation of input parameters and return values of a method using annotations.) Furthermore, artifacts like constraint validators were now injectable by CDI.

JSF 2.2 took steps to embrace CDI as well. One of the main features in JSF 2.0 was the so-called view scope. This scope made lots of JSF tasks much easier, but it had one huge problem; it worked only for the old native managed beans. This defect was somewhat solved by various utility libraries such as CODI and OmniFaces, but JSF 2.2 fixed this officially by introducing a CDI-compatible view scope itself. JSF furthermore embraced CDI by building its new Flows feature fully on CDI and making lots of its artifacts injectable by CDI.

On January 14, 2014, a tiny revision to the CDI 1.1 spec was started (a maintenance revision, aka MR) resulting in CDI 1.2. The change concerned resolving wording regarding how the cid parameter for the conversation scope was read. Antoine Sabot-Durand and not Pete Muir was the maintenance lead of this tiny revision.

And it wouldn't end at just being maintenance lead, as on March 15, 2014, Sabot-Durand announced he was going to be leading the CDI 2.0 specification together with Pete Muir. In an article called "Forward CDI 2.0," Sabot-Durand presented a wish list for 2.0. In this very long and detailed wish list were DeltaSpike-inspired features like "Java SE Bootstrapping" and the "BeanBuilder," for easily building Bean<T> instances in CDI extensions, but also modularization of the CDI architecture and the ability to programmatically apply interceptors and decorators to Bean<T> instances and beans returned from producer methods (which was a large gap in the existing CDI 1.1 SPI).

Almost exactly a year after Java EE 7 came out, on June 14, 2014, DeltaSpike 1.0 was released. Its signature features were @Transactional and @TransactionScoped annotations (which were already in Java EE 7), adding CDI support to Bean Validation (also in Java EE 7 already), a container controller to use CDI in Java SE, and various modules such as a security module, a JSF module (with things such as the ViewScope and WindowScope already in Java EE 7), a Data module (declarative queries on top of JPA), and a Servlet module (with things such as injecting a ServletRequest already in Java EE 7).

While DeltaSpike won the Duke's Choice Award later that year, the overall reception was not in line with the expectations of Seam 4. The main problem was perhaps that some of the functionality was already in Java EE 7, which had been out for a full year, and the time between the demise of Seam and the first release of DeltaSpike had been quite long. Additionally, its JSF module now faced (no pun) in a way competition from the OmniFaces project, for which the 1.0 version was released 2 years earlier on June 1, 2012, by JSF legend Bauke Scholtz (aka BalusC) and the very authors of this book (although practically they don't compete, as the feature set is quite different).

Another problem may be that the DeltaSpike security module did not natively support the existing security system of Java EE. For a framework that was supposed to be building on top of Java EE, it curiously ignored the EE SPIs for authentication (JASPIC) and authorization (JACC).

The DeltaSpike core module, however, did get a lot of praise and contained several gems such as its configuration feature and utilities for easily building beans (an area where the native CDI 1.1 SPI was seriously lacking and which Sabot-Durand had targeted for CDI 2.0), a mechanism for handling exceptions (`@ExceptionHandler`, based on Seam Catch), and much more. Worth mentioning is that the service handler proposal, which didn't make it into CDI itself, found its way into DeltaSpike as the `Partial-Bean` module.

Shortly after, on July 28, 2014, review for the new CDI 2.0 JSR started. The focus was on Java SE support and modularization of CDI, among which a minimal container that effectively just implements JSR 330. The Java EE 8 JSR review started about a month later, on August 26, 2014, and among others had an increased alignment with CDI as focus. JSF 2.3 started at the same day, with among others one of the authors of this book in its expert group. From the outset, the main spec lead, Ed Burns, made it clear that Oracle had very few resources available, and thus the JSF JSR was mostly up to the community to complete.

Also, starting that day was the somewhat controversial MVC spec. This spec was controversial since on the one hand it directly competed with JSF, which was also an MVC framework and already in Java EE, and on the other hand it was believed that client-side frameworks like Angular were the future, so a new, second MVC framework was really not needed. The MVC spec introduced controllers, which are essentially JAX-RS resources, but with an important difference; they *must* be CDI beans. Essentially this was the first step of correcting the (in hindsight) mistake of not using CDI for JAX-RS right away.

Shortly after, on October 13, 2014, JSF co-spec lead Manfred Riem did the first commit for JSF 2.3 where the so-called implicit objects were now being resolved by CDI and thus were also injectable by CDI. This marked the first step of JSF fully re-aligning on CDI.

On November 25, 2014, the review for a new Java EE 8 spec started: Java EE Security. One of the authors of this book, Arjan Tijms, was part of the EG and would eventually largely drive it. Tijms pushed dearly on for the EE Security artifacts to be CDI beans exclusively. Initially there was some resistance against that idea, and spec lead Alex Kosowski countered that not everything had to be CDI and proposed to use JNDI and `@Resource` instead. The matter was later resolved in the EG, and CDI was chosen as the preferred base.

When 2015 rolled around, the CDI EG was hard at work producing early drafts of the new CDI spec and discussing how best to implement the various feature requests. Even the partial beans from DeltaSpike were discussed again. One person was, however, curiously absent in most of this work and discussions, and that was the main spec lead Pete Muir.

It was therefore not a surprise that on July 30, 2015, Antoine Sabot-Durand announced on the CDI mailing list that Muir was stepping down as CDI spec lead and would take on new responsibilities within Red Hat. From then on, Sabot-Durand took over as the main spec lead. The EG reacted overwhelmingly positively to this news, and Muir made one last appearance where he said it's for the best that CDI was left in the capable hands of Sabot-Durand. After that, Muir would become a manager for the JBoss Developer Studio team and as such would largely (but not entirely) disappear from the public eye.

Trouble in Paradise

On September 30, 2015, InfoWorld published an article called "Insider: Oracle has lost interest in Java," in which it stated Oracle was winding down its efforts in Java and Java EE. Though Oracle didn't respond to it, in the months after it indeed became clear that Oracle had silently started to walk away from Java EE, and most specs that were tied to the Oracle spec leads being present started to wither.

In the year since Java EE 8 started, the JMS expert group had been working tirelessly to support CDI as a first-class citizen in JMS by crafting the API and spec to make CDI beans eligible to function as JMS listeners. However, on December 9, 2015, spec lead Nigel Deakin posted a worrying message in response to a casual question about the regular meetings being hosted:

> *"Unfortunately I can't host the next several JMS 2.1 meetings due to pressure of other work. I'll let everyone know when the situation changes."*

(The situation would, however, never change, and JMS 2.1 ended effectively right there and then.)

On April 29, 2016, independent JSF EG member Josh Juneau published the article "Java EE 8, What is the Current Status: Case Study for Completed Work Since Late 2015," which made it abundantly clear using various statistics that Oracle had quietly stopped working on most of the EE specs, something that the larger community still wasn't really aware of.

On May 25, 2016, Arjan Tijms deprecated all the native managed beans annotations for JSF 2.3, pointing them to their CDI equivalents. Though this didn't yet actually remove them, it was seen as a very important step toward that goal.

With all the uncertainty brought by Oracle silently walking away from its work on Java EE, the other EE vendors did not sit idle waiting for Oracle. Instead, a new initiative was started, and on June 27, 2016, at the DevNation conference in San Francisco, representatives from Payara, Red Hat, IBM, Tomitribe, and the London JUG announced a new collaboration called MicroProfile. MicroProfile builds on top of Java EE but creates new specifications and APIs, with the vendors creating their own implementations of those. As such, the process is Java EE like, except that it doesn't use the JCP process and is a lighter "code first" approach. This means there is a spec document, but the code (APIs and early implementations) take precedence. An important aspect of MicroProfile is that all the specs it produces should be CDI first.

During the keynote of the JavaOne conference in September 2016, Oracle announced it was going to finalize Java EE 8 but cancel JMS, MVC, and a lesser known spec called Management 2.0. Although the spec leads or other Oracle members had not done any work at all for JSF and Java EE Security during the last year, the fact that these two specs were largely community driven and not dependent on Oracle had kept them afloat, and luckily they weren't cancelled. CDI 2.0, not being an Oracle spec, was also not affected by the Oracle hiatus.

On October 26, 2016, CDI EG member and IBM Liberty architect Emily Jiang did the initial commit for the first spec that MicroProfile was going to deliver, MicroProfile Config. For the coming months, Jiang would be the main committer on this project. She was joined by Mark Struberg on January 18, 2017. Together they committed the bulk of the work, occasionally helped by various other committers.

Toward the end of 2016, several Oracle spec leads briefly returned to the JSF and EE Security specs, although not to do much or any new work but to make sure that the current snapshots of the specs were prepared for release.

On May 15, 2017, Antoine Sabot-Durand announced that CDI 2.0 had been released. The major new feature was, as planned, Java SE support, and the spec itself was more modular, split up into three parts (core, SE, and EE). The DeltaSpike inspired BeanBuilder API had indeed been included (now called Configurators), and a part of Sabot-Durand's original wish has been included as well; interceptors could now be (programmatically) applied to beans returned from producers. The ability for a `Bean<T>` implementation to find and apply its own decorators had, however, not made it into the 2.0 spec.

DeltaSpike did not only inspire CDI 2.0 but inspired MicroProfile as well. On July 25, 2017, Ondro Mihályi, an engineer working at Payara, released MicroProfile Config 1.0. MicroProfile Config was clearly based on DeltaSpike config and even used some of the same terms such as ConfigSource, which Struberg used all the way back in that December 2011 commit when DeltaSpike just started.

On August 17, 2017, David Delabassee, a software evangelist at Oracle, announced that Oracle wanted to move Java EE to an open source organization. A month later, on September 12, 2017, it was announced that this organization would be Eclipse, and shortly after that the project name was announced to be EE4J.

Java EE 8 was eventually released on September 18, 2017. It included among other things JSF 2.3 and EE Security 1.0. EE Security was fully built on CDI (and at a lower level JASPIC). Almost eight years after CDI 1.0 was released, there was now finally a spec that had been designed from the ground up with CDI in mind. Unfortunately, because of the hiatus, none of the further decoupling of services from EJB and moving those to CDI-based artifacts had been done.

On February 26, the official new name of the Java EE specification was chosen via community input to be Jakarta EE. A little later a logo was chosen, and step-by-step the source code was transferred from the Oracle owned "java-ee" organization on GitHub to the Eclipse owned "eclipse-ee4j."

A Brave New World

On March 26, 2018, Tijms contacted Lee to ask him about transferring JSR 330, which has been stagnant for close to a decade to Jakarta or merging it with CDI. Lee responded to definitely not wanting to merge it with CDI, but ignored the question about transferring it over to Jakarta.

On June 22, 2018, Stuart Douglas did the first commit for a new Red Hat project called Shamrock and Protean. The plan for this was to become a single one project framework (like Seam once was) that largely gives up on reflection and goes back to the code generation approach with which EJB once started, albeit in a much more automated way this time. This initial code commit contains a org.jboss.shamrock.codegen package with a BytecodeRecorder class, using JBoss ClassWriter, making it fairly obvious the core principal of this new framework was about code generation. On early description of Shamrock is:

"Shamrock is framework that allows you process Java EE and Microprofile metadata at build time, and use it to create low overhead jar files, as well as native images using Graal."

Red Hat is no stranger to this approach, as its CDI implementation Weld optionally makes use of Jandex, which can scan for annotations during build-time and store these in an index that Weld can consult at runtime.

While the Java EE transfer was still in progress and negotiations between Oracle and Eclipse were ongoing, Tijms kicked off the JSF 3.0 work on July 16, 2018. Among the plans was to fully remove the native managed bean system from JSF, including the ancient XML variant, and fully depend on CDI going forward. Around that same time, Tijms pitched the idea to Steve Millidge (Payara director) to turn HK2 into a full CDI compatible implementation. This idea was well received, as it would solve the problem of the Payara server internally using two DI frameworks; HK2 and CDI (Weld), which share the common AtInject annotations, and thus not rarely clash and cause various things such as scanning to be duplicated.

While all of this is happening Gavin King is still working on his Ceylon project, but after working on it for nearly 9 years, September 29, 2019 finally marked the date of King's last commit in the Ceylon repo. In the ensuing months King would gradually return to the Java EE scene.

Realising the Shamrock / Protean dualistic naming for Red Hat's new project is not entirely ideal, Shamrock was renamed to Quarkus on February 22, 2019. About two weeks later, on March 7, 2019, Jason Greene introduced Quarkus to the world. Utilising the build-time meta-data collection and code generation, and in combination with GraalVM, Quarkus was able to startup Java applications in a previously unheard-of mere milliseconds.

Specifically interesting was that Quarkus introduced a new DI implementation called Quarkus ArC. ArC implemented much of the CDI 2.0 API and behaviour but not everything. It wasn't based on Red Hat's CDI implementation Weld, but constituted a completely new, much leaner code base. Being build-time based, ArC was able to emit many of the typical CDI errors such as ambiguous resolution at build-time instead of runtime (startup time) as traditional CDI implementations did. ArC however did not support CDI portable extensions, but instead offered build-time variants to replace those. Because ArC was not an official CDI implementation, it took some liberties with introducing features that went beyond the CDI 2.0 APIs, such as making the usage of

`@Inject` optional if a qualifier is used; an idea that floated around a long time ago but never made it into the CDI spec.

Jonathan Coustick of Payara in an article co-authored with Arjan Tijms announced on June 06, 2019, nearly a year after Tijms pitched the initial idea, that Payara planned to turn HK2 into a full CDI implementation as an alternative to Weld sometime in the future.

On July 22, 2019, as part of the still ongoing Java EE transfer and the subsequent preparations for Jakarta EE 8, the CDI API and specification documents were officially transferred from Red Hat to the Eclipse EE4J repository on Github, where they sit together with all other transferred Java EE APIs which were rebranded to Jakarta EE.

The day after, on July 23, 2019, Scott Stark, a Red Hat engineer from Seattle, committed a fork of the JSR 330 API code to that same repo. Unfortunately no agreement with Lee or Johnson had been reached to transfer the original.

CHAPTER 2

Beans As the Component Model in EE

In the previous chapter, you got a glimpse of CDI's history and how CDI has been positioned as the default component model in Java EE. In this chapter, you'll take a closer look at this component model as we compare it to some of the other models that are still in Java EE.

What Is a Component Model?

The term *component* goes back a long time, and like the related word *module*, it's a term that's defined in several different ways. Sometimes the explanations overlap, and sometimes they clash with each other. For the sake of clarity, we'll define the model for a component, and hence for individual components, here. We won't pretend this is the canonical definition; it's merely intended to be the working definition for this book.

In Java EE, components are ultimately defined by classes, but compared to classes, most components are additionally the following:

- Managed
- Scoped
- Substitutable
- Interceptable
- Having a lifecycle
- Named

We'll explain what all these terms mean in the following sections.

J. Beernink and A. Tijms, *Pro CDI 2 in Java EE 8*, https://doi.org/10.1007/978-1-4842-4363-3_2

Managed

Managed in the context of components means that the developer doesn't instantiate classes that are components using Java's `new` operator. Instead, those classes are implicitly instantiated by a container (runtime) when the container determines an instance is needed (for example, to handle an incoming event such as a URL request) or when requested by the developer.

There are multiple ways in which developers can request such an instance.

The most explicit way is programmatically using the so-called service locator pattern. In that way, an instance of the desired component is typically obtained by calling a method on a class or instance. This class or instance then internally fetches the required instance from somewhere or, if no instance is available, creates one (and typically stores it for future reference).

The service locator pattern is slightly different from the factory pattern, so this might need to be clarified a little. On the surface they seem similar, as in both cases an instance is requested by calling a method on a class or instance (called a *factory* in the case of the factory pattern and a *service locator* in the case of the service locator pattern). The difference is that a factory creates a new instance, which is then owned by the code requesting it, while the service locator typically does a lookup for an existing instance, and only if no such instance is found, a new one is created. The instance returned from a service locator is subsequently *not* owned by the code requesting it. In particular, this means that same instance may be in use by another piece of code elsewhere (even simultaneously in another thread), and the requesting code should not try to destroy it.

As you'll see later in the chapter, there are some exceptions in CDI with `@Dependent` where the lines are blurred a little, but in general those differences hold up quite well.

The following are a few examples in Java EE:

EJB/JNDI

```
SomeService someService =
    (someService) new InitialContext().lookup("java:module/someService");
```

JSF

```
SomeService someService =
    FacesContext.getCurrentInstance()
                           .getApplication()
                           .evaluateExpressionGet(
```

```
                    FacesContext.getCurrentInstance(),
                    "#{someService}",
                    SomeService.class);
```

CDI

```
SomeService someService =
   CDI.current().select(SomeService.class).get()
```

Besides explicitly requesting instances using the service locator pattern, developers can request an instance using injection. In that case, the developer specifies the request in a more declarative way, and the container hands over the requested instance in response to that. There are two main variants of this. The first is using field injection, and the second is using parameter injection (practically, the parameter of a constructor or a method).

Using field injection, you almost always provide metadata in some way to declare your intent to the container so that when a new instance with injectable fields is created, the container knows those fields are to be injected. Historically, metadata was provided by XML deployment descriptors, but in recent years this has been mostly replaced by annotations.

Using parameter injection, you may not always have to provide metadata, or you can provide only a subset. In CDI, for instance, you mark the entire constructor with arguments as being injectable, and CDI will then provide instances for all constructor parameters (you don't have to mark every argument with `@Inject`; in fact, `@Inject` can not even target arguments). Note that there can be only one such injectable constructor, as CDI has no API for injection points to specify which constructor should be called, and CDI of course should not make an arbitrary choice.

With setter injection, CDI supports a specific subset of method injection. In this case, again the entire setter method is annotated with `@Inject` and not a single argument. These setters are then called by the CDI runtime after the bean is created, but before the `@PostConstruct` method is called. Injection in this way does not apply when setters are manually called. In most situations, they indeed should not be directly called, with testing environments a notable exception. Setter injection is largely identical to field injection but allows the bean developer to "intercept" the injection and perform additional logic if needed. This is largely the same principle as direct field assignment in an unmanaged simple Java class (aka POJO, for Plain Old Java Object) versus setter methods. However, perhaps remarkably, in CDI it's typically seen as best practice to use field injection and not setter injection, while in POJOs it's the other way around.

CDI also supports full method injection in all methods that are called by the runtime itself, which are producer methods, disposer methods, and event listeners (these will all be covered in more detail in later chapters). In these cases, the method is already clearly intended to be called by CDI, and you don't have to provide any `@Inject` annotation; for every (extra) argument in the method CDI will resolve an instance and pass that as a parameter.

In JAX-RS you see a similar thing for resource methods that are called by JAX-RS; however, this specification does require all extra arguments to be annotated with JAX-RS's `@Context` annotation or any of its other specific annotations.

Note that when using injection, the entire chain of object instances must be managed. In other words, field injection does not magically happen when an instance is created using Java's `new` operator. If you start a chain at a component that is called by the container in response to an event, there's no problem; the container will instantiate this initial component and will inject it. If those injected components have injection points, those will be injected too. This does present an interesting issue: if you can't have a component injected when using the `new` operator and the component isn't called (and therefore created) by the container, how do you bootstrap the sequence? The answer is to use the service locator pattern, as explained earlier, for this initial component to be created. That will result in a managed component, and subsequently all (transitive) injection points of said component will be resolved.

The following are a few examples in Java EE of annotation-based field injection:

EJB

```
@Stateless
public class SomeEJB {
   @EJB
   SomeService someService;
}
```

JSF

```
@ManagedBean
public class SomeJSFBean {
   @ManagedProperty(value = "#{someService}")
   SomeService someService;
```

```
    public void setSomeService(SomeService someService) {
        this.someService = someService;
    }
}
```

JAX-RS

```
@Path("/something/")
class SomeResource {
    @Context
    SomeService someService
}
```

CDI

```
public class SomeCDIBean {
    @Inject
    SomeService someService;
}
```

Note that the JSF version has a requirement for a setter method. This requirement is there because JSF's DI system was originally purely XML based, and the annotation variant was bolted on in 2.0. Specifically, this means that the line `@ManagedProperty SomeService` is not directly the injection point but just a marker that JSF picks up and then processes in the same way it would if it were defined using XML. Further, note that the JAX-RS `@Context` annotation is typically used to inject the various artifacts that JAX-RS itself provides. In the example, we used it to inject a custom object, but this would require proprietary (vendor-specific) code such as `InjectableProvider` in Jersey or `ContextProvider` in CFX.

The following are a few examples using parameter injection of various kinds (constructor and method):

CDI: Constructor injection

```
public class SomeCDIBean {
    @Inject
    public void SomeCDIBean(SomeService someService) {
    }
}
```

CDI: Setter method injection

```
public class SomeCDIBean {
    @Inject
    public void setSomeService(SomeService someService) {
    }
}
```

CDI: Producer method injection

```
public class SomeCDIBean {
    @Produces
    public Foo createFoo(SomeService someService) {
    }
}
```

CDI: Observer method injection

```
public class SomeCDIBean {
    public void listenTo(@Observes SomeEvent, SomeService someService) {
    }
}
```

JAX-RS

```
@Path("/something/")
public class SomeResource {
  @GET
  public Response getFoo(@Context HttpHeaders httpHeaders) {
  }
}
```

Scoped

In the context of components, *scoped* means that one or more instances of a component are being kept in the aforementioned conceptual repository, one for each instance (occurrence) of such scope. Depending on the context of the code requesting a component, a different instance from the matching scope is returned.

This might sound somewhat abstract, but an example should clear this up. Consider an HTTP request in a web application. There are often many simultaneous requests processed by such an application. Requests coming from a single browser can share a session, but of course there are many different clients, so there are many different browsers and many sessions. Finally, what all sessions share is that they are for the same application.

The scopes corresponding with this are respectively the classic request scope, session scope, and application scope. For a request-scoped component `foo`, if code that's running in one request wants to use that component, it gets an instance that's given only to code running in the context of that one request. Another request that also wants a `foo` gets a difference instance.

Not all components in Java EE support explicit scopes. Servlets, for example, don't, although they are effectively application-scoped. Stateless session beans and message-driven beans are a special case, in that respectively every call or message is potentially handled by a different instance.

Here are some examples of explicit scopes:

JSF

```
@javax.faces.bean.RequestScoped
@ManagedBean
public class SomeJSFBean {
}
```

CDI

```
@javax.enterprise.context.RequestScoped
public class SomeCDIBean {
}
```

Substitutable

Substitutable here means that components can be easily replaced by compatible components in a system, without the client code being aware of this. This can happen either through static (declarative) configuration or even more dynamically at runtime.

Naturally the substituted component would have to be compatible with the original component, which means it has to either implement the same interface (or a subinterface of that) or be a subclass of the original component. This does put constraints on the original component, of course; it indeed has to either implement an interface or, when not implementing any interfaces, not be a final class and not have final methods.

The original J2EE programming model was heavily focused on substitutable components, as basically everything was "ref'ed" (`mail-ref`, `resource-ref`, `role-ref`, `ejb-ref`, and so on). This meant developers were supposed to declare indirections (refs) and code against that. The refs were then intended to be mapped by a deployer when the application was deployed. The syntax used, however, was quite arcane, and the actual mapping had to be done in a server-specific way, which meant developers always had a hard time finding the right information for their servers.

The core problem here was that one *had* to map, instead of using defaults and then substitute only when required. The following gives an approximate example for EJB and GlassFish or Payara:

In `web.xml`

```
<ejb-ref>
   <ejb-ref-name>someEjb</ejb-ref-name>
</ejb-local-ref>
```

In `glassfish-web.xml`

```
<ejb-ref>
    <ejb-ref-name>someEjb</ejb-ref-name>
    <jndi-name>java:/somepath/someactualbean</jndi-name>
</ejb-ref>
```

The bean can then be looked up in a servlet via something like the following:

```
context.lookup("java:comp/env/someEjb");
```

By changing the JNDI name in `glassfish-web.xml`, you can transparently change what `java:comp/env/someEjb` refers to and hence what is being returned from the call shown earlier.

In CDI, however, things are quite a bit more elegant.

There is no excessive “ref-ing” of each and every little thing needed in CDI; hence, there’s no “ref-ing” at all in CDI. You define and inject dependencies directly, and when you need to change what’s being injected, you provide a so-called alternative. These alternatives are discussed in more detail later in this book, but a simple example looks as follows:

```
// This is used as the default
public class SomeCDIBean {
}

// This is a bean being injected with SomeCDIBean
public class SomeOtherCDIBean {
    @Inject
   SomeCDIBean someBean;

}

// Providing an alternative
@Dependent
@Alternative
@Priority(APPLICATION)
public class AlternativeProducer {
   @Produces
   public SomeCDIBean producer() {
        return new SubclassOfSomeCDIBean();
     }
}
```

Some critics may say that the CDI way doesn’t force the developer so much to think about substitution and that the default instance may appear in places where it should not if the override is forgotten or somehow isn’t being picked up (and thus silently ignored). While these concerns are somewhat valid, a mapping file like, for instance, `glassfish-web.xml` with a default version of a component can make it into production just as well. At any length, though, developers en masse choose for less ceremony, and the CDI approach has essentially won; “ref’ing” is now quite rare in real-world Java EE projects, and barely any new framework or Java EE API recently introduced has copied the excessive “ref” approach from old J2EE.

Interceptable

A component is said to be *interceptable* if the container or the developer can add implicit or explicit interceptors to the operations exposed by a component. An *interceptor* here is a piece of code that runs before or after (or both before and after) a call to an operation (method) without the caller having to notice that such interceptor is present. An interceptor is frequently capable of modifying the input parameters for a method, and is capable of modifying the return value (if any). Some types of interceptors can even retarget the call to another target component while keeping the interceptor chain.

Figure 2-1 shows a typical call sequence for an interceptor.

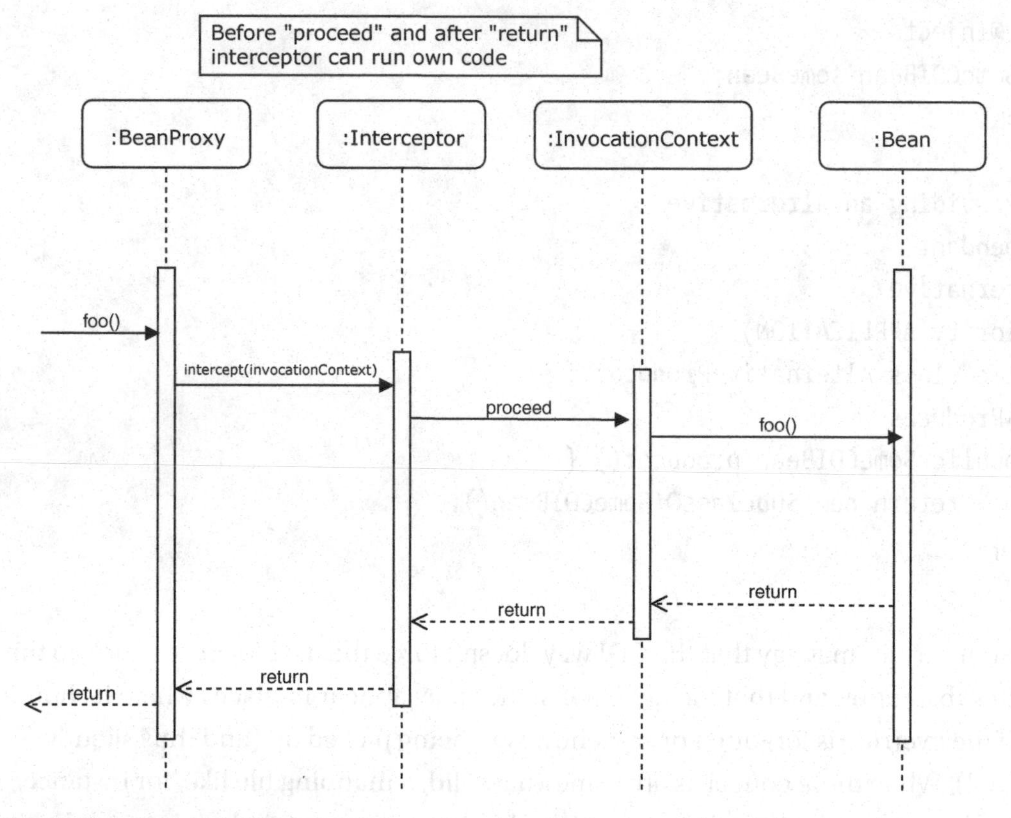

***Figure 2-1.** Call sequence for interceptor*

In Figure 2-1, a call is made on the (injected) bean proxy, which is a stand-in for the real bean that's going to be called. The proxy internally calls the interceptor(s), which as mentioned earlier can run code before and after the call to the actual bean. In the Interceptor spec, this real call is not done on the bean instance directly, but an

InvocationContext instance sits in between. This InvocationContext instance in turn helps the proxy to either invoke the next interceptor or eventually call the actual bean.

Interceptibility for components on which the developer does direct method calls (e.g., EJB and CDI beans, but not servlets or message-driven beans) typically implies substitutability, as the container has to return a modified instance that internally has a list of interceptors that are to be called and then finally calls the actual instance. Such a modified instance is called a *proxy* in Java EE. This is a compatible instance as explained earlier for "substitutable."

Components that aren't directly called can still have interceptors, such as the global JASPIC authentication module that is called for every HTTP request, or servlet filters, which are called for specified URL patterns or specified servlets.

The following are some examples (some examples are somewhat abbreviated):

JASPIC: **Servlet container profile**

```
public class SomeServerAuthModule implements ServerAuthModule {

   @Override
   public Class<?>[] getSupportedMessageTypes() {
       return new Class[] { HttpServletRequest.class, HttpServletResponse.
       class };
  }

   @Override
   public AuthStatus validateRequest(MessageInfo messageInfo, Subject
   clientSubject, Subject serviceSubject) {}

   @Override
   public AuthStatus secureResponse(MessageInfo messageInfo, Subject
   serviceSubject) {}
}
```

Servlet

```
@WebFilter("/someurl")
public class SomeFilter extends HttpFilter {
   @Override
   protected void doFilter(HttpServletRequest req, HttpServletResponse res,
   FilterChain chain) {}

}
```

EJB

```
@Stateless
public class SomeEJB {
  // Implicit container provided transaction interceptor applied here
  public void someMethod() {}

   // Container provided security interceptor applied here
   @RolesAllowed
   public void otherMethod() {}
}
```

CDI

```
// Define annotation
@Inherited
@InterceptorBinding
@Retention(RUNTIME)
@Target({ METHOD, TYPE })
public @interface SomeInterceptor {
}

// Define Interceptor
@Interceptor
@SomeInterceptor
@Priority(APPLICATION)
public class SomeInterceptorImpl {
   @AroundInvoke
   public Object doIntercept(InvocationContext context) throws Exception {

   }
}
// Use interceptor
public class SomeCDIBean {
   @SomeInterceptor
   public void someMethod() {
   }
}
```

Note that for EJB we showed only two of the built-in interceptors. For CDI we showed how to define a so-called interceptor binding, which is a CDI-specific construct to attach an interceptor to a CDI bean using an annotation.

The interceptor itself, including the @AroundInvoke and @Interceptor annotations and the InvocationContext type, however, is from Java EE's Interceptor spec and is not specifically tied to CDI (EJB can use the same interceptors). Interceptors in CDI are by default inactive but can be activated by either giving an interceptor a priority or, lacking such a priority, using CDI's beans.xml deployment descriptor. In the earlier example, we went for the annotation. The @Priority annotation that we used is from neither CDI nor the Interceptor spec but originates from the Common Annotations spec.

A special note for intercepting on object instances is that the this pointer in Java can't be intercepted. This is true for all different components in Java EE as it's an underlying Java restriction. Specifically, this means methods in a class calling themselves internally will not see interceptors being applied.

Here's an example in CDI:

```
// Use interceptor
public class SomeCDIBean {
    public void fooMethod() {
        someMethod();
    }

    @SomeInterceptor
    public void someMethod() {
    }
}
```

In this case, if an external class calls fooMethod() and, as shown, fooMethod() calls someMethod(), then the interceptor will not be called.

Interceptors and the closely related CDI-specific decorators will be discussed in more detail in Chapter 6.

Having a Lifecyle

Components in Java EE almost always have some kind of lifecycle. This follows from the *managed* aspect and means the container calls the component back at several logical moments, typically related to the construction, initialization, and destruction. Such a call is called a *lifecycle callback*.

These concerns are in fact so common that annotations for them have been added to common annotations, namely:

- `@PostConstruct`
- `@PreDestroy`

The annotations can be put on a method that's then being called back by the container at the appropriate time.

For `@PostConstruct`, that happens after injection into a component takes place but before it's put into service. The observant reader may ask why an `@PostConstruct` is necessary when Java already has a constructor. The answer is simply that a constructor is called before, or at the same time, the injection takes place (the latter if constructor injection is used). When an `@PostConstruct` annotated method is called, all injection (be it constructor or field based) is guaranteed to have been done.

The `@PreDestroy` method is called just before the component is taken out of service (and often, but not necessarily, made eligible for garbage collection). The difference from Java's finalizer should be clear here: finalizers are unreliable and should rarely if ever be used. The `@PreDestroy` annotated method, however, is called at a well-specified time and is much more dependable. Do note, however, that the reliability of the `@PreDestroy` annotated method depends somewhat on the scope being used for such a component, and it's typically called at the end of such scope. A request scope is often reliable, as most requests are of a short duration (there are exceptions, of course). The standard view scope from JSF, however, is less reliable, as it doesn't end automatically when the user navigates away using a simple GET request to a new view, meaning the `@PreDestroy` annotation won't be called in that case until the HTTP session associated with it times out or is explicitly closed.

A number of components in Java EE have their own initializer and destroy methods, which almost always predate the introduction of the common annotations mentioned. Some components, most notably servlets, actually support both their own initializer and their own destroy methods, as well as the common annotations. Unfortunately, the order in which those are called is not strictly specified. In the case of servlets, the `init()` method provides the all-important `ServletConfig` (which in turn provides the `ServletContext`), but even more unfortunate is that in practice `@PostConstruct` seems to be most often called before `init()`. This therefore means that when an `@PostConstruct` annotated method is called, the `ServletContext` isn't available yet. Since the Servlet spec doesn't make any of its own artifacts available for injection (it merely supports other artifacts being injected), there's also no way an `@PostConstruct` annotated method can get hold of this context. The result is that even for new code the Servlet `init()` method is still far more often used.

The following are some examples:

JASPIC

```
public class SomeServerAuthModule implements ServerAuthModule {
   private CallbackHandler handler;

   @Override
   public void initialize(MessagePolicy requestPolicy, MessagePolicy
   responsePolicy, CallbackHandler handler, Map options) {
       this.handler = handler;
   }
   @Override
   public AuthStatus validateRequest(MessageInfo messageInfo, Subject
   clientSubject, Subject serviceSubject) {}
}
```

Servlet

```
@WebServlet("/someurl")
public class SomeServlet extends HttpServlet {
   private static final long serialVersionUID = 1L;

    @PostConstruct
    public void myinit() {
      // getServletContext() may not work here
    }

    @Override
    public void init() {
        // getServletContext() works here
    }

    @Override
    public void doGet(HttpServletRequest request, HttpServletResponse
    response) {}

}
```

CDI

```
public class SomeCDIBean {
   @Inject
   SomeService someService;
   @PostConstruct
   public void init() {
        // someService injected here
   }
}
```

Named

Many components in Java EE are *named*, which means you can refer to them using a (string) name. Some components, such as JSF managed beans and servlets, use only names. Other components, such as EJB and CDI beans, can be referred to by both a name and a type.

The different component types in Java EE do not always share a namespace or naming system, though. In general, there are three naming systems in use.

- Component specific
- JNDI
- Expression language

Component-specific names are found, for instance, in the Servlet spec, which mostly shows up when using XML because that name is then used to map a servlet to a URL pattern.

```
<servlet>
    <servlet-name>Faces Servlet</servlet-name>
    <servlet-class>javax.faces.webapp.FacesServlet</servlet-class>
    <load-on-startup>1</load-on-startup>
</servlet>
<servlet-mapping>
    <servlet-name>Faces Servlet</servlet-name>
    <url-pattern>/faces/*</url-pattern>
</servlet-mapping>
```

The name, however, can also be used when looking up servlets programmatically.

EJB beans use both component-specific names, as well as JNDI names. By default these names are related, though. The component-specific name is called the *bean name*, which defaults to the simple class name of the bean. The portable JNDI name is derived from this name. Note that we said "portable JNDI name." This is because in the beginning of EJB the automatically generated JNDI names were always product-specific. Here's an example:

```
@Stateless
public class SomeService {}
```

In this case, the bean name is simply SomeService, and one of the JNDI names is the derived name java:module/SomeService.

You can also explicitly add a name.

```
@Stateless(name="foo")
public class SomeService {}
```

In that case, the bean name is foo, and the derived JNDI name is java:module/foo.

EJB beans can be injected using the EJB name as follows:

```
public class MyEJBBean {

   @EJB(beanName="foo")
   SomeService someService;
}
```

Or they can be injected using the JNDI name.

```
public class MyEJBBean {

   @EJB(lookup="java:module/foo")
   SomeService someService;
}
```

However, using all defaults, and when no names clash, names can be omitted.

```
public class MyEJBBean {
   @EJB
   SomeService someService;
}
```

The third naming system involves Java EE's expression language. Unlike JNDI, expression language is not a directory system; it consists more or less of a flat namespace representing objects. Like JNDI, though, you do resolve names against various contexts. In JNDI this is done via `InitialContext`, which you can point using parameters to various different JNDI trees, while with expression language you make use of an `ELContext` and specifically an `ELResolver`. The `ELResolver` for the CDI namespace, for instance, can be obtained from the CDI bean manager.

The JSF managed bean system is primarily named, and when defining names for beans, they end up being defined in JSF's own namespace. When a managed bean is defined in JSF without an explicit name declaration, the simple class name is used, just like in EJB, but this time with the first letter in lowercase.

Here's an example:

```
@ManagedBean
public class SomeJSFBean {
}
```

In that case, the bean name will be `someJSFBean`. Like EJB, again you can explicitly define the name as follows:

```
@ManagedBean(name = "foo")
public class SomeJSFBean {
}
```

As mentioned earlier, JSF managed beans can be injected using their name, as follows:

```
@ManagedBean
public class SomeJSFBean {
   @ManagedProperty(value = "#{foo}")
   SomeService someService;

   // + setter
}
```

Unlike EJB, there is no variant in JSF where the bean can be injected without specifying its name.

Note that when a bean is *referenced* using expression language, like in the `@ManagedProperty` annotation, it's not just a name that you can put there but an entire almost arbitrarily complex expression. When you *define* the bean, like in the `@ManagedBean` annotation, you use a simple name (an opaque string).

CDI in turn doesn't primarily use naming at all. Instead, components are fully identified by their Java type(s) and zero or more additional so-called qualifiers. You take a deeper look at those in a next chapter, but suffice to say here that these qualifiers are special annotations and therefore type-safe.

CDI, however, does have support for components to be named (it's even a first-class attribute on the metadata structure CDI uses internally to describe components), but naming a component in CDI is fully optional, and there's no default name for a component (called a CDI bean) when it's not explicitly named. A bean can be named using the `@Named` annotation or by directly constructing its metadata instance and setting the name attribute (as we'll discuss later). When you use the `@Named` annotation, you do get a default name, though, which is the same as in JSF: the bean's simple (unqualified) class name with the first letter in lowercase.

Why the Plethora of Different Component Models in Java EE?

Arguably one of the biggest issues in Java EE is a lack of a coherent component model. As was shown in the previous section, many specs/APIs in Java EE have their own model. This includes, and is not even limited to, the following:

- Servlets
- EJB session beans and message-driven beans
- Server auth modules
- JSF managed beans
- JSF artifacts such as converters, resource handlers, phase listeners, and so on
- JCA resource adapters
- JAX-RS resources

For those users who combine Java EE with the popular Spring framework, which is a more common combination than, say, Java EE and Guice, there's obviously the Spring component model and injection API in addition to those.

As we discussed in Chapter 1, most of this is historic; Java EE started with the EJB model, which was mostly aimed at developing high-level business components and not at all at developing various container services.

Another issue might have been that for a long time EJBs were the domain of expensive and closed-source products, while servlets were available for free and as open source in various products such as Tomcat and Jetty. If EJB had not been put on the market back then as such "exclusive" technology, servlets might have early on been based on it. By the time that EJB became more accessible (read: more widely available as in free and open source), servlets were already firmly established and difficult and unlikely to change.

While a lack of foresight in starting Java EE with a common and coherent component model has certainly played its part, it's not utterly for lack of trying. In the EJB spec, for instance, it was mentioned that components should not start threads themselves. For an eternity, this was logically interpreted by developers all over the world that EJB beans were not allowed to start threads but that it was fine to do that in servlets. Hence, numerous applications went through complicated gymnastics to delegate the creation of threads to a servlet and then somehow have code in EJB make use of them. However, legend has it that this constraint was never meant to apply solely to the EJB container but was intended to hold for the entire Java EE application server. Presumably, the writers of said constraints already had an entire platform in mind based on EJB components, which, as you know now, never came to be. The last and only attempt to base other specs to a degree on EJB was with JAX-RPC and JAX-RPC 2 (renamed to JAX-WS). In these specs, a web service component itself wasn't necessarily based on an EJB, but the reverse was, though. EJB beans added a new view next to the existing local and (binary) remote ones: the "web service client view." This was true to the philosophy of the time that other specs should not use EJB (in other words, build on EJB), but that EJB would be the facade for all other specs.

What hasn't helped for establishing a common component model is that despite Sun Microsystems leading the Java EE platform and even having a special steward role in the JCP, the process and organization overseeing the various Java specs have never been able to assert any iron-hand control over the platform in the same way that vendors like Microsoft and Interface 21/SpringSource/Pivotal automatically have over their own respective proprietary platforms. Instead, for the longest time, Java EE was a collection of several different more or less independent projects only loosely connected. The strong point of specs (input from many different stakeholders) also proved to be its weak point (many different opinions on where to move the platform).

Given that, it's perhaps somewhat ironic that the component model that is finally becoming the common one in Java EE did not come from Sun but from Red Hat (now IBM).

CDI Beans as the Component Model in Java EE

After a long journey, Java EE has finally arrived at the point where a common component model is being introduced in the platform, and that's by using CDI beans as the components.

Initially there was some confusion about *how* CDI would be used as this common component model, as there were basically two options.

- CDI as the facade for all other specs
- CDI as the core all other specs build on

Initially there was little agreement on the approach, and some people continued seeing CDI as just another type of EJB and included things like built-in beans for types owned by the Servlet spec such as `HttpServletRequest`, instead of convincing the Servlet spec to include them.

During the development of Java EE 7 and CDI 1.1, it became clear, however, that turning CDI into another EJB was the wrong approach, and a significant amount of CDI work in Java EE started to treat CDI as a way for uniting the Java EE component model and aligning specs around it to finally come to a more consistent platform. Specifically, in Java EE 7, a milestone was reached when Java EE's flagship feature, declarative transactions, was based on top of CDI and given ownership to the JTA spec. The importance of this milestone is in the fact that it showed that a low-level spec can ship contexts and interceptors based on CDI, without itself having to support every possible CDI implementation out there (thanks to portable extensions), without itself having to be based on CDI, and without CDI having to add anything specifically for this. (These have at some point in time all been used as objections why supposedly some specs would not be able to adopt CDI.)

To demonstrate, we'll show a fragment of the code used in Payara's JTA implementation.

The interceptor itself (slightly abbreviated) looks as follows:

```
/**
* Transactional annotation Interceptor class for Mandatory transaction
type, ie
 * javax.transaction.Transactional.TxType.MANDATORY If called outside a
transaction context,
 * TransactionRequiredException will be thrown If called inside a
transaction context, managed bean
 * method execution will then continue under that context.
* @author Paul Parkinson
 */
@Priority(PLATFORM_BEFORE + 200)
@Interceptor
@Transactional(MANDATORY)
public class TransactionalInterceptorMandatory extends
TransactionalInterceptorBase {
   @AroundInvoke
    public Object transactional(InvocationContext ctx) throws Exception {
       if (isLifeCycleMethod(ctx)) {
            return proceed(ctx);
        }
       setTransactionalTransactionOperationsManger(false);
       try {
            if (getTransactionManager().getTransaction() == null) {
                throw new TransactionalException(
                    "... from TxType.MANDATORY transactional interceptor.",
                        new TransactionRequiredException(
                            "Managed bean with Transactional annotation and
                            TxType of " +
                            "MANDATORY called outside of a transaction
                            context"));
            }
            return proceed(ctx);
```

```
        } finally {
            resetTransactionOperationsManager();
        }
    }
}
```

This interceptor is then added to the CDI runtime using a portable extension, as shown here:

```
/**
* The CDI Portable Extension for @Transactional.
*/
public class TransactionalExtension implements Extension {
   public void beforeBeanDiscovery(@Observes BeforeBeanDiscovery
   beforeBeanDiscoveryEvent, BeanManager beanManager) {
        AnnotatedType<TransactionalInterceptorMandatory> timat =
            beanManager.createAnnotatedType(TransactionalInterceptor
            Mandatory.class);
        beforeBeanDiscoveryEvent.addAnnotatedType(
            timat,
            TransactionalInterceptorMandatory.class.getName());
        // ...
    }
}
```

This code is basically everything that's needed for a low-level spec to make its services or artifacts available for consumption via CDI.

Besides JTA, JSF integrated in Java EE 7 with CDI by providing a CDI-compatible @ViewScoped in much the same way in which JTA also integrated with CDI but also provided a new scope, @FlowScoped, for which only a CDI scope was made available. Furthermore, the JMS 2 API and BeanValidation provided CDI support as well.

The hope, and partially indeed the plan, was for Java EE 8 to make very big steps toward being based on CDI, but in part because of the difficulties around Java EE's continuity (see Chapter 1), this didn't quite happen. JMS 2.1, for instance, was going to introduce CDI beans as being first-class message listeners (in addition to message-driven beans and Java SE programmatic listeners), and there were many discussions about basing additional EJB goodies like `@Asynchronous` and `@Timeout` on CDI. The in-progress Java Identity API (JSR 351) was slated to use CDI as well.

While all this didn't happen, community-driven specs like JSF did move the theme of being based on CDI forward, and the new EE Security API, community driven as well, was even fully based on CDI from the start.

As for the next revision of the platform, at the time of writing, plans are being drafted for JSF to completely drop its own managed bean system (which was deprecated in JSF 2.3/Java EE 8) and for JAX-RS to deprecate its own component type and its own `@Context`-based dependency injection and move over to CDI instead. Other plans include the EE Concurrency spec adopting the previously mentioned CDI versions of `@Asynchronous` and `@Timeout` annotations, among others.

Advantages of Using CDI by the Platform Internally

Some of the component models you've seen are solely user-facing, which means that only user applications base their logic on them, and the platform doesn't use them internally. Examples of such user-facing models are JSF's managed beans and EJB beans.

CDI, however, faces both the user and the system (platform), meaning that the platform can, and is even encouraged to, use the same APIs that the user code uses. What are the advantages of this? In this section, we'll go through some of them.

For the user, the fact that the platform is using CDI internally has the advantage that CDI is very dynamic. Beans and their methods can be wrapped by interceptors and decorators, which you can add programmatically to them using portable extensions. You can also replace beans fully by providing alternatives, or you can veto them.

The dynamic aspect means the platform itself becomes more programmable and that many types of platform behavior automatically become pluggable and extendable. For instance, in EE Security there exists something called `IdentityStoreHandler`, which determines how multiple identity stores get called. (Identity stores are user/credential databases that the platform uses to authenticate provided credentials against.) The default is that the platform calls them in order until one of them successfully authenticates, which is fine for most applications, but sometimes a different behavior is required, such as making sure that all authentication stores successfully authenticate instead of just a single one. Since internally `IdentityStoreHandler` is a CDI bean, it can be decorated or replaced by user code (either application code or that from a library) using the API that users are already familiar with.

The following is an abbreviated example from the Soteria implementation of EE Security of replacing the handler from an application:

```
@Alternative
@Priority(APPLICATION)
@ApplicationScoped
public class CustomIdentityStoreHandler implements IdentityStoreHandler {
    @Override
    public CredentialValidationResult validate(Credential credential) {
        CredentialValidationResult validationResult = null;

        // Check with all stores and abort when one fails to authenticate
        for (IdentityStore authenticationIdentityStore :
        validatingIdentityStores) {
            CredentialValidationResult temp = authenticationIdentityStore.
            validate(credential);
            switch (temp.getStatus()) {
                case NOT_VALIDATED:
                    break; // Don't do anything
                case INVALID:
                    return temp; // One fail == all fail
                case VALID:
                    validationResult = temp;
            }
        }

        if (validationResult == null) {
            return INVALID_RESULT; // not a single one validated
        }

        return validationResult; // valid result of last store
    }
}
```

The exact semantics of the EE Security API used in the previous example are outside the scope of this book, but what does matter here is that it shows the simplicity and elegance with which you can replace framework behavior using standard CDI primitives.

To summarize, the advantages for the platform using CDI for internal artifacts are as follows:

- You can modify platform behavior (not all specs have historically bothered to create their own plug-in system).
- The user doesn't have to learn any new API or config format.
- The spec/API designer and implementer of the platform doesn't have to define and implement yet another proprietary factory mechanism and/or deployment descriptor to allow for behavior plug-ins.

CHAPTER 3

Identifying Beans

One of the core responsibilities of CDI is to provide dependencies, which are beans in CDI. As you learned in the previous chapter, such beans can be obtained in various ways, namely, by having them injected in some way or by programmatic lookups. An important aspect of obtaining beans is that you need a way to specify which bean you want. In other words, you need to be able to identify beans. This raises the following questions: how are beans made identifiable, and how do you make sure someone can refer to your bean? How this works in CDI is the topic of this chapter.

What Is a Bean?

In the previous chapter, we stated that a component in CDI is called a *bean*. But what exactly constitutes a bean? Java has the concept of a JavaBean, which is often just called a bean as well, but a bean in CDI is much more abstract.

Technically, a bean in CDI is everything that can be represented by an instance of `javax.enterprise.inject.spi.Bean<T>`, which is an internal but user-accessible metadata structure that CDI stores internally for every bean it knows. This structure contains the core factory method `T create()` to actually create an instance of the bean. As you'll see in Chapter 4, CDI doesn't often call this factory method directly but does so in a controlled way via a contextual "caching layer." The `Bean<T>` structure also holds the so-called core bean attributes.

- Type
- Qualifier
- Name
- Scope
- Stereotypes
- Alternative (a Boolean indicating the bean is an alternative)

J. Beernink and A. Tijms, *Pro CDI 2 in Java EE 8*, https://doi.org/10.1007/978-1-4842-4363-3_3

Types, qualifiers, and names will be explained in this chapter. Scope will be explained in the next chapter.

Applications can, but don't have to, implement the `Bean<T>` interface for each bean. Actually, doing so is quite rare, as CDI implementations can generate `Bean<T>` implementations from three other, much easier to use artifacts.

- Managed beans
- Producer methods
- Producer fields

A managed bean itself is defined by the somewhat obscure managed bean specification, which is part of the Java EE umbrella spec. It even has its own annotation, `javax.annotation.ManagedBean`, which lives in yet another spec, namely, Common Annotations, and sits right next to the crucial CDI annotations `@PostConstruct` and `@PreDestroy`.

Managed beans are what most people would casually associate with a "CDI bean." This is simply a Java class (also called the *bean class*) that most closely resembles a JavaBean or a JSF managed bean. There are a few restrictions, though; for instance, inner classes or abstract classes can't be managed beans, and the bean class needs to have either a no-arg constructor or a single injectable constructor. The reason simply is that CDI has to be able to create instances of the class. Obviously, abstract classes can't be instantiated, and neither can classes with a constructor taking parameters that CDI doesn't know how to supply.

Since CDI creates a `Bean<T>` structure from a bean class and since `Bean<T>` has a `create()` method that returns instances of this class, you can say that a bean class is in fact a factory for its own type.

`Bean<T>` instances can also be created by CDI from something that is in a way a bit closer to the `Bean<T>` type, and that's from a producer method. A producer method is a method in a bean class annotated with the `@Produces` annotation. At a glance it looks like the `T create()` method of `Bean<T>`, but a producer method is a much higher-level artifact supporting annotations and method injection, where `T create()` is at a lower level and supports none of those things. As for restrictions, a producer method obviously can't be abstract (the CDI runtime has to call it after all), and if the return type is generic, it must have actual type parameters (no wildcards and only type variables in special circumstances discussed in the next chapter).

Finally, you have producer fields, which is an instance variable of a bean class annotated with `@Produces`. Such instance variables should typically be assigned right away at initialization, and CDI will then use the value of this instance field as the return value of the aforementioned `T create()` method of a `Bean<T>` instance.

We omitted two special cases of beans here, interceptors and decorators, which are in fact subtypes of `Bean<T>`. We'll discuss these in-depth in Chapter 6.

Directly creating `Bean<T>` instances, instead of letting CDI create them for you, is discussed in Chapter 8.

How Can You Identify a Bean?

We'll start by explaining how you use different terms associated with the identity of a bean. Like with the term *component* in Chapter 2, we don't put any claims on these being the canonical definitions, and different authors may use them slightly differently. By *obtaining*, we mean the general act of code wanting to use a bean and getting hold of that bean. A bean is obtained by *referring* to its identity, which means this identity is in some way given to the runtime. With the *identity* of a bean, we mean a unique combination of one or more attributes (of a bean) that you can use to let the runtime find this bean. Like principals in security (such as full name or Social Security number), a bean can have multiple identities. The process of finding a bean by the runtime is called *resolution,* which means matching the given identity to an actual bean instance.

In CDI there are several ways to refer to a bean or even to a collection of beans. Some overlap, and some supplement each other. The following list gives an overview:

- By type
- By type and qualifiers
- By name (expression language limitations)

We'll discuss each option in more detail in the following sections.

By Type

One thing that is central in CDI is the notion of type-safe resolution. In Java EE, this sets CDI apart from JSF and early versions of EJB, both of which have contributed ideas to CDI (see Chapter 1). While with EJB 3 it is possible to do type-safe injections to some degree using the @EJB annotation, CDI takes this concept much further and has it built in to its architecture as a core principle.

Type-safe resolution builds on the fact that the main ID of a bean is simply one of its classes or interfaces.

For instance, consider the following simple bean:

```
public class SomeCDIBean {
}
```

In this case, the bean has two types that can be used to refer to it, `SomeCDIBean.class` and `Object.class`. The latter is obviously overly general and not very useful as an identifier in practice.

Now consider the following types:

```
public interface SomeInterface {
}
public class SomeBaseBean implements SomeInterface {
}
public class SomeCDIBean extends SomeBaseBean {
}
```

Now `SomeCDIBean` has four types that can be used to refer to it: `SomeCDIBean.class` and `Object.class` as before, but now also `SomeBaseBean.class` and `SomeInterface.class`. You can basically obtain an instance of the bean using any of these. If you want a unique instance, you obviously need to use a unique identifier. This in turn means that you would have a need to obtain a bean based on the interface `SomeInterface`; there can be only one enabled bean implementing it. This is sometimes called the *highlander rule* (there can be only one).

Now, the observant reader may wonder what the use of an interface really is if it's allowed to be implemented only once. The answer lies in a subtlety: the actual emphasis for the restriction here is that only one "enabled" bean is allowed to implement said interface. An enabled bean is a bean that has not been disabled and that has not been "overridden" by another bean (via the "alternative" concept that we'll discuss later in the chapter). Simply put, it's the one bean CDI will choose to provide.

Furthermore, you can't use `SomeBaseBean.class` directly and without strings attached to get a unique instance of `SomeCDIBean` since obviously this identifier is used by `SomeBaseBean` as well. We'll explain how to deal with this in a short while.

Another bean can obtain a reference to SomeCDIBean by means of injection and by using the type of the injection point as a means to pass the identity of the requested bean to the runtime, as in the following examples:

```
public class AnotherBean {
    @Inject
    SomeCDIBean bean;
}
public class AnotherBean {
    @Inject
    SomeInterface bean;
}
```

The same thing can be done programmatically, either from a bean or from a class that's not a bean. Note that when a class is not a bean, you do have to be in a context in which CDI is initialized and in which the bean's scope is active. Such context initialization is largely implementation dependent, but in simple and practical terms, it means being in a thread where "CDI works." Scopes are discussed in full detail in the next chapter.

The following are some examples of doing this. Note that in the programmatic example, it's perhaps more obvious that the requesting code literally passes the identity of the requested bean to the runtime.

```
SomeCDIBean bean = CDI.current().select(SomeCDIBean.class).get();
SomeInterface bean = CDI.current().select(SomeInterface.class).get();
```

In many service lookup systems or APIs, the service has either full or at least some control over the identity it chooses to make public. In CDI this identity primarily comes from all the types a given bean has (its own type and all its ancestor types, also called its *transitive closure*). Should you change the type hierarchy of the bean just to influence which types become its identifiers? Is this even possible in all cases?

The answer to that is no. You don't have to do that. CDI has a mechanism to explicitly set the types a bean publishes as its identity via the @Typed annotation. Naturally these types should be types that are actually in the transitive closure of types the bean has.

For the SomeCDIBean example shown earlier, you can use @Typed for two different use cases.

The first case is when you, for example, want to ship SomeCDIBean in a library but expose only its interface to the outside world, leaving the implementation a private detail of your library. In that case, you'd annotate SomeCDIBean with @Typed as follows:

```
@Typed(SomeInterface.class)
public class SomeCDIBean extends SomeBaseBean {
}
```

Following this definition of SomeCDIBean, only SomeInterface.class and as a special case Object.class can be used to refer to the bean (Object.class can't be erased from the list of identities in this way).

The second example case is where you want to make a programmatic choice of which bean to supply for the SomeInterface.class identifier, perhaps via a producer. The producer should then uniquely correspond to this identifier, which means SomeCDIBean itself should not. One of the ways to accomplish this is by using @Typed again, this time to remove the interface from the list of identifiers.

```
@Typed(SomeCDIBean.class)
public class SomeCDIBean extends SomeBaseBean {
}
```

Following this definition, only SomeCDIBean.class can be used to refer to SomeCDIBean (and Object.class again).

This means you could now create a producer as follows:

```
public class SomeProducer {
    @Inject
    SomeCDIBean someCDIBean;
    @Inject
    SomeOtherCDIBean someOtherCDIBean;
    @Produces
    public SomeInterface produce() {
       if (...){
          return someCDIBean;
       }
       return someOtherCDIBean;
    }
}
```

In the previous example, the producer injects two beans, both implementing SomeInterface but not having SomeInterface.class among their identifiers, and therefore not clashing with the identifier of the producer. Based on some condition, either one or the other of the injected beans is returned.

In effect, code elsewhere in the application doing an @Inject SomeInterface will get an implementation either by SomeCDIBean or by SomeOtherCDIBean.

By Type and Qualifiers

A qualifier, initially called a *binding annotation* (@BindingType) in CDI (see Chapter 1), is a way to extend the identity of a bean beyond just its types. Qualifiers, like the @Inject annotation, are strictly spoken not in CDI itself but actually reside in the AtInject (JSR 330) spec. Like @Inject, qualifiers are, however, absolutely core to CDI, and CDI even adds its own behavior to them.

A qualifier is an annotation and therefore by itself type safe. The qualifier annotation may have zero or more attributes, and by default the value of each attribute adds to the identity of a bean. Additionally, a qualifier can have optional attributes that don't count toward the identity of a bean. These attributes have to be annotated with @NonBinding, which is a CDI annotation and thus specific to CDI. Note the similarity between the old CDI-specific name @BindingType and @NonBinding, which is probably not a coincidence.

In its definition, a bean can add zero or more qualifiers to extend its identity, and each qualifier can have zero or more (binding) attributes.

The full identifier of a bean then becomes this: "One of its types + all types of all its qualifiers + the value of the binding attributes of all its qualifiers."

For instance, consider SomeCDIBean again, but now with two qualifiers without attributes, as shown here:

```
@SomeQualifierOne @SomeQualifierTwo
public class SomeCDIBean extends SomeBaseBean {
}
```

Following that definition, one of the identifiers of this bean is now [SomeInterface.class, @SomeQualifierOne, @SomeQualifierTwo].

Another bean can obtain a reference to SomeCDIBean by means of injection and using the type of the injection point annotated with all the qualifiers as a means to pass the identity of the requested bean to the runtime, as in the following example:

```
public class AnotherBean {
    @Inject
    @SomeQualifierOne @SomeQualifierTwo
    SomeInterface bean;
}
```

The same thing can be done programmatically again. The following is an example of doing this. Note that in Java there's no syntax for annotation literals outside annotations themselves. You therefore have to create such an annotation instance yourself, which unfortunately is a bit of work. CDI provides the AnnotationLiteral to help with this. This works by subclassing AnnotationLiteral in a specified way. For the SomeQualifierOne qualifier, this would look as follows:

```
class SomeQualifierOneLiteral
    extends AnnotationLiteral<SomeQualifierOne>
    implements SomeQualifierOne {
    private static final long serialVersionUID = 1L;
}
```

Since this is still a lot of repetitive work to do in every project for every qualifier, CDI encourages a convention where qualifiers without attributes feature an inner class called Literal with a static member named INSTANCE to hold a preconstructed annotation instance for its outer class annotation. For SomeQualifierOne, the following shows what this looks like:

```
@Qualifier
@Retention(RUNTIME)
@Target({ TYPE, METHOD, FIELD, PARAMETER })
@Documented
public @interface SomeQualifierOne {
    public static final class Literal
        extends AnnotationLiteral<SomeQualifierOne>
        implements SomeQualifierOne {
```

```
        private static final long serialVersionUID = 1L;
        public static final Literal INSTANCE = new Literal();
    }
}
```

With that in place and assuming a similar definition for SomeQualifierTwo, you can now programmatically request an instance of SomeCDIBean as follows:

```
SomeCDIBean bean =
    CDI.current()
       .select(
           SomeCDIBean.class,
           SomeQualifierOne.Literal.INSTANCE,
           SomeQualifierTwo.Literal.INSTANCE
       )
       .get();

SomeInterface bean =
    CDI.current()
       .select(
           SomeInterface.class,
           SomeQualifierOne.Literal.INSTANCE,
           SomeQualifierTwo.Literal.INSTANCE
       )
       .get();
```

Up to now you have been looking at qualifiers with no attributes. As mentioned earlier, qualifiers can have attributes as well, and these contribute to the identifier. You do have to realize, though, that using attributes is not necessarily type safe, as you can use, for example, string-based attributes that are prone to typing mistakes.

For qualifiers with attributes, the simple convention of having an INSTANCE for their associated literals is not enough, of course, as you need to provide the values for the attributes in some way. If some of the (binding) attributes don't have a default value, it doesn't make much sense to provide an INSTANCE anyway, as you must provide defaults then. These defaults could be meaningless or just unclear. CDI has a convention for this too, though, and that's to provide a static factory method in the same inner Literal class called of.

In the following example, where you add a single enum-based attribute, this is demonstrated:

```
@Qualifier
@Retention(RUNTIME)
@Target({ TYPE, METHOD, FIELD, PARAMETER })
@Documented
public @interface SomeQualifierOne {
    TimeUnit value() default DAYS;
    public static final class Literal
        extends AnnotationLiteral<SomeQualifierOne>
        implements SomeQualifierOne {
        private static final long serialVersionUID = 1L;
        public static final Literal INSTANCE = of(DAYS);
        private final TimeUnit value;
        public static Literal of(TimeUnit value) {
            return new Literal(value);
        }
        private Literal(TimeUnit value) {
            this.value = value;
        }
        public TimeUnit value() {
            return value;
        }
    }
}
```

In the case of this example, the single attribute (`value`) has a default value (`DAYS`), so you are able to create an `INSTANCE` here. If there would not have been such a default, you would have simply omitted it and provided only the `of` method. The pattern being used here is applicable to basically all qualifiers; the static `of` method takes values for all qualifier attributes and calls the private constructor with those values. The private constructor sets a final instance variable for each annotation attribute, and getter-like methods with the same name as the attribute return these.

With this qualifier in place, the bean definition can now look like this:

```
@SomeQualifierOne(HOURS) @SomeQualifierTwo
public class SomeCDIBean extends SomeBaseBean {
}
```

You can request an instance of this bean using injection with the following code:

```
public class AnotherBean {
    @Inject
    @SomeQualifierOne(HOURS)
    @SomeQualifierTwo
    SomeInterface bean;
}
```

And here it is programmatically:

```
SomeInterface bean =
    CDI.current()
        .select(
            SomeInterface.class,
            SomeQualifierOne.Literal.of(HOURS),
            SomeQualifierTwo.Literal.INSTANCE
        )
        .get();
```

Note that for the runtime resolution to work (meaning, for the right bean to be found), the attribute value *must* match exactly, and if there are multiple attributes, they must all match exactly. You can, however, supply extra information in attributes that is not used at all for the resolution. Such attributes then have to be annotated with the `@NonBinding` annotation. This extra information can subsequently be used, for instance, by producers in some dynamic and custom way.

Here is how you first extend your qualifier with the new nonbinding attribute:

```
@Qualifier
@Retention(RUNTIME)
@Target({ TYPE, METHOD, FIELD, PARAMETER })
@Documented
public @interface SomeQualifierOne {
```

```
    TimeUnit value() default DAYS;
    @Nonbinding String key() default "";
    public static final class Literal
    extends AnnotationLiteral<SomeQualifierOne>
    implements SomeQualifierOne {
        private static final long serialVersionUID = 1L;
        public static final Literal INSTANCE = of(DAYS, "");
        private final TimeUnit value;
        private final String key;
        public static Literal of(TimeUnit value, String key) {
           return new Literal(value, key);
        }
        private Literal(TimeUnit value, String key) {
            this.value = value;
            this.key = key;
        }
        public TimeUnit value() {
            return value;
        }
        public String key() {
            return key;
        }
    }
}
```

As you can see, we've added a new attribute called key, which is `@NonBinding`. This same attribute had to be added to the inner class `Literal` as well. With this qualifier in place, you can now define the following producer that makes use of the extra information:

```
public class SomeProducer {
    @Inject
    SomeCDIBean someCDIBean;

    @Produces
    @SomeQualifierOne(HOURS) @SomeQualifierTwo
    public SomeInterface produce(InjectionPoint injectionPoint) {
```

```
        String key =
            injectionPoint.getAnnotated()
                          .getAnnotation(SomeQualifierOne.class)
                          .key();
        if (key == ..) {
            // do something special with someCDIBean
        }
        return someCDIBean;
    }
}
```

For clarity, in the @SomeQualifierOne annotation, we have not provided an explicit value for the key attribute here. We did this to emphasize it's not being used for the resolution. If we had provided a value for key, though, it would simply have been ignored by the runtime (just as the default value, "", now is).

Getting a hold of this extra information does bring up a weak point of CDI; there's no universal way to get a reference to the annotations that were used in the resolution (you'll later see a similar issue when we discuss interceptors). What you can do, though, is have a so-called InjectionPoint instance injected. Recall from Chapter 2 that this is an example of method injection, for which you don't need to use any @Inject annotation; every extra parameter in the producer is provided by CDI here.

An InjectionPoint represents the point where the @Inject annotation is used and contains all metadata such as the name of the method or field in which injection took place, its annotations, and so on. In this situation, you're after the annotations, which are most easily obtained from the "javax.enterprise.inject.spi.Annotated," which represents the entity on which the annotations reside.

You might question that if you're using an InjectionPoint to obtain the annotations, how does that work when you do a programmatic lookup for a bean? There's no injection point in that case, of course. The somewhat disappointing answer is that it doesn't work with programmatic lookup. Retrieving a bean via injection and via lookup are thus not entirely symmetrical. It's a limitation, or perhaps an oversight, in the CDI API, which initially focused most on the declarative injection and less on the programmatic lookups.

When indeed using injection, though, things are straightforward, as shown here:

```
public class AnotherBean {
    @Inject
    @SomeQualifierOne(value = HOURS, key = "test")
    @SomeQualifierTwo
    SomeInterface bean;
}
```

SomeInterface.class, SomeQualifierOne.class, SomeQualifierTwo.class, and SomeQualifierOne.value == HOURS are all used for the resolution, while key == "test" is there as extra information.

Why Do You Actually Need Qualifiers?

Although you've seen various examples so far, a central question has remained unanswered; why do we have qualifiers in the first place, and why can't we just use extra interfaces to express the same thing?

To begin with, let's take a look at an example that's often used to explain qualifiers: the use of interfaces combined with the desire to have a specific implementation.

For instance, consider an interface for executing jobs shown here:

```
public interface JobExecutor {
    void executeJob(Job job);
}
```

Now suppose you have two implementations of this interface—one job executor that works in parallel and one that works sequentially.

```
public class ParallelJobExecutor implements JobExecutor {
    public void executeJob(Job job) {
        // ...
    }
}
public class SequentialJobExecutor implements JobExecutor {
    public void executeJob(Job job) {
        // ...
    }
}
```

Now suppose a bean wants to use the parallel or sequential executor (or maybe even both). How would that work? This is where qualifiers are often brought in, and you could have, for example, an @Parallel qualifier and an @Sequential qualifier.

```
@Parallel
public class ParallelJobExecutor implements JobExecutor {
    public void executeJob(Job job) {
        // ...
    }
}
@Sequential
public class SequentialJobExecutor implements JobExecutor {
    public void executeJob(Job job) {
        // ...
    }
}
```

A bean can now obtain a reference to any of these in the usual way, as shown here:

```
public class AnotherBean {
    @Inject
    @Parallel
    JobExecutor executor;
}
```

The big question here, though, is why didn't we just inject ParallelJobExecutor instead of @Parallel JobExecutor?

While we certainly could have done that in this simple case, in practice it might be the difference between a defined public API and an implementation jar. In that case, @Parallel, @Sequential and the interface JobExecutor would be types in the public API, but ParallelJobExecutor and SequentialJobExecutor types in the implementation jar.

In general applications should only depend on types from a public API, and not on private types from an implementation. Adhering to this general rule means you can easily switch the implementation jar to an another implementation, without any need to change the application's code.

This is illustrated in Figure 3-1.

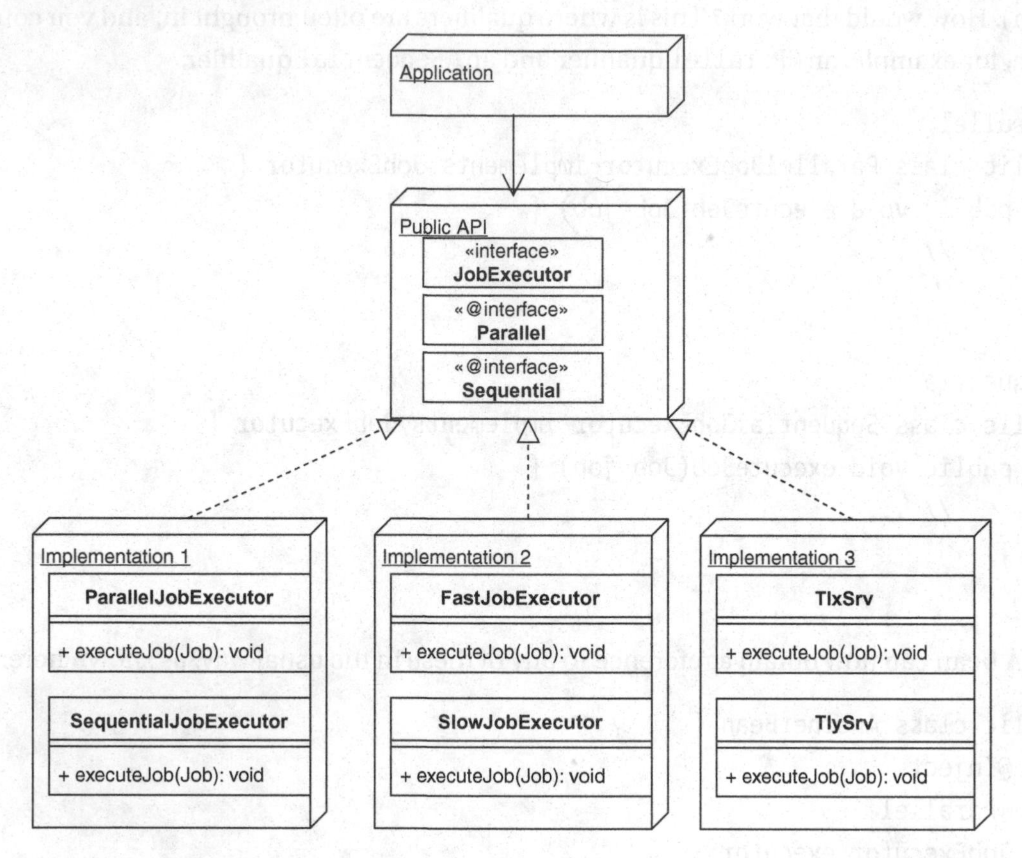

Figure 3-1. *Public API with multiple implementations*

Another question you could ask yourself is, why not simply use extra interfaces instead of those extra qualifiers? For example, the API referred to earlier could have defined two interfaces such as this:

```
public interface ParallelJobExecutor extends JobExecutor {
}
public interface SequentialJobExecutor extends JobExecutor {
}
```

Each (private) implementation could then implement one of these interfaces, and the injection point and lookup would even be simpler, as they'd only have to refer to that single interface and not to an interface plus qualifiers. In other words, it would then be as follows:

```
JobExecutor executor =
    CDI.current()
       .select(
           ParallelJobExecutor.class
       )
       .get();
```

Instead of this:

```
JobExecutor executor =
    CDI.current()
       .select(
           JobExecutor.class,
           Parallel.Literal.INSTANCE
       )
       .get();
```

While that would certainly get the job done, an interface with no methods (called a *marker interface*) is generally somewhat frowned upon. A full discussion is outside the scope of this book, but in short, the fact of the matter is that a marker interface mixes the purpose of an interface, which is declaring the operations that a class supports, with an implicit contract that is not expressed through such operations.

Another reason to favor qualifiers in this particular example is that as you saw earlier you can provide extra data in qualifiers. In the case of the `@Parallel` annotation, you could use this, for example, to configure some execution settings:

```
public class AnotherBean {
    @Inject
    @Parallel(minThreads=1, maxThreads=10)
    JobExecutor executor;
}
```

Without using qualifiers, and purely using types, the workaround for configuration type data would, for instance, be to inject a factory type, set your configuration parameters on that, and then obtain your bean from it. In some cases, the injected bean may support configuration settings.

Here's an example of using a factory:

```
public class AnotherBean {
    @Inject
    JobExecutorFactory executorFactory;
    JobExecutor executor;
    @PostConstruct
    public void init() {
        executor = executorFactory.create(1, 10);
    }
}
```

This example uses a bean that supports postcreate initialization:

```
public class AnotherBean {
    @Inject
    JobExecutor executor;
    @PostConstruct
    public void init() {
        executor.setMinThreads(1);
        executor.setMaxThreads(10);
    }
}
```

Arguably, using the configuration data in the qualifier is a cleaner approach and abstracts you from the producer using a factory behind the scenes or configuring the bean while or after creating it.

Qualifiers also have an edge when multiple ones are to be combined. For example, imagine that next to the mutually exclusive `@Parallel/@Sequential` you also had a `@Local/@Remote` annotation to execute jobs strictly local or on a remote server, and a `@Stateful/@Stateless` annotation for executors that persist or do not persist the job progress.

Using qualifiers, you could ask for a bean that's `@Parallel @Remote @Stateful` *or* `@Parallel @Local @Stateful`, and so on. Creating (marker) interfaces for every possible combination can become quite tedious and awkward looking.

```
interface ParallelLocalStatefulJobExecutor extends JobExecutor {}
interface ParallelRemoteStatefulJobExecutor extends JobExecutor {}
interface ParallelLocalStatelessJobExecutor extends JobExecutor {}
interface ParallelRemoteStatelessJobExecutor extends JobExecutor {}
interface SequentialLocalStatefulJobExecutor extends JobExecutor {}
interface SequentialRemoteStatefulJobExecutor extends JobExecutor {}
interface SequentialkLocalStatelessJobExecutor extends JobExecutor {}
interface SequentialRemoteStatelessJobExecutor extends JobExecutor {}
```

Note, though, that even though multiple qualifiers are possible in CDI, in practice one should not go over the top with this, as it still makes the code look dense and difficult to use. There is unfortunately no easy-to-use mechanism in CDI to combine multiple qualifiers into one. CDI does have a limited option to combine (mostly) interceptor binding annotations (called `StereoTypes`), which we'll look at later.

One situation where qualifiers are particularly useful, or even unavoidable, is when producers produce (general) types that they, or the library they are part of, don't own. For instance, JSF obviously doesn't own the Java SE `Map` type, so any producers it ships with that produce this type pretty much have to be qualified to avoid ambiguity with any other producers that produce this same type, even its own. For example, JSF allows you to inject the so-called header map and request parameter map, which contain HTTP request headers and HTTP request parameters, respectively. Both are a `Map` (specifically a `Map<String, String>`), so JSF uses qualifiers for these. The following is an example of this:

```
public class AnotherBean {
    @Inject
    @HeaderMap
    Map<String, String> headers;
    @Inject
    @RequestParameterMap
    Map<String, String> parameters;
}
```

Without the qualifiers used here, you'd get some kind of ambiguous resolution exception.

For library or component writers, one additional usage of qualifiers is to use "internal producers." In this case, a producer (or possibly even a bean) is qualified with a private qualifier (for instance, a qualifier with default access, i.e., "package private"). When using such a private qualifier, the risk that client code accidentally uses the internal producer is greatly reduced.

By Name

Besides a `typesafe` identifier formed by one of its types and zero or more qualifiers, beans in CDI have another optional and parallel identifier: a flat string-based name. This name is fully optional, and beans don't need to have it. Furthermore, the name can be totally independent of the main identifier and can be as simple or complex as it needs to be, though there are certain restrictions.

The flat name is not intended for regular usage but for integration with string-based environments and in Java EE specifically for integration with the platform's Expression Language (EL). Practically, most of the time you can read "bean name" as "EL name."

The previously mentioned restrictions on the name further strengthen the bean name being an Expression Language name, as the bean name has to be at least a valid Expression Language name. In addition, it can be a concatenation of valid Expression Language identifiers with a period in between. However, in practice such pseudo-namespaced names are discouraged as they can be quite confusing when used in actual expression language.

For bean classes and producer methods, a bean name is set by a perhaps somewhat peculiar special use of a built-in qualifier called `@Named`. This usage is peculiar since despite being an actual qualifier annotation, it's not really used as an actual qualifier. It mostly has a mechanism to set that bean name, which is specially recognized by the CDI runtime. In general, when designing an API, you try to avoid giving things implicit second or hard-coded semantics, but obviously this is not always easy, and the initial CDI designers probably had to compromise here in some way. In the metadata structure `javax.enterprise.inject.spi.Bean<T>`, via its super interface `BeanAttributes`, the bean name does have its own property, though, and that's simply the read-only "name" property (via the `getName()` getter method).

When using this "fake" qualifier, you can either provide the name yourself or have the name defaulted. When applied to bean classes, the default name is the simple class name with the first letter lowercase. For instance, for `com.example.Foo`, the default bean name when using `@Named` without an attribute is `foo`. When applied to a producer method, the default name is the name of the method verbatim, unless the method name starts with get in which case the bean name is the method name without get and the first letter lowercase. For instance, for public Foo getFoo(), the default name would be foo again, while for public Foo produceFoo() it would be produceFoo.

The following is an example of applying @Named to a bean class:

```
@Named
public class SomeCDIBean {
}
```

and to a producer method:

```
public class SomeProducer {
    @Produces
    @Named("someInterface")
    public SomeInterface produce() {
        // ...
    }
}
```

Beans can be retrieved via expression language using these names in contexts where the EL-to-CDI bean resolving is already defined to be active, such as in JSF and in EE Security. Beans can also be retrieved directly via the expression language API using the ELResolver that can be obtained from a BeanManager.

The following example demonstrates the latter:

```
public class SomeCDIBean {
    @Inject
    BeanManager beanManager;
    public void someMethod() {
        ELProcessor elProcessor = new ELProcessor();
        elProcessor.getELManager()
                   .addELResolver(
                       beanManager.getELResolver());
       SomeCDIBean someCDIBean =
           elProcessor.getValue(
               "someCDIBean", SomeCDIBean.class);
    }
}
```

Note that in this example SomeCDIBean.class that is passed in as the second argument of the getValue() method is not used for the resolution; you could have passed in Object.class as well. Instead, that argument is used for coercing (converting) the value that results from the evaluation of the expression (someCDIBean here) and the subsequent resolution by the CDI runtime.

Alternatively, you can use @Named as an actual qualifier for lookups, although this is greatly discouraged as bean names and @Named are not supposed to be used for this. Nevertheless, for completeness, the following is an example:

```
SomeCDIBean bean = (SomeCDIBean)
    CDI.current()
       .select(Object.class, NamedLiteral.of("someCDIBean"))
       .get();
```

Since @Named originates from AtInject (JSR 330) and literals are a CDI construct, the actual annotation could not be updated to comply with the CDI convention. Instead, CDI includes a separate literal for @Named called NamedLiteral, which is used in the previous code.

Identifying and Retrieving Multiple Beans

In CDI you are not limited to retrieving only a single bean instance; you can retrieve collections of beans as well. You can do this both when injecting and when retrieving beans programmatically.

Doing this programmatically has been shown already in a way, as it's just the return value of the select() method. Calling get() on this is what actually reduces it to a single bean (if it's possible to reduce it).

Before we show more detailed examples of how to retrieve collections of beans, it's important to be aware of two built-in qualifiers: @Default and @Any.

When a bean has no explicit real qualifiers added to it, it gets one default qualifier aptly named @Default. As soon as any explicit qualifiers are added to it (@Named doesn't count), the @Default qualifier is removed.

When you're just injecting a bean without any qualifiers at the injection point or when you're retrieving a bean programmatically and have no qualifiers in the select() method, the CDI runtime in actuality does a lookup for type + @Default.

Next to @Default, every bean always has the @Any qualifier in its set of qualifiers. Following the normal CDI conventions, this qualifier is never removed (as you see in a following chapter, you could remove it when you're creating or manipulating the bean metadata directly via the Bean<T> structures).

Furthermore, when composing the identity of a bean to retrieve it and supplying the qualifiers, the resolution rules actually say that all qualifiers you add to the identity should be present on the bean, but the other way around is not the case. Not all qualifiers that a bean has need to be matched in order for the resolution to succeed. Sometimes it may not seem that way, since if you're using an identifier of just "type" for a bean that has a qualifier, the resolution doesn't work; the CDI runtime won't find the bean. But remember, what you're *actually* asking for is a bean with identifier type + @Default, and @Default is removed whenever you add explicit qualifiers. So, initially, it may seem like using subsets of the identifier doesn't work, but in reality, it does. Consider, for instance, a bean with two qualifiers, @SomeQualifierOne and @SomeQualifierTwo. If you just compose an identifier of type + @SomeQualifierOne, you can use this to indeed retrieve this bean.

In a way, with the addition of the two special qualifiers @Default and @Any, you effectively have a small and simple "bean query language."

Let's now see some examples of what this looks like in practice. Consider the following three beans:

```
@SomeQualifierOne
@SomeQualifierTwo
public class SomeCDIBean implements SomeInterface {
}

@SomeQualifierOne
public class AnotherBean implements SomeInterface {
}

public class YetAnotherBean implements SomeInterface {
}
```

You can now retrieve both beans having the @SomeQualifierOne annotation via the following "query":

```
Instance<SomeInterface> someInterfaceBeans =
    CDI.current()
       .select(
           SomeInterface.class,
           SomeQualifierOne.Literal.INSTANCE)
```

The Instance container is a special CDI type that encapsulates the result of your initial query, and subsequently allows you to make subselects, and to test whether you have a single "resolvable" result (a single bean that would be eligible for injection). You subsequently obtain that result and various methods to iterate over the collection.

Given the previous query, asking it whether it's resolvable returns false, as you should have two beans.

```
boolean isResolvable = someInterfaceBeans.isResolvable();
```

You can do a subselection on the result by calling a select() method again, as follows:

```
Instance<SomeInterface> withTwoBeans =
    someInterfaceBeans.select(
        SomeQualifierTwo.Literal.INSTANCE);
```

From the result that you already have (which are the two beans defined earlier, which both have @SomeQualifierOne), you do a subselect asking it for all beans that have @SomeQualifierTwo. This will result in a new Instance, this time only referencing SomeCDIBean. Since you have only one bean now, the following will now return true:

```
boolean resolvable = withTwoBeans.isResolvable();
```

If you want to have a collection of all beans implementing SomeInterface, you can use the following query, making use of the special @Any qualifier:

```
Instance<SomeInterface> allInterfaceBeans =
    CDI.current()
       .select(
           SomeInterface.class,
           Any.Literal.INSTANCE);
```

The allInterfaceBeans instance will now refer to all three beans defined earlier.

Now suppose that from this collection you'd like to select the one bean without any qualifiers. As mentioned, this means that bean has the implicit @Default qualifier, so you can use that one for a subselect again.

```
Instance<SomeInterface> defaultBeans =
    allInterfaceBeans.select(
        Default.Literal.INSTANCE);
```

As mentioned, besides selecting from and testing the result, you can also iterate over it. An Instance is itself an Iterable, so you can use it directly in a for-each loop, but you can also get a general Stream from it. The following example shows how you can, for example, convert the result to a regular List using the Stream:

```
List<SomeInterface> someInterfaces =
    allInterfaceBeans.stream()
                     .collect(toList());
```

Retrieving multiple beans is not limited to the programmatic API in CDI. Using injection, you can achieve the same result. In that case, the injection point has to be of type Instance, with the requested type as a generic parameter and the requested qualifiers present as annotations. The following is an example of this:

```
public class MultipleInjectionBean {
    @Inject
    @SomeQualifierOne
    Instance<SomeInterface> someInterfaceBeans;
}
```

Retrieving Beans via Custom Method Parameter Injection

Besides injection into fields, CDI has the notion of injection into methods and into the constructor of a class. Just like with injection into fields, injection into methods is supported only when CDI is in control of calling such a method or constructor.

As you saw in Chapter 2, injection into a constructor is done by annotating the constructor itself with @Inject. Contrary to some other frameworks, it's not necessary (or even possible) to annotate the individual parameters with @Inject. It is of course possible to qualify the injection by annotating any of the parameters with one or more qualifier annotations.

Let's look at an example. Consider bean SomeBean.

```
@RequestScoped
@SomeQualifierOne
public class SomeBean {
   public String hi() {
       return "Hello from someBean";
   }
}
```

Consider the following constructor injection in AnotherBean:

```
@RequestScoped
public class AnotherBean {
   @Inject
   public AnotherBean (@SomeQualifierOne SomeBean someBean) {
       // ... do something with someBean
   }
}
```

It should be noted that constructor injection naturally happens *before* field injection takes place. Meaning, if AnotherBean also specifies injection into instance variables, these will still be null at the time the constructor is called.

Method injection is also allowed in producers. These are injectable by default so don't have to marked as such using @Inject. The following is an example:

```
@ApplicationScoped
public class ProducerBean {

   @Produces
   public String produce(@SomeQualifierOne SomeBean someBean) {
       return someBean.hi();
   }
}
```

Whenever that producer method is called (for instance, when @Inject String string appears in the code), CDI will provide (inject) an instance of SomeBean as an argument with the request qualifier.

Observer methods, being also methods that are called by CDI, are injectable as well. An observer method like a producer method is injectable by default, so the @Inject annotation is also not needed here. Consider the following example:

```
public class ListenerBean {
   public void listen(
       @Observes @SomeQualifierOne EventObject eventObject,
       SomeBean someBean) {
      // ...
   }
}
```

Such an observer method listens to an event thrown by code like the following:

```
beanManager.fireEvent(
    new EventObject(this),
    SomeQualifierOne.Literal.INSTANCE);
```

As you can see, no SomeBean instance is provided there. The observant reader may notice we used a qualifier on the event here. Like beans, events can be qualified as well in a fairly similar way, and although it's not often explained like this, an observer method lookup is fairly similar to a bean lookup, where "event type + qualifiers" forms the identifier of an observer method, and the CDI runtime subsequently looks up all observers that correspond to this identifier. Events are discussed in more detail in Chapter 5.

Practical Example: Implementing Custom Method Injection

This section is a larger hands-on example, demonstrating how to use the CDI programmatic API to develop your own custom features, and is intended to give some insight in how to develop a CDI utility library.

Readers who are mainly interested in learning about CDI itself for direct usage in applications may want to skip over this section or skim it.

Sometimes you may want to allow for injection in your own custom methods, in other words, methods that are not directly being called by CDI. CDI doesn't have direct support for this, but using the CDI APIs explained in the previous sections of this chapter, you can implement something like that yourself. The general approach is to loop over the formal parameters of a Method, which is a Java SE class reflectively representing a Java method and for each parameter recording the type and optionally all the qualifier annotations. For each such recorded type and qualifier annotation, CDI.current().select(...) can then be used to obtain a bean and pass that into the method being called, demonstrating a particular practical use case for the programmatic API explained earlier.

The following code is an example of this:

```
@SuppressWarnings("unchecked")
public <T> T callMethod(
    BeanManager beanManager,
    Object bean, Method method, Map<Integer, Object> providedValues) {
    List<Object> parameterValues = new ArrayList<>();
    Parameter[] methodParameters = method.getParameters();
    for (int i=0; i < methodParameters.length ; i++) {
        if (providedValues.containsKey(i)) {
            parameterValues.add(providedValues.get(i));
        } else {
            Annotation[] qualifiers =
                stream(methodParameters[i].getAnnotations())
                  .filter(
                      e -> beanManager.isQualifier(e.annotationType()))
                  .collect(toList())
                  .toArray(new Annotation[0]);
            parameterValues.add(
                CDI.current()
                  .select(
                      methodParameters[i].getType(),
                      qualifiers)
                  .get()
            );
        }
    }
    try {
        return (T)
            method.invoke(bean, parameterValues.toArray());
```

```
        } catch (
            IllegalAccessException |
            IllegalArgumentException |
            InvocationTargetException e) {
            throw new RuntimeException(e);
        }
    }
```

The example shown here uses a Map with positional parameters so the call site can provide its own parameters as well. The rest will then be injected by CDI. The isQualifier method of the beanManager is used here to determine whether a given annotation is a qualifier.

For convenience you can put the method presented earlier in a bean like the following:

```
@ApplicationScoped
public class MethodParamInjector {
    @Inject
    private BeanManager beanManager;

    public <T> T callMethod(Object bean, Method method) {
        return callMethod(beanManager, bean, method, emptyMap());
    }
    public <T> T callMethod(
        Object bean, Method method,
        Map<Integer, Object> providedValues) {
        return callMethod(
            beanManager, bean, method, providedValues);
    }

    @SuppressWarnings("unchecked")
    public <T> T callMethod(BeanManager beanManager,
        Object bean, Method method,
        Map<Integer, Object> providedValues) { … }
}
```

Now consider the following version of SomeBean:

```
@RequestScoped
public class SomeBean {
   public String getHello(HttpServletRequest request) {
        return
            "Hello from foo in request " +
            request.getRequestURI();
   }
}
```

You can now call the getHello() method via the parameter injector in the following way:

```
@Inject
private SomeBean someBean;
@Inject
private MethodParamInjector methodParamInjector;
public String getHello() throws Throwable {
   return methodParamInjector.callMethod(
       someBean,
       someBean.getClass()
              .getMethod(
                 "getHello",
                 HttpServletRequest.class));
}
```

Notice that the method name is in a String. While this is typical, it's not entirely ideal. The method name may be misspelled, and the compiler of course won't catch it. Or the method itself may be refactored, causing the name here to get out of sync. What you'd really need here is a "method literal" (a literal representing a method such as SomeBean.class represents a class), but unfortunately Java doesn't support them.

Java does support "method references," though. These aren't so much a representation of a method but more a way to call a certain method in combination with an instance of the class to which that method belongs (for nonstatic methods). Via a trick you can recover the actual method to which a method reference resolves. This trick involves using an InvocationHandler, which is a handler that's called when a method on a proxy is to be invoked. This handler can store the Method instance that's about to be invoked and thus gives you access to an actual representation of the method. Such a handler is shown here:

```
class InterceptingMethodHandler implements InvocationHandler {

      private Method interceptedMethod;
      @Override
      public Object invoke(
         Object proxy, Method method, Object[] args)
         throws Throwable {
          interceptedMethod = method;
          return null;
      }
      Method getInterceptedMethod() {
          return interceptedMethod;
      }
}
```

The next step is to generate a dynamic proxy for the bean class. This proxy will be of the same type as the original bean class, which means it can be passed into the method reference, and the method reference will try to call the intended method on it.

We'll be using the well-known ByteBuddy library to generate this dynamic proxy. The JDK does have a dynamic proxy facility itself, but it's only capable of generating proxies for interfaces, making it too limited for this use case.

The proxy generating method is shown here:

```
private static <T> T createProxy(
   Class<T> beanClass, InvocationHandler invocationHandler,
   int arguments) {
      try {
          return new ByteBuddy()
              .subclass(beanClass, DEFAULT_CONSTRUCTOR)
              .method(
                   isMethod()
                  .and(takesArguments(arguments))
                  .and(not(isDeclaredBy(Object.class))))
```

```
                .intercept(InvocationHandlerAdapter.of(invocationHandler))
                .make()
                .load(MethodParamInjector.class.getClassLoader())
                .getLoaded()
                .newInstance();
        } catch (
            IllegalAccessError |
            InstantiationException |
            IllegalAccessException e){
            throw new RuntimeException(e);
        }
    }
```

Having these two key components in place, we'll define a small glue method that instantiates the handler and the proxy and delegates the actual call on the proxy to a consumer.

```
public static <T> Method findMethod(
    Class<T> beanClass, int arguments, Consumer<T> consumer) {
    InterceptingMethodHandler interceptingMethodHandler =
        new InterceptingMethodHandler();
    consumer.accept(
        createProxy(
            beanClass, interceptingMethodHandler, arguments));
   return interceptingMethodHandler.getInterceptedMethod();
}
```

The final step is to write the method that accepts a method reference and does a call on it in such a way that the proxy ends up being invoked. This, however, can't be a single method, as a method reference has to be assigned to a "matching" functional interface. Specifically, this means you need to have functional interfaces covering a wide range of possible bean methods and for each such functional interface a matching method that accepts it. These possible bean methods are broadly divided into two sets: those that have a return value and those that don't. For each of them, you then need variants accepting zero method arguments, one method argument, two method arguments, and so on.

Here are three examples of the variant with a return value:

```
@FunctionalInterface
public interface Return0Arg<T, R> {
    R invoke(T bean);
}

@FunctionalInterface
public interface Return1Arg<T, R, W> {
    R invoke(T bean, W arg0);
}

@FunctionalInterface
public interface Return2Arg<T, R, W, X> {
    R invoke(T bean, W arg0, X arg1);
}
```

Likewise, you need three methods matching these:

```
public static <T> Method findMethod(
     Class<T> beanClass, Return0Arg<T, ?> return1arg) {
        return findMethod(
            beanClass, 0,
            proxy -> return1arg.invoke(proxy));
}

public static <T> Method findMethod(
    Class<T> beanClass, Return1Arg<T, ?, ?> return1arg) {
        return findMethod(
            beanClass, 1,
            proxy -> return1arg.invoke(proxy, null));
}

public static <T> Method findMethod(
    Class<T> beanClass, Return2Arg<T, ?, ?, ?> return1arg) {
        return findMethod(
            beanClass, 2,
            proxy -> return1arg.invoke(proxy, null, null));
}
```

Note that in an actual library you would likely use code generation to create a large enough number of variants.

With the previous code in place, you can now replace the getHello() method shown previously with the following variant:

```
public String getHello() {
    Return1Arg<SomeBean, String, HttpServletRequest> helloReference =
        SomeBean::getHello;
   return methodParamInjector.callMethod(
       someBean,
       findMethod(
           SomeBean.class, helloReference));
}
```

It's important to note that you can't directly pass SomeBean::getHello into findMethod as the wildcards are not exact enough to fully determine which actual method SomeBean::getHello is referencing. Because of overloads, there can be many variants, and Java uses the left-side type to determine which one you want. The separate assignment can be omitted, though, but then a cast is needed, which is arguably not making the code any prettier.

CHAPTER 4

Scopes and Contexts

Because the CDI container is responsible for the creation and destruction of beans in a CDI-enabled application, it essentially is responsible for the lifecycle of the beans it manages. This means the container should be made aware when it is safe to create and destroy each bean. If a bean is created too late, code depending on that bean may fail. If the bean is destroyed too late, memory may become clogged up with old, obsolete objects, leading to longer garbage collection pauses and eventually out-of-memory errors. Another issue with the lifecycle management of a bean is the sharing of bean instances between different beans. For example, it could be too costly to create multiple instances of a certain bean. A bean could also be mutable, and any changes should be directly visible to all other beans that depend on that bean. If a bean contains or manages any privacy-sensitive data, an application may also want to limit the visibility of this bean to other beans.

Consider the example of an application that processes incoming HTTP requests. You may want to pass an HTTP request object, containing all the data from the incoming request, to each method that performs some part of the request processing. Without dependency injection, the only way to do this is to pass the request object as a method argument to each method. Every method in the call chain processing this request needs to pass this request object to the next method processing the request, even if it's not relevant to the processor. With dependency injection, it becomes possible to avoid passing the request object around and to directly inject it in any bean that needs access instead. When the request object is injected instead of passed around, the CDI container needs to be aware that once the request completes, the bean can be destroyed. If this doesn't happen, the request objects and all the data (indirectly) from the request objects keep piling up until the JVM runs out of memory. Depending on the HTTP application, the HTTP request object may also contain user-specific information such as names, addresses, or credit card details. It would be quite bad if a bean dealing with one HTTP request were able to see the contents of a request from a different user. Figure 4-1 illustrates what would happen if two users performed a request at a similar time.

J. Beernink and A. Tijms, *Pro CDI 2 in Java EE 8*, https://doi.org/10.1007/978-1-4842-4363-3_4

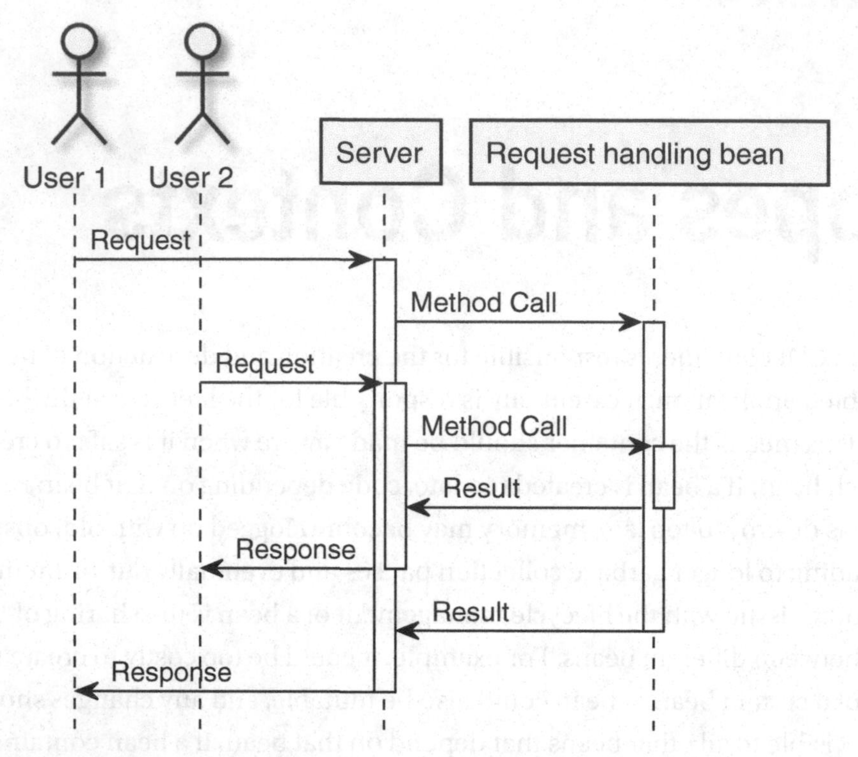

***Figure 4-1.** Concurrent user requests*

In this figure, you have only a single instance of the request handling bean to handle all requests. When the first user performs a request, a call is made to the request handling bean. While the request from the first user is still being processed, a second request from another user is performed. The server once again calls the same instance of the request handling bean to handle this new request. If you were to directly inject the request object into the request handling bean, the thread handling the first user's request should not be able to see data from the second user's request, and vice versa. Even if you have multiple instances of the request handling bean, you need to be sure that you have the data from the current request visible only in the thread that handles that request.

To solve this issue, the CDI specification allows beans to have *scopes*. You can define an explicit scope for each bean. When a scope is defined for a bean, the lifecycle of that bean is tied to an instance of that scope. *Contexts* are the second part of the solution. You can use contexts to create and destroy scopes; this is one of the most important parts of the CDI specification (the *C* in CDI stands for "contexts"). Contexts are responsible for managing scope instances. They are responsible for both the creation and destruction of scope instances and for the creation and destruction of bean instances that are tied to these scope instances.

Let's apply this to the previous HTTP request handling example. The request object could be tied to an instance of a request-specific scope. When an HTTP request is received, the thread that is handling the request is assigned a new instance of the request-specific scope by the context corresponding to that scope. The request object is tied to this instance of the request-specific scope so that all other beans that are invoked in the same thread can inject the instance of the request object. Once the handling of the request is complete, the context deactivates and destroys the request-specific scope. Once a new request comes in, this cycle is repeated with a new instance of the request-specific scope. As the request-specific scope here is destroyed at the end of handling the request, it is no longer possible to inject or otherwise obtain the request object. This prevents details from one request from being accidentally leaked to the next request that is handled by the same thread. Other threads will receive a different instance of the request-specific scope, preventing concurrent requests from observing details from other requests that are happening at the same time.

In this chapter, we'll cover each of the built-in scopes and how and when they can be used. We'll also cover how to create a custom scope, utilizing most of the features available to scopes. Finally, we'll cover how a custom scope can override or redefine the lifecycle of any of the built-in scopes.

Using Scopes

For a bean instance to be tied to a scope, there first must be a way to declare the scope of a bean. CDI achieves this through the use of scope annotations. Each scope is associated with a single scope annotation, which usually is named in such a way that it describes the scope. For example, a scope that is tied to a specific thread would most likely have an `@ThreadScoped` annotation. In most cases, the class of the bean itself must be annotated with the scope annotation. However, if the bean is produced by a producer, the scope annotation must be applied to the producer method instead.

When a bean is scoped, there is no limit to where it is injected, as long as an instance of the corresponding scope is active when the injected bean is called. A bean with a certain scope can be injected into other beans that have a much wider scope. For example, a bean that is scoped to a given thread can be injected into a bean that is scoped to the entire application. Multiple threads accessing this application-scoped bean will see different instances of the thread-scoped bean, even if the thread-scoped bean is injected into a field of the application-scoped bean. CDI achieves this by not injecting scoped beans directly but by injecting a proxy instance instead. Whenever a method is called on this injected proxy, it performs a lookup for the actual bean instance for the currently active scope. If that bean does not exist, one is created at that time. The bean is essentially being resolved at invocation time instead of at injection time. However, if the corresponding scope is not active, any method call to the proxy will fail. As the scope is not active, there is no bean instance that the method call will be delegated to, and the proxy will throw an `IllegalStateException` instead.

The use of a proxy has a number of consequences for any scoped bean. The first is that scoped beans are usually created lazily. Only when the first method call is performed to a bean or when an event is dispatched to the bean will it be created. The benefit of this is that the scope of the bean does not need to be active when the proxy is being injected into another bean when the corresponding scope is not yet active. Another consequence of the use of a proxy is that the proxy only implements the type that is defined at the injection point. Say you have an interface A and a class B that implements this interface. When you inject B into a field of the interface type A, the injected proxy will only implement interface A but will not extend class B. Any methods that are declared on B are unavailable, and any attempt to cast the proxy to type B will fail.

The type being proxied must also be either an interface or a nonfinal class where all public methods are nonfinal. This is because if the proxied type is a class, the proxy must extend this class. Any fields and methods of the original type are inherited, and all methods must be overridden to allow the delegation to the actual type to happen. If the methods are final, the proxy cannot delegate the method calls to the actual bean as they would be executed on the proxy instance instead. This has another consequence that the proxied type should not have any publicly accessible fields as they must be encapsulated instead. Another similar issue is that the scoped type should not have any publicly accessible fields. Reading from and writing to public fields cannot be delegated to the actual bean instance and so the values would be read from or written to the proxy instance. The fields most likely only contain a default value, and the actual bean instance would not be able to read any modified values. Instead, it is practically a requirement to encapsulate any fields using getter and setter methods.

Because of these restrictions, CDI containers will fail the deployment of the application and refuse to launch upon encountering a bean with an explicitly declared scope when that bean either is a final class or has any final methods. The only exception to this is if that bean implements any interfaces and is injected only as the type of that interface. For example, if you have a final class Foo that implements FooInterface, there is no problem as long as all the applicable injection points use FooInterface instead of Foo. Remember that the injected proxy will only be of type FooInterface, not of type Foo. This allows the container to still intercept methods to a bean with a final class or any final methods.

Scoped beans can also be destroyed, just like any other bean. However, a scoped bean could theoretically be destroyed while the corresponding scope is still active. If this happens, any further method calls on a reference to the bean will trigger a new instance to be created. For example, if in the request scope example the request object is destroyed, any further calls to the request object during that scope will trigger a new request object to be created. One example where this could be useful is when a bean instance throws an exception that may have left the instance in a corrupt state. In this case, it might be better to destroy the bean instance and continue using a new instance instead of using the "corrupted" instance, which may lead to any kind of bug.

To be able to apply a scope, a scope type must be created. The scope type is an annotation that usually has a name that describes the scope and ends in Scoped. For example, for the request-specific scope mentioned earlier, there would be a corresponding @RequestScoped annotation. Declaring a scope for a bean is as simple as declaring the annotation on the bean, depending on how the bean is created.

Let's say you have a number of beans that you would like to keep scoped to a single thread. To do this, a special thread scope is available with a corresponding @ThreadScoped annotation. This thread scope makes beans visible to only a single thread, and any beans in this scope are destroyed once the thread stops executing. Let's say the first bean you have is defined in a bean class named Bar. To declare instances of Bar as having the thread scope, you only have to declare the @ThreadScoped on your Bar class.

```
@ThreadScoped
public class Bar {

    // Bar implemented here
}
```

In this application, you also want to have beans of type Bar2. However, Bar2 was not designed for use with CDI and does not have a default constructor, and any constructor parameters cannot be injected directly. In this situation, you could use a producer method to create the Bar2 instance for injection. You can make the Bar2 instance produced by this method thread-scoped by annotating the producer method with @ThreadScoped.

```
@Produces
@ThreadScoped
public static Bar2 createBar2() {
    return new Bar2("Constructor argument");
}
```

Lastly, there is a Bar3 type that has the same problem as Bar2. If you have another thread-scoped Foo class that creates and uses an instance of Bar3 internally, you don't have to create a producer method for the Bar3 method. By applying the @Produces and @ThreadScoped annotations directly to the field, the field becomes a producer field, which is directly available for injection by the CDI container. When using this approach, it is important that the bean that creates Bar3 does so before any other bean in the same scope tries to use an injected Bar3 reference. If the Bar3 instance is not created before then, this may result in errors as the bean instance is not yet available.

```
@Produces
@ThreadScoped
private Bar3 bar3;
```

Note A bean must have only a single scope defined on it. It is illegal for beans to have multiple scope annotations applied to them. A CDI container must fail the deployment if a bean with two declared scopes is encountered. However, it is possible for different producer methods with the same return type to have a different scope, as long as each method has a single scope and a unique qualifier.

Built-in Scopes

In theory it would be possible for every CDI-based application to use only custom scopes. However, this would lead to a waste of engineering resources, as many applications have similar requirements and would need similar scopes. Only allowing custom scopes would also make the work for CDI containers and other Java EE components harder. If all scopes are custom, then containers and CDI components would not be able to depend on an application using a certain scope. As a result, CDI specifies a number of scopes that would be common to most (web) applications and must be made available by every CDI container. These scopes have specific predefined lifecycles so that applications can be easily switched from one CDI container to another. The following scopes are defined by CDI:

- The application scope
- The session scope
- The conversation scope
- The request scope
- The dependent scope

Application Scope

The first predefined scope is the application scope, which can be applied using the `@ApplicationScoped` annotation. The application scope is linked to the lifecycle of the application. This means that any application-scoped bean is essentially a singleton during the life of an application, unless it is explicitly destroyed, at which point a new instance may be created. As the name implies, the application scope and any corresponding application-scoped beans will be destroyed at the end of the lifecycle of the application itself. Figure 4-2 shows the typical application scope lifecycle in a server.

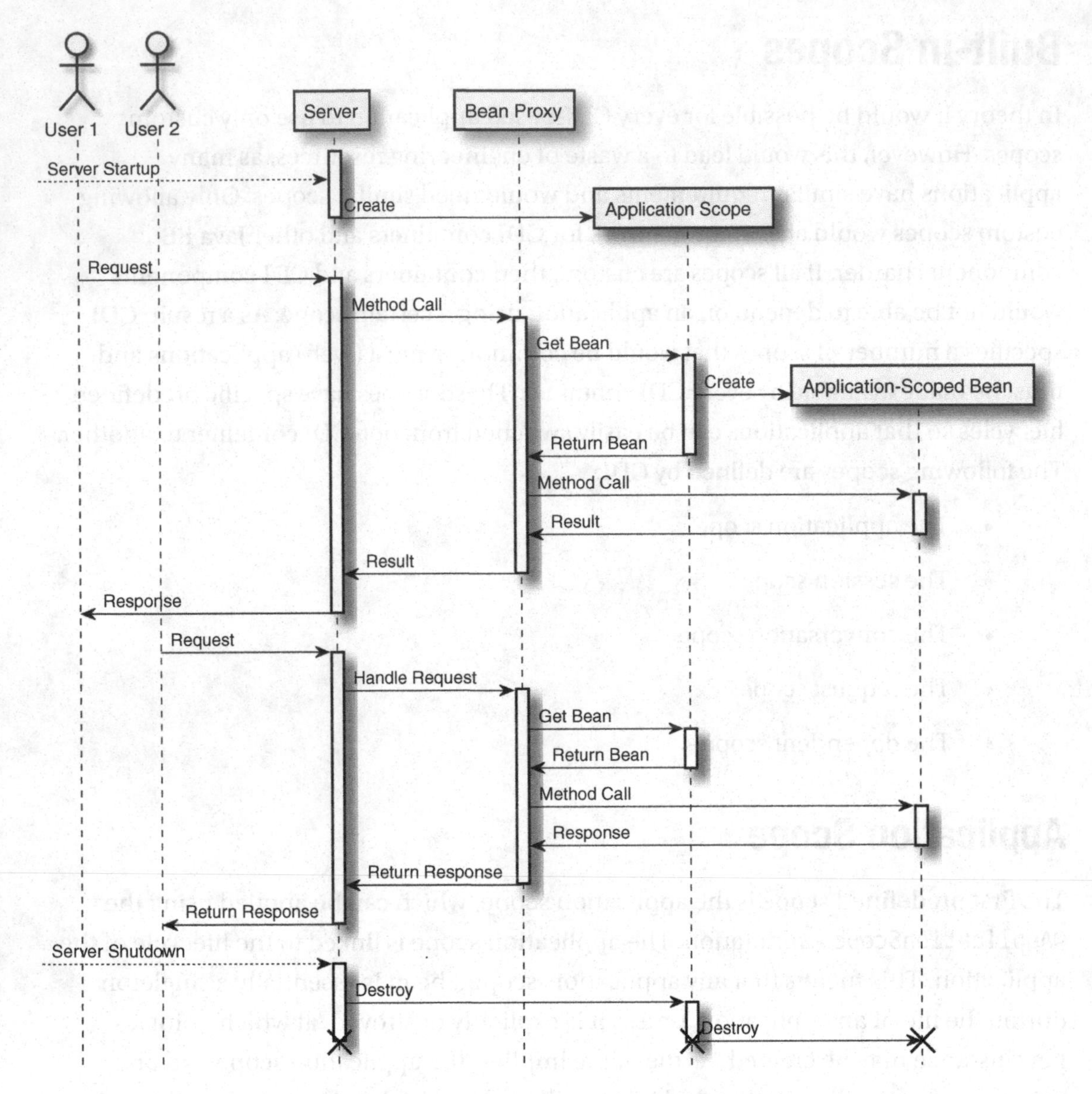

***Figure 4-2.** Typical application scope lifecycle in a server*

The application scope is created at server startup, but the application-scoped beans will typically not be created until the first time they are used. If you had an application-scoped bean that handles individual user requests, the bean would be created only the first time a call was made to one of the methods on the bean's proxy. Each individual request would be handled by the same bean, regardless of the user performing the request, even if the requests go through different proxy instances. When the server is shut down, the application scope and all beans belonging to it are destroyed.

Session Scope

The session scope is tied to a single user session and can be applied using the @SessionScoped annotation. The session scope can be used to keep bean instances restricted to a single user. For example, a web application may want to display the username of the current user in a corner of the screen. The username could be maintained by an @SessionScoped bean, which would ensure that the username was not accidentally displayed to a different user. The session scope also does not require a user to be logged in, so it's also suitable, for example, to tracking the items a non-logged-in user placed in their shopping cart in a web shop. In Java EE, the session scope is tied to a single HTTP session and can span multiple requests. The session scope is active during each call to the `service()` method, during the `doFilter()` method of any servlet filter, and during any call to an `HttpSessionListener`, `AsyncListener`, or `ServletRequestListener`.

In Java EE, when an HTTP session times out, the session scope is automatically destroyed. This will happen only after all `HttpSessionListeners` for that session have been destroyed so that the session scope is still available to these listeners. The session scope is also destroyed at the end of the processing of any request in which the session was invalidated. In that case, the session scope will also be destroyed only after all the `ServletRequestListeners` have been called. Figure 4-3 shows an example of the session scope lifecycle.

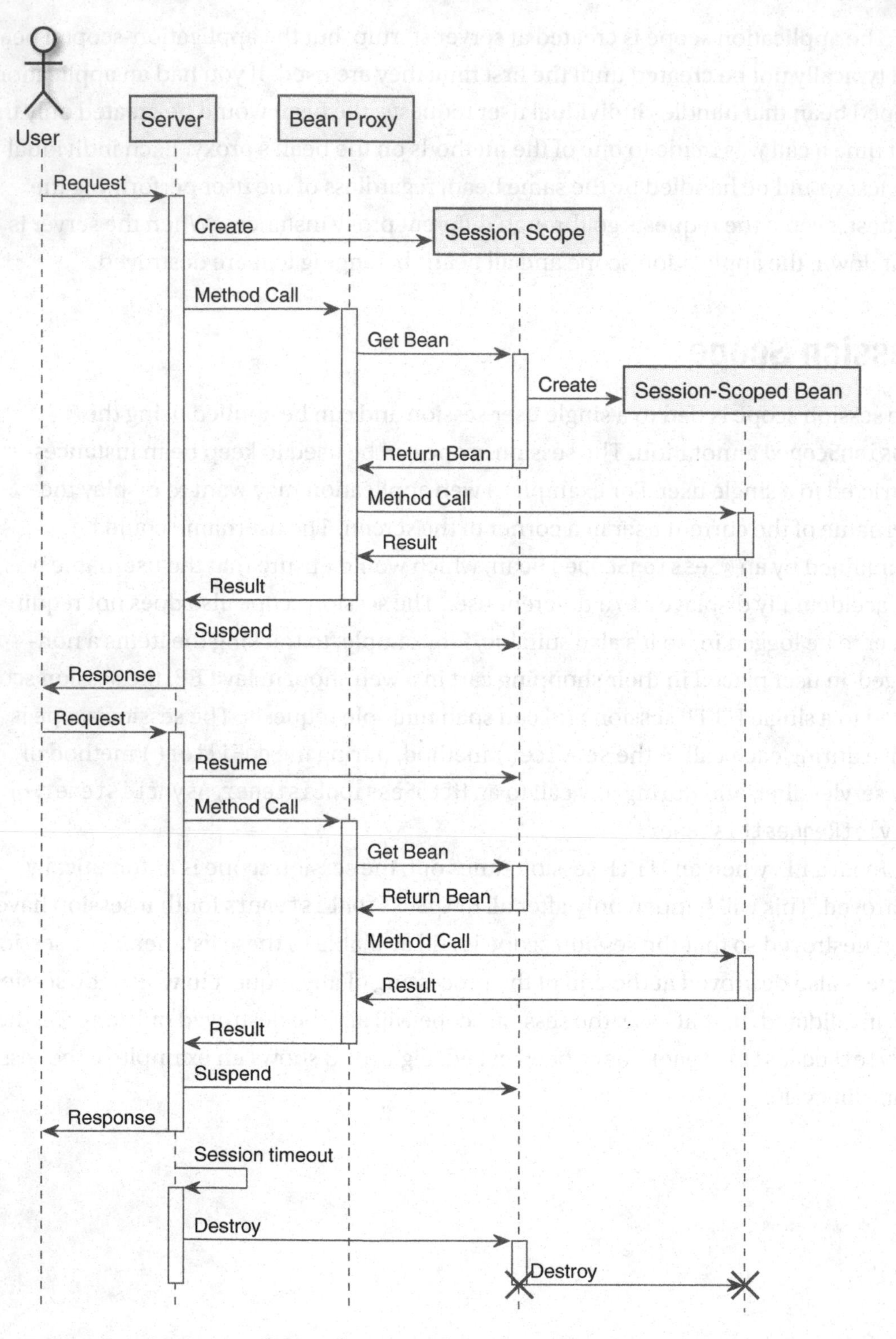

***Figure 4-3.** Session scope lifecycle example*

As soon as the request ends, the scope is suspended and then resumed again on the next request. While the scope is active, all beans in that scope remain active. After the session times out, the session scope and all its beans are actively destroyed.

Request Scope

CDI also defines a request scope, which can be applied using the `@RequestScoped` annotation. The request scope is generally active during any external user request. In Java EE, the request scope is supported by servlets, web services, and EJBs. For web application, the request scope is active during any call to `service()` on a servlet or `doFilter()` on a servlet filter. Any web services, whether it is a JAX-WS or JAX-RS, will have a request scope active during the handling of a single web service invocation. For EJBs, any remote EJB invocation will cause the request scope to be activated during the handling of that invocation by the EJB. At the end of each of these types of requests, the request scope, and all the beans belonging to that scope, will be destroyed.

The request scope will also be active in a number of other situations, even when the current thread is not processing an incoming request. One example of this is during the call to a bean's `@PostConstruct` method. If no existing request scope is active at that time, a new request scope is activated for the duration of the call to the `@PostConstruct` method. After the method has completed, that request scope is then destroyed, along with all the beans in that scope. A new request scope is also created for each time an event is dispatched to an asynchronous observer method and destroyed after the call to the observer method is completed. Figure 4-4 shows a typical request scope lifecycle.

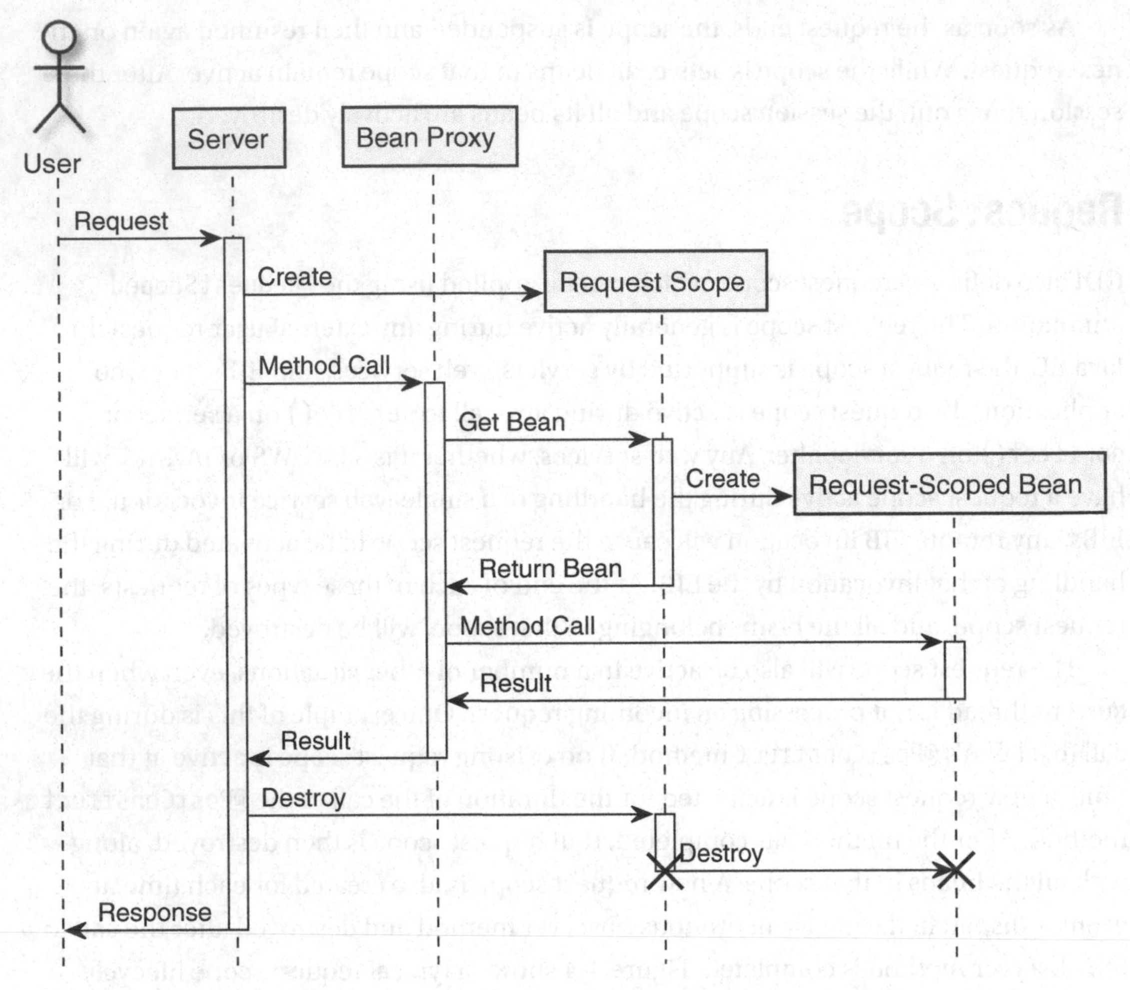

Figure 4-4. *Typical request scope lifecycle*

At the start of handling each request, a new request scope is created and will remain active while the request is being handled. When the request handling completes and the response is returned to the user, the request scope and all the beans belonging to that scope are destroyed.

The request scope can also be created and destroyed by application code. Consider an application that doesn't rely on servlets, any standardized web services, or remote EJBs to handle incoming requests. For example, an application could receive incoming requests through an alternative communication channel like e-mail. An application may also require a request scope to temporarily be activated during processing on a background thread, when the request scope would normally not be active. For these use cases, the CDI specification provides a special API to manage the request scope.

CDI provides a built-in bean named RequestScopeController. Instances of this type can be injected into any other bean. The RequestScopeController class defines two methods, activate and deactivate. Calling the activate() method will trigger a new request scope to be started, if one is not already active. This method will also return a Boolean to indicate whether a new request scope was started. Conversely, the deactivate() method will deactivate any request scope started by the same instance of the RequestScopeController. This means the activate() method is called when a request scope is already active, and calling the deactivate() method will do nothing, as long as the request scope is still active. If, however, the request scope is no longer active, the deactivate() method will throw a ContextNotActiveException instead.

Say you have a request-scoped bean you want to call a method on but the request scope is not currently active. You can call the activate() method to activate the request scope and then perform the method call to the request-scoped bean in a try block. In the corresponding finally block, you call the deactivate() method to deactivate and destroy the request scope. You use a finally block here so that if the method call throws an exception, the request scope is always cleanly deactivated. Note that you call the deactivate() method even if the activate() method returned false. If a scope is already active when you call activate(), the deactivate() call will have no effect.

```
public class ProgrammaticRequestScopeActivation {

    private static final Logger logger = Logger.getLogger("foo.logger");

    @Inject
    private MyRequestScopedBean myRequestScopedBean;

    @Inject
    private RequestContextController requestContextController;

    public void doSomethingWithRequestScope() {
        boolean activated = requestContextController.activate();

        if (activated) {
            logger.info("New request scope activated");
        }
```

```
        try {
            myRequestScopedBean.doSomething();
        }
        finally {
            requestContextController.deactivate();
        }
    }
}
```

In addition to the RequestScopeController, CDI offers an interceptor that activates the request scope during a method call. Interceptors will be covered in more detail in Chapter 6, but for now it's enough to know that applying an annotation corresponding to an interceptor to a method or bean will activate the interceptor for that method or all methods on that bean. The annotation to use to have the request scope activated during a method call is @ActivateRequestContext. When a method that this interceptor has been applied to is called, the interceptor will activate the request scope just before the actual method is called. Once the method call completes, the interceptor will deactivate the request scope. Like the RequestScopeController, if a request scope is already active, the interceptor will effectively do nothing. Using the @ActivateRequestContextannotation, you can drastically simplify the previous example.

```
public class InterceptorRequestScopeActivation {

    @Inject
    private MyRequestScopedBean myRequestScopedBean;

    @ActivateRequestContext
    public void doSomethingWithRequestScope() {
        myRequestScopedBean.doSomething();
    }
}
```

Conversation Scope

The next scope is the conversation scope, which can be applied using the `@ConversationScoped` annotation. The conversation scope is most suited for cases where interactions span a number of requests. Unlike the request scope, the conversation scope has no predefined lifecycle by itself. Instead, the application can exert some influence into when a new conversation context is created and when it is destroyed. As the conversation scope covers multiple requests, it is great for implementing wizards or other sorts of conversations between the user and the system. A web shop, for example, may have a wizard-like set of steps when the customer decides to place this order. This wizard-like interface would take the customer's address, shipment preferences, and payment details before allowing the customer to finally confirm the order. The web shop may choose to keep this information only if the customer decides to confirm the order. A conversation-scoped bean would be a good option to temporarily store this information. The conversation scope could be started as soon as the customer starts the order process and be destroyed once the customer finalizes the order and the order has been saved.

There are two types of conversation scope: the long-running conversation scope, spanning multiple subsequent requests, and the transient conversation scope. A transient conversation scope lasts for only a single request; the scope is destroyed at the same time the request scope is destroyed. In Java EE, a transient conversation scope is active by default during the processing of each servlet request and will last only for the duration of a single request. However, the transient conversation scope can be transformed into a long-running conversation scope. Figure 4-5 shows a typical conversation scope lifecycle.

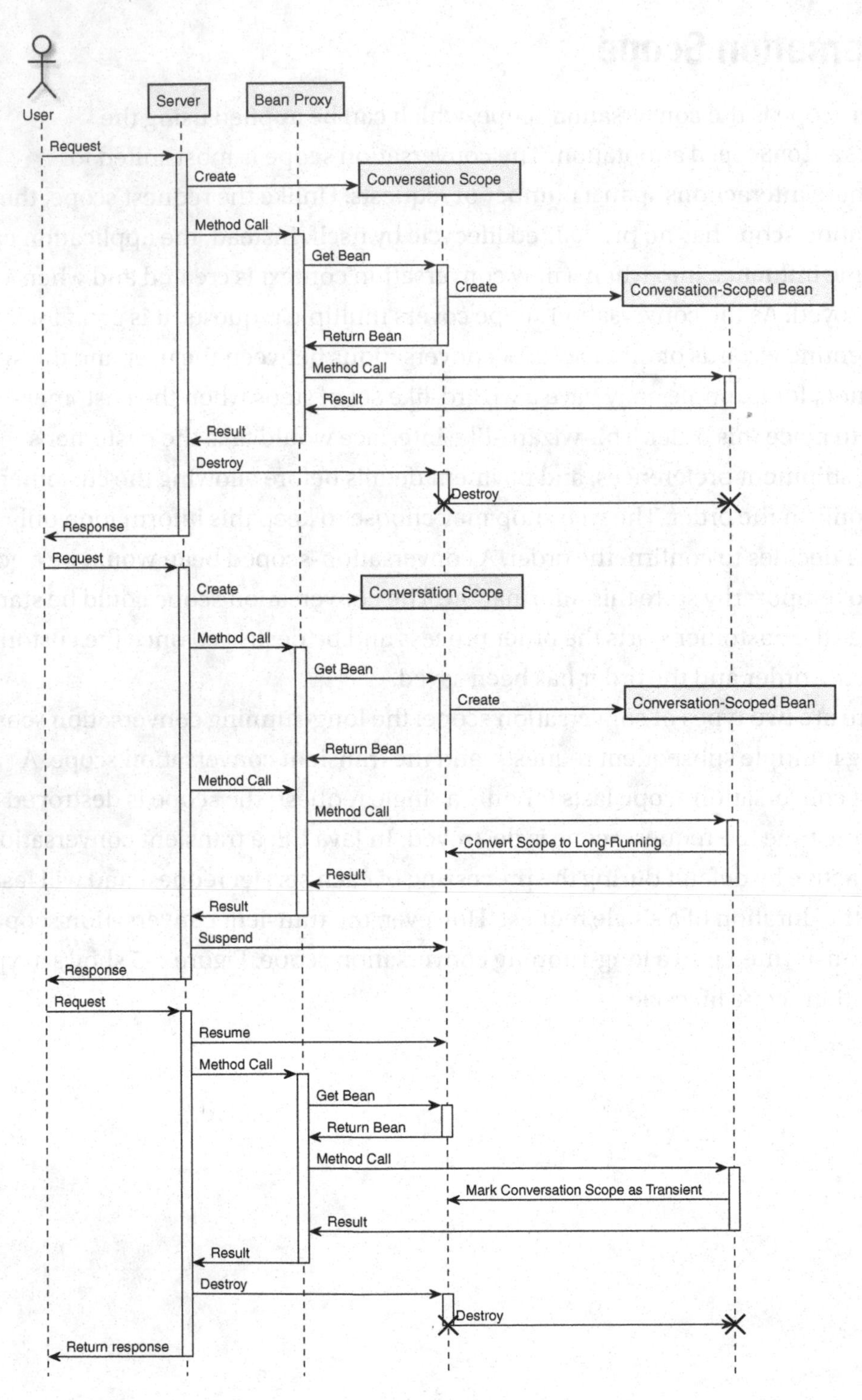

***Figure 4-5.** A typical conversation scope lifecycle*

By default, the conversation scope will act in the same way as the request scope and will be destroyed at the end of the request. However, if the conversation scope is converted to a long-running scope, it will be automatically resumed on the next request. When the conversation ends, the conversation scope is converted back to a transient conversation scope and deleted at the end of the request.

To manage the conversation scope, CDI provides a request-scoped bean of type `javax.enterprise.context.Conversation`. This `Conversation` bean offers the following methods:

- `void begin()`
- `void begin(String id)`
- `void end()`
- `String getId()`
- `long getTimeout()`
- `boolean isTransient()`
- `void setTimeout(long milliseconds)`

The `begin()` and `begin(String id)` methods transform a transient conversation scope into a long-running conversation scope. After calling one of these methods, the same conversation scope will be active on every subsequent request, until the conversation scope is ended. The `begin()` method without a parameter will cause the container to generate a unique ID for the conversation scope. This ID can then be retrieved using the `getID()` method, which will return the ID the container generated. In some cases, the application may want to assign an ID to the conversation scope instead; for example, the ID could be set to the generated ID for the user's shopping cart in a web shop. The application can specify the ID for the long-running conversation scope by calling `begin(String id)` with the generated ID as a parameter instead. Keep in mind that when the application generates an ID, that it still must be unique over all conversations in the running application. If the application already generates a unique number for the conversation, then this would be a good choice. In a web shop, an order number would be a good example of a good ID for a conversation scope as the order number will be unique to a specific order. Also note that both begin methods can be called only when a transient conversation scope is active; if they are called when no conversation scope is active or when a long-running conversation scope is active, an `IllegalStateException` will be thrown.

When the conversation scope has been transformed in a long-running conversation scope, some way of identifying which existing conversation scope is required is needed for subsequent requests. A user of a web site may be going through different wizards on a web site on separate tabs. Even though they would both be for the same user, each of these wizards will require a separate conversation scope. This could lead to bugs if the user suddenly switched from one active conversation scope to another in a single wizard. For web applications, the exact conversation context to use can be controlled by adding an HTTP request parameter to the URL named `cid`. This parameter must be set to the conversation scope ID of the conversation scope to use. In the case of the web shop example from earlier on, the `cid` parameter would be set to the order number of the order. If the application uses JSF, propagating the conversation scope to the next request is even easier. By default, JSF will ensure that the conversation scope ID is propagated to the next request, either by using a hidden form field or by adding the `cid` parameter to each URL.

Calling the `end()` method will mark the current long-running conversation scope as transient again. This means that the conversation scope will end as soon as the current request scope ends. The container can also clean up long-running conversation scopes automatically. Consider the case that in a web shop, the user does start the order process but closes their browser before finalizing the order. Without automatic cleanup, the conversation would be started but never destroyed. All data collected from the customer and all items placed in the shopping will be stored in conversation-scoped beans that will remain active indefinitely. Each conversation scope has a timeout in milliseconds, which indicates how much time must expire after the last time the scope is active before the scope is destroyed. Applications can access the current timeout value by calling the `getTimeout()` method on the `Conversation` instance. If the application needs a long-running conversation scope to have a longer or even shorter timeout, the timeout can be changed by calling `setTimeout(long milliseconds)` with the new timeout value. Please note that the timeout is only a hint to the CDI container; the container may decide to destroy the conversation before or long after the timeout has expired.

Dependent Scopes

The last scope is the dependent scope. The dependent scope can be applied using the `@Dependent` annotation. However, the dependent scope is also the default scope for all beans if no scope annotations are present, so it's not necessary to apply the annotation.

The dependent scope differs quite a bit from the other predefined scopes. Unlike the beans that are scoped with any of the other predefined scopes, dependent-scoped beans do not have a predefined lifecycle. Instead, beans that are dependent-scoped inherit the lifecycle of the bean they are injected into. For example, if a dependent-scoped bean is injected into a request-scoped bean, it will be destroyed at the end of the request scope. A bean injected into another dependent-scoped bean will inherit the scope of the bean that bean has been injected into, until a scoped bean is fined.

Instances of dependent-scoped beans can also be created programmatically through the `BeanManager`. The lifecycle of these instances depends on the bean into which the `BeanManager` was injected, similar to directly injecting dependent-scoped beans. However, if the `BeanManager` was retrieved programmatically using the CDI API, then the dependent bean will automatically be application-scoped. This happens as objects that are not CDI beans may create beans using this API. There is no scope to inherit, so the safest scope that can be given to the created bean is the application scope.

The inheritance of the surrounding scope also leads to another difference between dependent-scoped beans and beans with other scopes. Dependent-scoped bean instances are not shared between different beans. For example, when injecting a dependent-scoped bean of type X into an application-scoped bean and a request scoped bean, the bean of type X would need to have two different lifecycles, which is not possible. This has another consequence for dependent-scoped beans: unlike beans with any of the other scopes, they are not proxied by default. This means that dependent-scoped beans do not have the same restrictions as beans for other scopes and that dependent-scoped beans can final classes or have final methods.

Exposing Nonproxyable Types as Scoped Beans

One possible use for the dependent scope is to make a type that is final or has final methods available under another scope. Say you have a type that you want to make available as a scoped bean from an external library that you have no control over, but this bean has a final method. For example, a type from an external library may not be designed for CDI and have final methods. To make the final type available using a scope, you can hand-write a scoped proxy class that delegates calls to an injected instance of the actual class. Say you have a final class `FinalFoo`, which you would like to make available as an `@RequestScoped` bean. You would write a request-scoped `FooProxy` class, into which a dependent-scoped `FinalFoo` is injected. By implementing similar methods on your proxy, you can delegate these method calls to the FinalFoo instance. Instead of injecting the FinalFoo into your beans, you inject your FooProxy instead. As this FooProxy has the request scope, the dependent-scoped FinalFoo instance will also inherit the request scope and be destroyed at the end of the request.

```
@RequestScoped
public class FooProxy {

    @Inject
    private FinalFoo dependentScopedBean;

    public void foo() {
        dependentScopedBean.foo();
    }
}
```

A handwritten proxy or wrapper can also be used to scope the result of a producer method if it is of a nonproxyable type. The result of a producer method that returns the username of the currently active user as a string should have the narrowest scope possible, which most likely is a scope that starts just after the user's credentials have been validated but is destroyed when the user logs out. The session scope is not suitable, as this will still be active once the user logs out, and you no longer want to display the username at this point. The request scope is also not suitable. The processing of any response pages sent back to the user happens in the same request, but for these pages the user should already be effectively logged out. As the String class is a final class, it is nonproxyable, and scopes cannot be applied to it. To allow the username string to be injected as a scoped bean, it must be wrapped in a custom wrapper or proxy first.

Passivating Scopes

Unlike the application and request scopes, the conversation and session scopes are passivating scopes. While bean instances of nonpassivating scopes are kept in memory until they or the corresponding scope instance is destroyed, the same is not necessarily true for passivating scopes. Passivating scopes and the corresponding beans can be temporarily transferred from memory to temporary storage. This can happen, for example, if a long-running scope hasn't been active in a while but will most likely become active again in the future. After the scope and its beans are passivated, the scope needs to be activated again, which in turn will load all the corresponding beans from the secondary storage.

Passivating scopes like the conversation scope can be applied only to beans that are passivation capable. A nonpassivation capable bean that is declared to have a passivating scope will be considered a deployment problem and will prevent the application from starting. For a bean to be passivation capable, the bean must be `Serializable`, and all its interceptors and decorators must be passivation capable too. In addition to this, all fields of this bean must be passivation capable or transient. To aid with this, all bean proxies provided by the container must be passivation capable. This way it is possible to inject a nonpassivation capable bean instance into a passivation capable bean instance, as long as the nonpassivation capable bean has a scope other than the dependent scope. Any dependent-scoped beans injected into a passivation capable bean must also be `Serializable`.

Other Scopes Defined in Java EE

Java EE 8 is comprised of multiple separate specifications. Like any normal library or application, each of these may have a need for specific scopes that aren't covered by the built-in scopes. Just like with normal libraries or applications, these other specifications can also define their own custom scopes. In Java EE 8, both the Java Servlet Faces (JSF) and Java Transaction API (JTA) specification define their own scopes.

The JSF specification defines two scopes on top of CDI. The first is the view scope. The view scope, declared using the `@ViewScoped` annotation, lasts for the duration of a single JSF view. In JSF, multiple requests can be for the same view, for example when performing Ajax requests. Having a scope that lasts for the lifetime of that view allows requests for that view to have some state that persists across requests. For example, in a modern web application, the content of a table may be loaded only when it is needed, like when the user scrolls to the bottom of the table. Each time the next few rows of data are fetched, a new request must be sent from the client to the server, but all these requests belong to the same view. If the table contents are filled from a certain user query, this user query and possibly the index of the next data to fetch could be stored in the view scope.

The flow scope, defined by `@FlowScoped`, can be thought of as similar to the conversation scope in CDI. Like the view scope, it covers multiple requests that are all part of a workflow the user takes in a web application. These workflows must have clear entry and exit points. Consider again the example of an online store. When the user decides to purchase the contents of their shopping cart, they start the order flow, which completes once the user has completed and submitted the order. To do so, the user typically would have to go through multiple steps where they enter their personal details, their shipping preferences, and, probably most importantly, their payment information. Each of these steps would be part of the same flow.

JTA is used to enable distributed transactions in Java EE. The scope defined by JTA is the transaction scope. This scope can be applied to beans using the `javax.transaction.TransactionScoped` annotation. The transaction scope is active during the lifecycle of a single JTA transaction. Different transactions within the same application that are active at the same time will have a different transaction scope associated with them. This means that the transaction scope is most suited to beans that need to keep track of something during a single transaction. An example of a transaction-scoped bean is a bean that keeps track of the database changes that are made during a transaction and then stores them in a transaction log at the end of the transaction.

Scope init Events

Each of the built-in scopes will fire an event at the start and end of the lifecycle of a scope. We won't cover events and observer methods here in too much detail; this will be handled more in-depth in Chapter 5. Beans can opt in to be notified of when a scope context is initialized, when it is about to be destroyed, and when it actually has been destroyed. For this, CDI offers three qualifier annotations: `javax.enterprise.context.Initialized`, `javax.enterprise.context.BeforeDestroyed`, and `javax.enterprise.context.Destroyed`. Each of these annotations has a value parameter, which must be set to the class of the scope annotation. To make a bean opt in to these lifecycle events, a `void` returning method takes a single parameter that is annotated with `@Observes` and the qualifier annotation for the event the bean wants to listen to. The type of this parameter depends on the actual scope events the bean listens to but can be an object. This parameter would need to be annotated with the `@Observes` and the required annotations. Each type of event the bean wants to opt in to will require a separate observer method. It's not possible to have a single method that listens for the initialization of the request and application scopes at the same time or that listens for the initialization and destruction of the application scope.

```
@ApplicationScoped
public class RequestScopeEvents {

    public void onInitialization(@Observes
      @Initialized(RequestScoped.class) Object o) {
        System.out.println("Request scope initialized");
    }

    public void onBeforeDestruction(@Observes
      @BeforeDestroyed(RequestScoped.class) Object o) {
        System.out.println("Request scope about to be destroyed");
    }
    public void onDestroyed(@Observes
      @Destroyed(RequestScoped.class) Object o) {
        System.out.println("Request scope destroyed");
    }

}
```

Note that only scoped beans can opt in to these lifecycle events; dependent-scoped beans cannot receive these events directly. Scoped beans will also only receive these events as long as their scope is active. A request-scoped bean, for example, will never be able to receive the `@Destroyed(RequestScoped.class)` event, as the request scope is no longer active at that point, and the bean itself will already have been destroyed.

Custom Scopes

Each application is unique and as a result may have requirements for scopes that fall outside the scopes made available by CDI and the other Java EE specifications. Consider something like a chat application that allows group chats with multiple different users. Such an application may require a scope for each group chat, which would allow messages in that group chat to be delivered to all members. It would be impossible to cover all possible use cases for scopes in the CDI specification itself. CDI doesn't even cover all the use cases within Java EE 8. This is where custom scopes come in. Applications and libraries extend CDI with custom scopes. Defining custom scopes is done through the use of portable extensions. Portable extensions allow the extension of CDI features in many ways and are by far one of the most powerful features in CDI.

We won't cover them in too much detail in this chapter, as Chapter 7 will cover portable extensions.

Before starting to write a custom scope, there are a number of design decisions that need to be considered first. These design decisions will play an important part in how the scope works and to which beans it is suitable to apply the scope to. The most important decisions to make when designing a custom scope are when the scope is created and when it is destroyed. This determines when the beans with that scope can be used. For example, if you decide to create a scope for threads from a certain thread pool, the beans with that scope could not be used by any other threads. Another related design decision is if the scope should be suspendable or not. An application, for example, could have a user scope that is active when handling requests for that user, which is destroyed only once the user logs out. Any thread that handles a user request may handle requests for multiple users. This thread could then unsuspend the scope, handle the request, and then suspend the scope again so that it is free to handle a request from any other user.

One of the most important aspects in the design of a custom scope is if it will be shared between threads. Scopes like the request scope are dedicated to a single thread, but scopes like the application scope are shared between all threads in an application. Sharing a scope between threads will mean that any beans that are declared with that scope will also have to be thread safe. If not, any number of concurrency-related bugs may occur.

A follow-up consideration is if a scope should be propagated to other threads as well. Take, for example, the request scope, while the default request scope is not propagated to other threads at all, there are use cases where it might make more sense to propagate the scope to a different thread. Say you receive an HTTP request and you submit a task that will handle that request asynchronously; then it would be useful to propagate the scope to the background thread as well. However, the same caveats will most likely apply as with any other scope that is shared between multiple threads in that beans should thread safe to avoid any weird bugs.

Another important question is whether the scope should be passivating. For shorter-lived scopes, it may not make sense to declare the scope as passivating as passivation may never occur and because it adds a number of restrictions on the beans the scope can be applied to. If a scope is potentially long-running and may consume a lot of memory, either in a small number of large instances or in many smaller ones, it is worth it to consider making your custom scope passivation capable. However, as mentioned previously, passivation capable scopes also add extra requirements on any beans with that scope. In some cases, it may not be possible to make a bean passivation capable, which rules out applying a passivating scope to that bean. If you have a producer method or field that produces a nonserializable bean from a library outside your control, it isn't possible to apply a passivating scope to that bean.

Lastly, scopes can be made stackable or not. Say, for example, that you have a method invocation scope. This scope could be active for any invocation of a method. However, if another method is called that has the same scope, the original scope should be suspended while the second method is executing. This is considered stacking the scopes; the new scope is stacked upon the original scope and replaces it. Once the new scope is either suspended or destroyed, the original scope automatically becomes active again until it is also suspended or destroyed.

To create a custom scope, you need to do three things.

1. Create an annotation for the new scope.
2. Implement a scope context for the scope.
3. Register the new scope in a CDI extension.

The scope annotation will identify the scope and allow it to be applied to beans. The scope context will contain the logic for the scope and determines when the scope is active and which beans are active in a given instance of that scope. Lastly, the custom extension allows you to register the new scope with the CDI container.

Custom Scope Annotation

You'll start off creating your new scope by creating an annotation for your scope. The convention for the name of the annotation is to have something descriptive for the scope and end the name with `Scoped`. For example, the annotation for a `Foo` scope would be `@FooScoped`. It is important to note that this is only a convention; there are no restrictions on the name of the annotation other than the restrictions for class names. However, not following the naming conventions could be confusing to developers who need to apply the scope, as they would have to remember the name of the annotation. It also makes the annotation harder to discover as users will need to consult the documentation to find the name of the annotation. Contrast that to something like the `@RequestScoped` and `@ApplicationScoped` annotations, which are easy to find using autocomplete in any IDE.

Now that you have your scope annotation, you need to configure it by applying other annotations to it. If you are familiar with writing annotations, you may be aware that annotations by default have only class-level retention. This means the annotation is stored in the class file of any class it is used in but that it is not possible to access the annotation at runtime. For CDI to be able to apply the scope to a bean, it must be able to detect the annotation at runtime. To enable this, you need to apply the `@Retention` annotation to your annotation. `@Retention` has a single value parameter, which you set to the value `RetentionPolicy.RUNTIME` to allow CDI to access the annotation at runtime.

You should also define the `@Target` annotation. The `@Target` annotation controls which source code elements the annotation can be applied to. For the scope annotation, you should only be able to apply it to bean classes, producer fields, and producer methods. It does not make sense to apply a scope annotation to a method parameter, for example. The `@Target` annotation has an array of `ElementType` as the only parameter, which you need to set to `{ElementType.TYPE, ElementType.METHOD, ElementType.FIELD}`.

Lastly, you need to declare your annotation to be a scope annotation. You can do this by declaring one of two annotations. For pseudoscopes like the dependent scope, you would apply the `@Scopeannotation`. Pseudoscopes are rare, so most scope creators should never need to use this annotation. The `@NormalScope` annotation should be used instead for all other scopes. This annotation has a single Boolean parameter named passivating, which is set to `false` by default. This parameter controls if the scope will be a passivating scope. To make a scope passivating, simply set the parameter value to `true`.

After all this, a nonpassivating `Foo` scope annotation would look something like this:

```
@NormalScope
@Retention(RUNTIME)
@Target({TYPE, FIELD, METHOD})
public @interface FooScoped {
}
```

There are a few other annotations you could apply to the scope annotation to further configure it. You may want to have the scope annotation automatically also apply to subclasses of a class with that scope or on producer methods that override a producer method with that scope. This can be done by applying the `@Inherited` annotation to the scope annotation. Care should be taken when doing this, as this will make it impossible to give subclasses or overriding producer methods a different scope. Usually an inherited annotation can be overridden by applying the same annotation on the class or method that inherited it. Different scopes, however, have different annotations. Applying a different scope annotation would end up in the bean type, producer method, or producer field having more than one scope defined, which is a deployment problem. To avoid these issues, however, it's usually best to use the `@Inherited` annotation for scope annotations.

Another thing you can do is to make the scope appear in the Javadoc generated for a type. This is generally a good practice as this will allow a developer browsing the Javadoc to easily see what scope is declared for a bean. To do this, the `@Documented` annotation should be applied to the scope annotation.

Context

Once the annotation for the scope is defined, it's time to move on to the next part of implementing a scope, the context. The context has a number of responsibilities and is the most important part of implementing a scope. The context is both responsible for determining whether the scope is active for a given thread and for responsible for managing all bean instances for that scope. It may be surprising to learn that the CDI container itself does not keep track of which bean instance is associated with each scope and delegates this responsibility to the context. However, this allows the context implementations more flexibility in their implementation. For example, the context can now decide to temporarily suspend a scope without destroying any of the beam instances for that scope.

The heart of the context is the context object. Each different scope will have exactly one instance of the scope object, which is shared between all scope instances of that scope. To implement a context object, you need to implement the `javax.enterprise.context.spi.Context` interface. This interface defines the following methods:

- `boolean isActive()`
- `Class<? extends Annotation> getScope()`
- `T get(Contextual contextual)`
- `T get(Contextual contextual, CreationalContext creationalContext)`

This interface looks deceptively simple but allows a lot of flexibility in the implementation of a scope. We'll discuss each of these methods separately before diving deeper into the implementation of a `Context` object.

The `isActive()` method returns a Boolean to indicate whether the scope this context belongs to is active for the current thread. As you would expect, this method must return `true` if the scope is active and `false` if it is not. When a thread attempts to call a method on a proxy object for a scoped bean, the CDI container will call `isActive()` to determine whether the scope is active. Only if this scope is active will the container attempt to get an instance of the scoped bean. This call will happen on every single method invocation on the proxy, so it is possible for a scope to be activated or deactivated in between successive calls, depending on the implementation of the context.

The `getScope()` method is fairly straightforward and must return the class of the scope annotation associated with the current context. This is mainly used by the CDI container to determine which annotation and context object belong together. For example, the built-in request scope would return the `@RequestScoped` annotation. A context object must always return the same annotation, as it's not possible to switch the associated annotation halfway through running a CDI application. For most context implementations, it should be sufficient to return a hard-coded annotation from this method.

Both the methods named `get` are where most of the logic in a CDI context implementation can be found. The first method, `get(Contextual<T> contextual)`, returns an existing bean instance for a given contextual. A *contextual* is a descriptor for a given bean type that has been resolved by the CDI container and that offers methods to allow bean instances for the given bean type to be created or destroyed. Each bean type will have a unique contextual. The bean type here consists of the actual type of the bean instance and the qualifier annotation that is applied to the bean type. For example, an `@Foo Foo` bean will have a different contextual from an `@Bar Foo`. Having different contextuals for different qualifier annotations is what allows qualifier annotations to work. The context itself does not need keep track of the qualifier annotations, but instead can just rely on the contextual. It's important to note that this method must never create a new instance of a bean matching a contextual. If there is no existing instance for the current active scope instance, then this method must return `null` to indicate so. Like the `isActive()` method, this method is called on each invocation on a proxy of a scoped type. This makes it possible to switch different scope instances between successive method invocations, depending on how the context is implemented.

The other method, `get(Contextual<T> contextual, CreationalContext<T> creationalContext)`, is the method that may create new instances of a bean matching a contextual. Like the previous method, this method must also return an existing bean instance for the current scope instance, if there is one available. If there is no existing bean, this method must instead create a new instance. Creating a bean instance in CDI is not as simple as calling the relevant constructor. The created bean may be also have dependencies that need to be injected by CDI, or the bean may have interceptors that need to be applied to it. This is where the second argument to this method, `CreationalContext<T>`, comes in. The `CreationalContext<T>` argument can be used with the `Contextual<T>` to create or destroy an instance of a bean. Creating the bean instance is simple; just call the `create()` method on the contextual and pass the creational context as an argument.

```
T bean = contextual.create(creationalContext);
```

It is important that if the `get(Contextual<T> contextual, CreationalContext<T> creationalContext)` method creates a new bean instance, this must be done using the given contextual and creational context instances. You may be wondering why `CreationalContext` must be passed as an argument here. The main reason for this is that this associates the given bean instance with the creational context. The `CreationalContext` interface has a `release()` method, which triggers all beans associated with that creational context to be destroyed. This is primarily used to destroy any `@Dependent`-scoped beans. These are associated with the creational context of the instance they are injected in. When that instance is destroyed, `release()` is called on `CreationalContext`, which causes the `@Dependent`-scoped beans to be destroyed.

You may notice that the `Context` interface does not have any methods to start, suspend, or destroy a scope instance. The main reason for this is that the methods in the `Context` interface are meant to be called only by the CDI container. Starting, suspending, or destroying a scope instance depends on the implementation of the scope and as such is not a concern of the CDI container. This does not mean that the context object can't have methods that control the scope. On the contrary, if such methods are needed, the context object is the most logical place to put them as the context object is responsible for maintaining the scope. However, as these methods are called by library or application code and different scopes may have different requirements for such methods, these methods are not defined in the `Context` interface.

Extension

The last part of implementing a scope is to define a portable extension that registers the scope with the container. Portable extensions are a topic for a later chapter, so we will not dive too deeply into them at this point. The portable extension will have two responsibilities. The first is to register the scope annotation with the CDI container. The second responsibility is to register the instance of the context object with the container.

To create a portable extension, you must create a new class that implements the javax.enterprise.inject.spi.Extension interface. This interface is a marker interface; it marks classes as portable extensions but does not define any methods. To register your scope annotation, you must declare a single method that will be called before the CDI container scans all the JAR files for beans. The name of this method is not important; you can name it anything you want, as long as you declare the method with a certain signature. The method's return type must be void, and it must accept a single argument of type javax.enterprise.inject.spi.BeforeBeanDiscovery. This argument must also be annotated with @Observes. This lets the container know that this method should be called before the container scans all the JAR files on the class (or module paths) to discover which beans they contain. The BeforeBeanDiscovery object will have an addScope() method that can be used to register your scope annotation. This method has three arguments: the scope annotation class, a Boolean indicating if the scope is a normal scope, and a Boolean indicating if the scope is a passivating scope. If you have a normal nonpassivating scope with an @FooScoped annotation, the method could look something like this:

```
public void beforeBeanDiscovery(@Observes BeforeBeanDiscovery bbd) {
    bbd.addScope(FooScoped.class, true, false);
}
```

Next, you need to register the context object as well. Registering the context object is similar to registering the scope annotation, but you'll need to add a second method for this. This method will take an instance of javax.enterprise.inject.spi.AfterBeanDiscovery as a single argument instead of BeforeBeanDiscovery. As the name would suggest, the CDI container will call this method once it has completed the process of bean discovery. To register the context object, you simply pass an instance of it to AfterBeanDiscovery.addContext(). Let's say you name your context class FooContext; then your AfterBeanDiscovery method could look something like this:

```
public void beforeBeanDiscovery(@Observes BeforeBeanDiscovery bbd) {
    bbd.addScope(FooScoped.class, true, false);
}
```

As you may notice, you directly pass in the instance of the context object instead of registering the class, like you did with the scope annotation. The result of this is that there will be only a single instance of the context object for your scope.

Lastly, you need to make sure the CDI container is aware of your portable extension. CDI discovers which portable extensions are available at startup using the `ServiceLoader` mechanism. If you are unfamiliar with `ServiceLoader`, it allows for dynamic loading of service provider classes. Service provider classes are classes that implement a predefined interface or extend a predefined class. In essence, this allows libraries and applications to dynamically load other classes as plugins. The portable extension class is such a service provider class, but you need to register it with the `ServiceLoader` first. To do so, you need to add a file under `META-INF/services` that is named after the fully qualified name of the `Extension` interface. The only contents this class will have is the fully qualified name of your portable extension class. If you're building your project with Maven or Gradle, the file should be located at `src/main/resources/META-INF/services/javax.enterprise.inject.spi.Extension`. Now let's say your portable extension class is named `bar.foo.PortableExtension`; then the contents of this file would be this:

```
com.foo.PortableExtension
```

Now that we have covered how to create and register a scope, you can learn how to implement a simple scope. Let's assume for a moment that the application scope doesn't exist, but you need something like it for your application. In real code, you would never need to implement a scope like this, but this allows us to cover the simplest scope implementation possible and expand from there.

To start the new custom application scope, you first need to define your scope annotation, which you'll name `@MyApplicationScoped`. This annotation will be a fairly straightforward annotation. Let's name the annotation `@CustomAppScoped` and mark it as the annotation of a nonpassivating scope. Its definition should look something like the following:

```
@NormalScope
@Retention(RUNTIME)
@Target({TYPE, FIELD, METHOD})
public @interface CustomAppScoped {
}
```

Next, you'll implement the context object. Implementing the `isActive()` and `getScope()` methods is fairly trivial. As you want the custom application scope to be active at all times, you simply return `true` from the `isActive()` method. The `getScope()` method should always return the class of your scope annotation, so it should always return `CustomAppScoped`.

At this point, you need to implement the core logic for your scope in both the `get()` methods. To implement the `get()` methods, you will first need a way to cache any bean instances that are created by your context object. It's important to remember at this point that there's only a single context object for a given scope. This means that multiple threads may be asking for a bean instance for a `Contextual` at the same time. The simplest way to implement a cache would be to use a map with `Contextual<T>` as the map key and the instance as the value. The thread-safety requirements mean that `ConcurrentHashMap` is the most suitable map implementation for the cache. An added benefit of using `ConcurrentHashMap` for your instance cache is that you can use the `computeIfAbsent()` method to make sure that no two threads will try to create a bean instance for the same `Contextual<T>` at the same time. When you put everything together, the implementation of the scope method will look something like the following code:

```
public class CustomAppScopeContext implements Context {

    private final ConcurrentHashMap<Contextual<?>, Object> instances =
      new ConcurrentHashMap<>();

    @Override
    public Class<? extends Annotation> getScope() {
        return CustomAppScoped.class;
    }
    @Override
    public boolean isActive() {
        return true;
    }

    @Override
    public <T> T get(Contextual<T> contextual, CreationalContext<T>
      creationalContext) {
        @SuppressWarnings("unchecked")
        T instance = (T) instances.computeIfAbsent(contextual,
          c -> contextual.create(creationalContext));

        return instance;
    }
```

```
    @Override
    public <T> T get(Contextual<T> contextual) {
        @SuppressWarnings("unchecked")
        T instance = (T) instances.get(contextual);
        return instance;
    }
}
```

Lastly, you need to write your portable extension and register it with the `ServiceLoader`. The portable extension is fairly straightforward; you only need to register your scope annotation and context object in it.

```
public class CustomAppScopeExtension implements Extension {

    public void beforeBeanDiscovery(@Observes BeforeBeanDiscovery bbd) {
        bbd.addScope(CustomAppScoped.class, true, false);
    }

    public void afterBeanDiscovery(@Observes AfterBeanDiscovery abd) {
        abd.addContext(new CustomAppScopeContext());
    }
}
```

Now all that is left is to annotate beans and producer methods with your scope annotation so you can use your new scope. In practice, having a scope that is always active and shares instances between all threads is not very useful, as the application scope already covers that requirement. A more typical situation is that the scope can be created and suspended or destroyed at will. Typically, the control of the scope falls to an interceptor (which will be covered in a later chapter) or, less commonly, to a bean class. However, as noted previously, the `Context` interface does not declare any methods to control the lifecycle of a scope. You can fix this by defining these methods yourself.

Let's try to create a scope that can be started, suspended, resumed, and even destroyed. To be able to resume your scope, you should first pick a type that can be used as an identifier that can be used to resume your scope. A good practice would be to use an immutable type for this. You will use this identifier as a map key. A mutable type may have a hash code that may change because of changes to its value.

The context object will need to keep track of this identifier for each thread with an active scope. The most suitable way to do this is to define a thread local in your scope and store the String in it. However, writing directly to a ThreadLocal is a fairly expensive operation. Instead, you can use an AtomicReference instance as the value in your thread-local variable and update this instead. To implement your isActive() method, you simply need to check whether AtomicReference in the thread-local variable for the current thread contains null or not. If it contains anything other than null, the scope is active and isActive() will return true.

You will name the methods to start and suspend your scope, start() and suspend(), respectively. In the start() method, you should check whether there is not already a scope instance active for the current thread, as your scope is not a stackable scope. You would lose the identifier of whatever scope was active if you allow a new scope to be started while one is already active, so you need to throw an exception if this happens. When suspending the scope, you need to do a similar check; only then will you need to throw an exception if no scope instance is currently active for the thread. Attempting to suspend a scope when none is active is an indicator of a bug in your code somewhere.

```
private static final ThreadLocal<AtomicReference<String>>
  ACTIVE_SCOPE_THREAD_LOCAL = ThreadLocal.withInitial(AtomicReference::new);

@Override
public boolean isActive() {
    return ACTIVE_SCOPE_THREAD_LOCAL.get().get() != null;
}

public void start(String scopeId) {
    AtomicReference<String> activeScope = ACTIVE_SCOPE_THREAD_LOCAL.get();
    if (activeScope.get() != null) {
        throw new IllegalStateException(
          "An instance of the scope is already active");
    }
    activeScope.set(scopeId);
}

public void suspend() {
    AtomicReference<String> activeScope = ACTIVE_SCOPE_THREAD_LOCAL.get();
```

```
    if (activeScope.get() == null) {
        throw new IllegalStateException("Scope not currently active!");
    }

    activeScope.set(null);
}
```

Before you get to writing the rest of the context object, you need to consider how to destroy bean instances. In the custom application scope, the scope was always active, so destroying bean instances was not a necessary design consideration. However, if you start and suspend scopes as required by the application, you may eventually run out of memory if you don't clean up the scopes that are no longer in use. When you destroy a scope instance, you also need to destroy each individual bean instance associated with that scope instance. As mentioned previously, `Contextualinterface` has a `destroy` method that can be used to destroy bean instances. However, the `destroy()` method takes both the bean instance and `CreationalContext<T>` as arguments. `CreationalContext<T>` is passed only to `get(Contextual<T>, CreationalContext<T>)` and used to create the bean instance. As you are defining your own destroy method, the `CreationalContext` will not be available. To be able to destroy beans, you will need to cache the context that is passed into this method as well. To do this, you will define a custom type to use in your instance map called `BeanInstance`. This class will basically be a wrapper around your bean instance that also stores the associated `Contextual<T>` and `CreationalContext<T>`. You will need to define a method here that returns the actual bean instance so that the context object is able to access it. As you already have everything you need to destroy a bean instance, you can add a destroy method here as well. This method calls `Contextual.destroy()` with the current bean instance and associated `CreationalContext<T>`.

```
final class BeanInstance<T> {

    private final T instance;
    private final Contextual<T> contextual;
    private final CreationalContext<T> creationalContext;

    BeanInstance(T instance, Contextual<T> contextual,
      CreationalContext<T> creationalContext) {
        this.instance = instance;
        this.contextual = contextual;
```

```
        this.creationalContext = creationalContext;
    }

    T get() {
        return instance;
    }

    void destroy() {
        contextual.destroy(instance, creationalContext);
    }
}
```

For the previous scope, you had a single ConcurrentHashMap containing all the bean instances for your scope. Unlike the previous scope, your new scope will have multiple different instances, meaning that a single map for your instance cache will no longer suffice. Instead, you can use a ConcurrentHashMap with your identifier as the map key and for each value another ConcurrentHashMap containing the instances. When implementing the get(Contextual<T>) method, there's one other thing you need to consider. The previous scope you wrote was active at all times, but this scope won't be. The contract for get(Contextual<T>) demands that if a scope is not active for the current thread, the current thread should throw a ContextNotActiveException. At the start of get(Contextual<T>), you should check whether the scope is actually active. You can do this by checking whether AtomicReference stored in the thread-local you defined contains a scope ID or null. If it is set to null, the scope is not active, and you need to throw the ContextNotActiveException.

If the scope ID is not active, you can then use the scope ID to get the map of bean instances for this scope. As this might be the first call, the map of all scopes may not contain a map of instances for the current scope instance yet. Your first instinct may be to use Map.computeIfAbsent() to create the map, but there's a better option. As the get(Contextual<T>) method doesn't create any instances, you don't actually need the map to be created at this point. Instead, you can use Map.getOrDefault() in combination with the new static Map.of() method introduced in JDK 9 to return an empty immutable map if there is no instance map available for the current scope yet. Calling Map.of() without any arguments should always return the same empty map, so you avoid the overhead of creating a new map until you need to. Once you have the map, you can check whether the Contextual<T> you are looking for is present in the map and return the corresponding bean instance.

```
private final
  ConcurrentHashMap<String, Map<Contextual<?>, BeanInstance<?>>>
    cache = new ConcurrentHashMap<>();

@Override
public <T> T get(Contextual<T> contextual) {
    String scopeId = ACTIVE_SCOPE_THREAD_LOCAL.get().get();

    if (scopeId == null) {
        throw new ContextNotActiveException();
    }

    @SuppressWarnings("unchecked")
    BeanInstance<T> instance = (BeanInstance<T>)
      cache.getOrDefault(scopeId, Map.of()).get(contextual);

    if (instance == null) {
        return null;
    }

    return instance.get();
}
```

The `get(Contextual<T>, CreationalContext<T>)` method will follow a similar approach as the `get(Contextual<T>)` method, with a few small differences. As you need to create a bean instance if it does not exist, you need to have a map instance for your scope, so you need to create one using `Map.computeIfAbsent()`. The instance map should be a `ConcurrentHashMap`, just like the surrounding scope map, as the instance map may be accessed and even modified by multiple concurrent threads at the same time, depending on when the scope is active. When you need to create a bean instance, you wrap it in the `BeanInstance` class you created earlier. This allows you to easily destroy the scope at a later point.

```
@Override
public <T> T get(Contextual<T> contextual,
  CreationalContext<T> creationalContext) {
    String scopeId = ACTIVE_SCOPE_THREAD_LOCAL.get().get();
```

```
    if (scopeId == null) {
        throw new ContextNotActiveException();
    }

    @SuppressWarnings("unchecked")
    T instance = (T) cache
      .computeIfAbsent(scopeId, s -> new ConcurrentHashMap<>())
      .computeIfAbsent(contextual,
         c -> new BeanInstance<>(
            contextual.create(creationalContext), contextual,
            creationalContext))
      .get();

    return instance;
}
```

The last thing you need to do is to create a method that destroys a given scope. This is needed so you can clean up any instances you don't need anymore. You should first remove the instance map from the scope map and check whether the remove operation returned `null`. This is primarily to prevent two threads from concurrently destroying the scope instance. If this were to happen, only one thread would be able successfully remove the instance map from the scope map. To make sure that you have indeed successfully removed the instance map from the scope map, you should check whether the instance map is `null`. If it's `null`, then another thread tried to delete the scope instance at the same time, and you don't need to take any further action. If the instance map is not `null`, the next thing you need to do is delete all the individual bean instances. You can do this by iterating over the values in the instance map and calling the `destroy()` method that you added to `BeanInstance` class you defined earlier. The scope and all its beans have now been deleted. Note that if the scope is active during the deletion or if it becomes active again after deletion, it will essentially be a new scope. Any attempt to access a bean from a destroyed scope will lead to a new bean instance being created. The destroy method is called in the same way as the `start()` method you declared earlier.

```
public void destroy(String scopeId) {
    Map<Contextual<?>, BeanInstance<?>> instances = cache.remove(scopeId);
```

```
        if (instances != null) {
            instances.values()
                .forEach(BeanInstance::destroy);
        }
    }
```

You can now use your custom scope. To do so, you need to have access to your context object. The BeanManager defines a getContext() method, which returns the corresponding context object when given a scope annotation class. This method has Context as return type, so you will need to cast the returned context object to the correct type. You can then use the returned context object to manage the lifecycle of your scope. The following example will start a new instance of your scope, suspend it after use, and finally destroy it:

```
CustomScopeContext context = (CustomScopeContext) beanManager.
getContext(CustomScope.class);

 context.start(scopeId);
 try {
     // Use scoped beans

     context.suspend();
 } finally {
     context.destroy(scopeId);
 }
```

Passivation-Capable Scope

Passivation-capable scopes are similar to non-passivation-capable scopes. CDI does not define how and when a scope must be passivated, so this needs to be decided at the time of implementing the context object. In most cases, the context object will keep track of which scopes are active and decide when and which scope to passivate. Usually this would be done by tracking which scope hasn't been used recently and then passivating these, for example, through a periodic cleanup job.

You can adapt your custom scope from the previous example to become a passivating scope. To do this, you need to add two private methods to the context, writeToStorage() and loadFromStorage(). The implementations of both methods are left to you, as they entirely depend on what kind of underlying storage mechanism is used to store the scope. We'll have the load method return the scope wrapped in an optional; the reason for this will become clear soon.

Now you need to add a method that passivates the scope. In a real passivation-capable context object, scopes would most likely be periodically passivated based on which scope was most recently active. For the purposes of this example, however, you'll define a `passivate()` method that passivates a scope based on the ID of the scope. To make sure that none of the beans for that scope can be accessed during passivation, you will need to use the `Map.compute()` method to serialize the scope and remove it from the scope map. The `compute()` method takes a lambda as an argument, which calculates a value for a given key, or returns null if the key is to be removed from the map. As you're using a `ConcurrentHashMap` for the scope map, the call to `compute()` should happen as a single atomic operation. If another thread were to attempt to access a bean from a scope that is being passivated at that time, this thread would block until passivation has been completed and the scope is removed from the scope map.

```
public void passivate(String scopeId) {
    cache.compute(scopeId, (id, instanceMap) -> {
        writeToStorage(id, instanceMap);

        // TODO check if beans need to be destroyed
        instanceMap.values().forEach(BeanInstance::destroy);

        // Return null to remove the instance map from the cache
        return null;
    });
}
```

The implementation of `get(Contextual<T>)` is fairly similar to a nonpassivating scope. The main difference is that, if the scope hasn't been found in the scope map, you need to attempt to load it from storage. If the scope is present in storage, then you also need to update the scope map with it. You can use the `computeIfAbsent()` method again to accomplish this task in a thread-safe manner. However, if the scope is a new scope or has already been destroyed, then the scope will not be found in the storage. In this case, the load method will return an empty `Optional`. You can use this optional value to return a lazily created new `ConcurrentHashMap` when the map hasn't been found in storage. The same general approach also applies to the `get(Contextual<T>, CreationalContext<T>)` method.

```
@Override
public <T> T get(Contextual<T> contextual) {
    String scopeId = ACTIVE_SCOPE_THREAD_LOCAL.get().get();

    if (scopeId == null) {
        throw new ContextNotActiveException();
    }

    @SuppressWarnings("unchecked")
    BeanInstance<T> instance =
      (BeanInstance<T>) cache.computeIfAbsent(scopeId,
        id -> loadFromStorage(id).orElseGet(ConcurrentHashMap::new))
        .get(contextual);

    if (instance == null) {
        return null;
    }

    return instance.get();
}

@Override
public <T> T get(Contextual<T> contextual, CreationalContext<T>
creationalContext) {
    String scopeId = ACTIVE_SCOPE_THREAD_LOCAL.get().get();
    if (scopeId == null) {
        throw new ContextNotActiveException();
    }

    @SuppressWarnings("unchecked")
    T instance = (T) cache.computeIfAbsent(scopeId,
      id -> loadFromStorage(id).orElseGet(ConcurrentHashMap::new))
      .computeIfAbsent(contextual,
         c -> new BeanInstance<>(contextual.create(creationalContext),
           contextual, creationalContext))
      .get();

    return instance;
}
```

As a last step, you should also update the destroy method to delete the scope from the underlying storage, if it has been saved there.

Overriding Built-in Scopes

Another possibility of creating a custom scope is to override a built-in scope. This is mostly the same as writing a normal custom scope, but with a few small but important differences. The annotation the context object is associated with must be the annotation of the scope that is to be overridden. Another important thing to note is that the custom scope must never be active at the same time as the built-in scope. The CDI container will throw an exception if two different context objects report having an active scope for the same annotation. For some scopes, overriding the built-in scope may not make much sense. Consider the request scope, which can already be managed from application code without overriding the scope. However, for the `SessionScope`, for example, no lifecycle has been defined for its use in Java SE applications. A consequence of this is that, by default, a Java SE CDI application would not be able to depend on any beans that are session-scoped.

To override a built-in scope, you can create a context object like for a regular scope. The main difference is that you need to return the scope annotation of the scope you want to override from your context object. To register the overridden scope, you now only need to register the custom context object in the portable extesnion. As you use an existing scope annotation that has already been registered previously, you don't need to register it again. A (nonpassivating) implementation of a custom session scope could look something like the following example:

```
public class CustomSessionScopeContext implements Context {

    private static final ThreadLocal<AtomicReference<String>>
      ACTIVE_SCOPE_THREAD_LOCAL =
        ThreadLocal.withInitial(AtomicReference::new);

    @Override
    public boolean isActive() {
        return ACTIVE_SCOPE_THREAD_LOCAL.get().get() != null;
    }
```

```
public void start(String scopeId) {
    AtomicReference<String> activeScope = ACTIVE_SCOPE_THREAD_LOCAL.get();

    if (activeScope.get() != null) {
        throw new IllegalStateException(
          "An instance of the scope is already active");
    }

    activeScope.set(scopeId);
}

public void suspend() {
    AtomicReference<String> activeScope = ACTIVE_SCOPE_THREAD_LOCAL.get();

    if (activeScope.get() == null) {
        throw new IllegalStateException("Scope not currently active!");
    }

    activeScope.set(null);
}

@Override
public Class<? extends Annotation> getScope() {
    return SessionScoped.class;
}
private final
  ConcurrentHashMap<String, Map<Contextual<?>, BeanInstance<?>>>
    cache = new ConcurrentHashMap<>();
@Override
public <T> T get(Contextual<T> contextual) {
    String scopeId = ACTIVE_SCOPE_THREAD_LOCAL.get().get();

    if (scopeId == null) {
        throw new ContextNotActiveException();
    }

    @SuppressWarnings("unchecked")
    BeanInstance<T> instance =
      (BeanInstance<T>) cache.getOrDefault(scopeId, Map.of())
      .get(contextual);
```

```
        if (instance == null) {
            return null;
        }

        return instance.get();
    }

    @Override
    public <T> T get(Contextual<T> contextual,
      CreationalContext<T> creationalContext) {
        String scopeId = ACTIVE_SCOPE_THREAD_LOCAL.get().get();
        if (scopeId == null) {
            throw new ContextNotActiveException();
        }

        @SuppressWarnings("unchecked")
        T instance = (T) cache.computeIfAbsent(scopeId,
          s -> new ConcurrentHashMap<>())
          .computeIfAbsent(contextual,
            c -> new BeanInstance<>(contextual.create(creationalContext),
            contextual, creationalContext))
          .get();

        return instance;
    }

    public void destroy(String scopeId) {
        Map<Contextual<?>, BeanInstance<?>> instances = cache.remove(scopeId);

        if (instances != null) {
            instances.values().forEach(BeanInstance::destroy);
        }
    }
}
```

CHAPTER 5

Events

The observer pattern is a common design pattern used in many applications. It allows an object to notify any number of other objects of changes or other events, without a strong coupling between the subject and the observer. Consider the alternative, where the observee needs to individually call each observer separately. This does not scale well to a large number of observers and strongly couples the subject that is being observed to the observers.

CDI supports the observer pattern through events. Events can be fired from any CDI bean, and almost any CDI bean can observe events. Each fired event has a payload, which can be any primitive type or Java object.

By the end of this chapter, you will be familiar with firing and receiving events in CDI. You will know how to control what events a bean will receive and when. You will also know the differences between synchronous and asynchronous events and should be comfortable using both.

Event Types

Each CDI event is associated with an event object. Similar to beans, each event can also optionally be associated with a qualifier. Event listeners listen to events of a type and with an optional qualifier. CDI determines which event listeners to notify by trying to match the qualifier and type of the event with the qualifier and type of the events the event listener listens to. The qualifier must be absent for both the event and listener or must match exactly otherwise, following the same rules for qualifiers as for regular beans. The type of an event listener listens to must be the same as the event object's type or be a supertype of the event object's type. Let's take an example where there is one bean producing integers and firing these as events without a qualifier. Assume there are two unqualified event listeners, one that listens for events of type `Object` and one that listens for events of type `Integer`. When the event is fired, CDI will try to find

J. Beernink and A. Tijms, *Pro CDI 2 in Java EE 8*, https://doi.org/10.1007/978-1-4842-4363-3_5

the appropriate event listeners at runtime. In this case, the event object is an `Integer`, which, like all other objects in Java, is a subtype of `Object`. In this case, both these event listeners are notified of the event. Both match the qualifier of the event, which isn't present. Figure 5-1 shows how events can be delivered based on the event type.

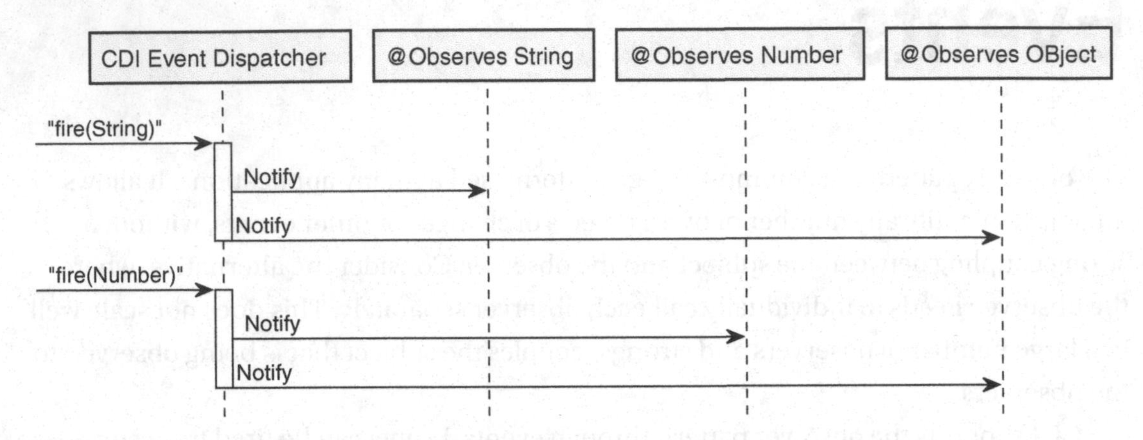

***Figure 5-1.** Example of event delivery based on type*

In this example, there are three different observers; one observes events of type `String`, one observes events of type `Number`, and the last observes events of type `Object`. You first fire an event of type `String`. As `String` is a subtype of `Object`, CDI will dispatch this event to both the observers for events of type `String` and `Object`. The same goes when you then fire an event of type `Number`. CDI will deliver this event to both the observer expecting events of type `Number` and the observer expecting events of type `Object`.

Event Observers

Any scoped bean can listen for CDI events by providing observer methods. Observer methods are invoked when an event is fired that matches the event type and qualifiers the observer method listens for. An observer method may have any valid method name and may be declared as any level of visibility, even private. To declare a method as an observer method, exactly one of the parameters of that method must be annotated with `@Observes`. This parameter is the event parameter and is the payload of the event. The type of the event parameter determines the event type that the observer method will listen to. This type may have generic type parameters or wildcards, so it's possible to listen to events of type `List<String>` or `List<?>`. An observer method with multiple parameters with `@Observes` annotations is forbidden and will lead to errors at deployment time.

The event parameter may also have one or more qualifiers defined upon it. If no qualifiers are defined on the event parameter, the observer method is notified for every event with a type that can be assigned to the event parameter, regardless of the event's qualifiers. If one or more qualifiers is defined, then the observer method will be notified of the event only if the qualifiers on the event parameter are a subset of the qualifiers of the event. Say you have two observer methods with event parameters of type `String`. The first method has no qualifiers on its event parameter, but the second defines `@X` and `@Y` as parameters. If an event is fired of type `String` with `@Y` as a qualifier, only the method without qualifiers will be notified. If, instead, you fire an event with `@X`, `@Y`, and `@Z` as qualifiers, both observer methods will be notified, even though the qualifiers didn't exactly match.

Let's assume you have a bean that fires events of `@X String`. You can implement an observer method for these types of events by declaring a method that has an `@Observes @X String` parameter. The observer method declaration would look like the following:

```
private void onXEvent(@Observes @X String event) {
    // Handle event here
}
```

By default, observer methods without any qualifiers will be notified for every event with a matching type, regardless of the qualifiers defined on that type. However, it is possible to restrict an observer method to listen only for events without qualifiers by applying the `@Default` qualifier. For beans and injection points without a defined qualifier, the `@Default` qualifier is automatically applied. The same goes for events; when an event doesn't have an explicit qualifier, it has the `@Default` qualifier. By specifying the default qualifier explicitly, the observer method will only be notified for events that have the `@Default` qualifier. This means that only events without any qualifiers or events that also have the `@Default` qualifier explicitly applied to them will trigger the observer method to be notified.

```
public void onEventWithoutQualifiers(@Observes @Default String event) {
    // Handle event here
}
```

Conditional Event Observers

As stated previously, when an event is fired, it is delivered to any observer that is part of a scope that is active at that point. Because of the lazy initialization of CDI beans, a bean listening to an event may not yet have been initialized for one of these scopes. If a bean observing an event has not been created yet at the time of the event, CDI will, by default, create an instance of this bean. Sometimes it may not be desirable for a bean to be created during event notification if it does not exist. For example, the observing bean may be expensive to create and may only need to observe events after some other condition is met. To prevent CDI from creating a bean instance just to deliver a method, a conditional observer method can be declared instead of a regular observer method using the `notifyObserver` field of the `@Observes` annotation. This field can accept one of two values, `IF_EXISTS` and `ALWAYS`, which is the default. When `notifyObserver` is set to `ALWAYS`, CDI will always create a new instance of the bean if it doesn't exist yet for a given active scope. If the `notifyObserver` field is set to `IF_EXISTS` instead, the observer method will be notified only if the bean already exists within the active scope it is associated with. The following is an example of a conditional event observer:

```
public void onEvent(@Observes(notifyObserver = IF_EXISTS) String event) {
    // Handle event here
}
```

Observer Ordering

By default, the order in which observers are called is undetermined and depends on the container implementation. However, since CDI 2.0, it is possible to influence the order in which observers are called using the `@javax.annotation.Priority` annotation. This annotation must be applied to the event parameter and defines a single `int` field that determines the order in which the observer method is invoked. The smaller the number, the earlier the observer will be notified. Libraries and CDI or Java EE containers can also register observer methods. These might need to run either before or after application observers are notified. To define a clear ordering for container, library, and application observers, each category has its own base priority. For example, container observers running before application observers have a base priority of 0, while library observers running before application observers have a base priority of 1000, and application observers have a base priority of 2000. This means that for library observers that run before application code, any value between 1000 and 1999 is a valid priority. Luckily, you don't have to memorize these numbers. The `javax.interceptor.Interceptor.Priority` class defines the following constants for the base priorities:

- PLATFORM_BEFORE
- LIBRARY_BEFORE
- APPLICATION
- LIBRARY_AFTER
- PLATFORM_AFTER

For observers defined by an application, any priority between `APPLICATION` and `LIBRARY_AFTER` is available. To use these constants to help define a priority for the event observer, simply use these constants and add an offset to them to define the order. If the observer does not define the `@Priority` annotation, a priority of `APPLICATION + 500` is used automatically. Say, for example, that you have three application-defined observer methods, where the first one must always be run first, the second must run somewhere after that, and the third one defines no priority. For the first observer, you can define the priority as `APPLICATION`. For the second, you can pick any low number and add it to the `APPLICATION` constant. As the third observer has no annotation, it automatically uses `APPLICATION + 500` and will be invoked last of the three observer methods. The following shows the `Observer` ordering:

```
public void firstObserver(@Observes @Priority(
  Interceptor.Priority.APPLICATION) Object eventObject) {
    System.out.println("Called first: " + eventObject);
}

public void secondObserver(@Observes @Priority(
  Interceptor.Priority.APPLICATION + 5) Object eventObject) {
    System.out.println("Called second: " + eventObject);
}

public void thirdObserver(@Observes Object eventObject) {
    System.out.println("Called third: " + eventObject);
}
```

Note If two different observer methods have the same priority, the order they are invoked in is undefined.

For any library authors who need to provide observer methods, the LIBRARY_BEFORE and LIBRARY_AFTER constants can be used in much the same way. As the name implies, the LIBRARY_BEFORE base priority will ensure the observer method will be invoked before any application-defined observer methods, and LIBRARY_AFTER will be invoked after application-defined observer methods. The following shows library-defined observer ordering:

```
public void libraryBeforeObserver(@Observes @Priority(
  Interceptor.Priority.LIBRARY_BEFORE) Object eventObject) {
    System.out.println("Called before application: " + eventObject);
}

public void libraryAfterObserver(@Observes @Priority(
  Interceptor.Priority.LIBRARY_AFTER) Object eventObject) {
    System.out.println("Called after application: " + eventObject);
}
```

In general, most developers will never need to use the platform-level priorities. These are primarily used for Java EE and CDI containers for observers that are defined by the platform specifications.

Event Metadata

In some cases, it might be necessary to obtain additional information about the event fired. For example, it might be necessary to handle an event differently based on the nonbinding parameters defined in one or more of the qualifiers, or it might be necessary to get information about the injection point the event was fired from. To help achieve this, it's possible to inject an javax.enterprise.inject.spi.EventMetadata object into an observer method as an additional parameter. The EventMetadata defines the following methods:

- Set getQualifiers();
- InjectionPoint getInjectionPoint();
- Type getType();

The getQualifiers() method can be used to get the set of qualifiers of the event. This makes it possible to inspect each qualifier and potentially extract values from one or more of them. If, for example, you have a ParameterizedQualifier declared on your event, with a nonbinding single field that you want to extract and use in the handling of the event, you would use the getQualifiers() method to get the set of qualifiers and then attempt to find the qualifier you need from there. When you have this qualifier, you can then extract any value you need from it.

```
public void observerWithMetadata(
  @Observes @ParameterizedQualifier(name = "") String event,
    EventMetadata eventMetadata) {
    ParameterizedQualifier qualifier =
      eventMetadata.getQualifiers()
        .stream()
        .filter(
          annotation -> annotation instanceof ParameterizedQualifier)
        .map(ParameterizedQualifier.class::cast)
        .findFirst()
        .orElseThrow();

    String name = qualifier.name();
    System.out.println(
      "Event " + event + " with name " + name + " observed.");
}
```

The getInjectionPoint() method returns information about the injection point from which the event was fired. This includes not just information about the injection point itself but also the bean the injection point belongs to, including the type, qualifiers, and even scope of that bean. This is mainly useful if there is a need to determine where the event was fired from. If the event was fired through the BeanManager, the getInjectionPoint() method will return null as there likely may not be any injection point in this case.

```
public void observe(@Observes @MyQualifier String event,
  EventMetadata eventMetadata) {
    Bean<?> bean = eventMetadata.getInjectionPoint().getBean();
    String scope = bean.getScope().getName();
    String beanClassName = bean.getBeanClass().getName();
```

```
    System.out.println(
        "Event " + event + " fired from bean " + beanClassName +
            " with scope " + scope);
}
```

The getType() method returns information about the runtime type of the event object. This will usually return the same as calling getClass() on the event parameter itself.

Firing an Event

Like observing events, firing events is fairly straightforward. The primary way to fire an event is through an instance of the javax.enterprise.event.Event interface. The Event interface has a generic type parameter, which denotes the types of events the Event instance can fire. For example, an Event<String> can fire events of type String.

The primary way to obtain an instance of the Event interface is through injection. In fact, Event instances are injected almost exactly like regular beans, with one small difference. Just like with injected beans, one or more optional qualifiers can be declared for the injected Event. Unlike beans, however, the qualifier does not determine which instance is injected. Instead, the qualifier will determine the qualifier of the event that is fired. If one or more qualifiers is declared, when the event is fired, it will have that given set of qualifiers. If no qualifier is declared, the event will carry the default qualifier only. To inject an Event to fire events without any qualifiers, you simply annotate it with @Inject without any qualifiers.

```
@Inject
private Event<String> unqualifiedEvent;
```

An Event that can fire events with one or more qualifiers can be injected in the same way. Simply declare the @Inject annotation and all the required qualifiers on the Event to inject it.

```
@Inject
@FirstQualifier @SecondQualifier
private Event<String> qualifiedEvent;
```

The Event interface defines a fire(T event) method that can be used to fire events. To fire an event, simply pass an object that matches the type of the event. Say you have a bean that wants to fire an event of type String with qualifier @Foo any time a certain method is called. You can inject an Event<String> in a field annotated with @Inject and @Foo. By passing the String you want to fire as an event to the fire() method, it is fired as an event of type String with qualifier @Foo. Once fired, any observer method that listens for events of type String without qualifiers or defining @Foo as the qualifier will be notified.

```
public class EventFiringBean {

    @Inject
    @Foo
    private Event<String> event;

    public void fireEvent(String string) {
        event.fire(string);
    }

}
```

An alternative method of obtaining an Event instance is through the BeanManager. The getEvent() method of the BeanManager returns an unqualified Event<Object>. This may seem restrictive, but the Event interface defines a number of select() methods that allow you to narrow down the generic type of the event and to define qualifiers. These methods are not restricted to Event instances obtained through the BeanManager but are also available on injected instances. These methods work in a similar way as to the select() methods defined on the Instance interface. There are three variants: one that accepts zero or more annotations, one that accepts a class and zero or more annotations, and one that accepts a type literal and zero or more annotations. It's important to note that only the annotations will affect where the event will be delivered. The class and type literal will both not affect event delivery as event delivery is determined at runtime by the actual type of the event object.

Let's say you want to obtain an Event instance for firing events of type String and with @Foo as the qualifier. You can obtain these through the BeanManager by using the select() method and passing along String.class and an instance of the @Foo annotation. Creating an instance of an annotation is fairly cumbersome; for this you first need to create an abstract class that extends the AnnotationLiteral class and implements the annotation type itself as an interface. Once that is done, you can create an instance of @Foo by creating an instance of the anonymous class you just created. The following is an example of obtaining an event instance through the BeanManager:

```
public abstract class FooLiteral extends AnnotationLiteral<Foo>
  implements Foo {
}

@Inject
private BeanManager beanManager;

public void fireEvent() {
    Event<String> event = beanManager.getEvent()
      .select(String.class, new FooLiteral() {
    });

    event.fire("Event object obtained through BeanManager");
}
```

As you can see, this is a fairly verbose way to fire an event. For this reason, it's best to avoid obtaining the Event instance through the BeanManager if possible. Use this only if you want to dynamically select the qualifiers of your event at runtime or if it's not possible to inject the Eventinstance directly.

The BeanManager also has a fireEvent() method that can be used to fire events without obtaining an Event instance first. However, this method has been deprecated in CDI 2.0 and should not be used.

We can put the previous together to show how an event is fired and handled. In a web shop, payments may be validated asynchronously. Say you have an OrderService bean that manages a single order. Another bean may actually be responsible for accepting the payment confirmation. You could use events to notify your order service of the successful payment from the point the payment is received. To achieve this, you first need to define your event class. Let's name your event class Order. The exact contents of this class aren't too important; the only important aspect is that you have an order ID field in it, which allows you to uniquely identify an order. See the following for a rough example of such an event bean, but please note that most of the details have been omitted. The following is an example for an order class:

```
public class Order {

    private String orderId;

    // Order details ommitted for brevity
}
```

However, your order type may not be enough to uniquely identify your event type. In fact, it's not hard to imagine that there may be multiple different types of events fired with the same Order object. For example, there may be an event for an order being cancelled, shipped, or even the payment failing. To make sure you listen only for the exact event you want, you should introduce a qualifier. As you want to listen only for successful payments, you will define the @PaymentReceived qualifier annotation. The following snippet shows this qualifier annotation for successful payment events:

```
@Qualifier
@Retention(RUNTIME)
@Target({ElementType.FIELD, PARAMETER})
public @interface PaymentReceived {
}
```

Now that you have both your event type and the qualifier for your event, you can start writing the bean that will fire the event and the bean that will consume it. However, you first do have to make sure that when you fire the event, the bean that will consume it will be in scope. To do this, let's assume for a second that you have an order scope, defined by an @OrderScoped annotation, and that when an external payment notification is received, the order scope is automatically started before the method that will fire the event is called. Let's assume you have a PaymentService that will receive the payment confirmation. If you inject an Event<Order> in this bean, annotated with @PaymentSuccessful, you can use this to fire the event for firing the payment.

```
public class PaymentService {

    @Inject
    @PaymentReceived
    private Event<Order> paymentSuccesfulEvent;

    public void processPayment(Order order) {
        // This method will only be called when the order scope is active.
        paymentSuccesfulEvent.fire(order);
    }
}
```

You can now implement your `OrderService`, which will listen for the successfull payment events and will update the order status. To listen for the events, you need to add a method that takes an `Order` instance as its main parameter. To listen to the correct type of events, you'll annotate the observer method with both `@Observes` and `@PaymentSuccessful`. There may be other listeners as well that depend on being called only after the order state has already been updated, so you'll need to make sure that your bean is notified as one of the first beans. As this is an application-defined bean, you can have your bean run early by giving it the priority `APPLICATION + 5`. This makes your observer one of the first ones to be called but still allows some space for other observers to be defined later that should be called first. Here's the event observer bean:

```
@OrderScoped
public class OrderService {

    public void onSuccessfulPayment(
      @Observes(during = AFTER_SUCCESS)
      @Priority(APPLICATION + 5)
      @PaymentReceived Order order) {
        updateOrderStatus(order);
    }

    private void updateOrderStatus(Order order) {
        // TODO update the order status
    }
}
```

Once your application receives a successful payment, the payment service will file a bean. CDI will then attempt to deliver the bean and will first resolve all the listeners, using the type of the event (the `Order` class) and any qualifier annotations defined on it. As your `OrderService` has a method that matches both the type of the event object and the annotations defined on the event, CDI passes along the event to your observer.

Generic Event Types

One thing to keep in mind is that event listener resolution happens entirely at runtime. For types with generics, like `List` and `Set`, the generic type information is available only at compile time, not at runtime. This means that, for these types, the generic parameters cannot be resolved at runtime. If an event is of type `List<String>`, this is seen as just

List at runtime, without the generic type parameter. An event of type List<String> is completely indistinguishable from an event of type List<Number>. As such, trying to fire an event of a generic type could lead to it being passed to a listener with an incompatible generic type, which would lead to unexpected ClassCastExceptions being thrown at runtime. This means that, unlike for observer methods, CDI explicitly forbids firing events of types that have generic type parameters that are unresolvable at runtime.

However, this does not mean that event types cannot use generics. Say you have a class X, which is defined as class X implements List<String>. The generic type parameter X defined for the Listinterface is available at runtime as it is part of the class' signature. This means that CDI is able to correctly inject class X into listeners that listen for events of type List<String>. Generic type parameters are allowed in observer method declarations, as these parameters are resolved at runtime.

```
public class StringList implements List<String> {

private final List<String> list;

public StringList(List<String> list) {
    this.list = list;
}

// Delegation method declarations here
}
```

This also provides a solution in the case you absolutely need to fire events with a generic type. If the generic type implements an interface, you can create a wrapper class that implements the same interface but has the generic type parameter hard-coded as part of its class signature. To avoid having to re-implement the original interface, this wrapper class simply wraps and delegates to the original implementation.

Observer Exceptions

It can occasionally happen that an observer method throws an exception during its execution. This could be for a variety of reasons like a resource it depends on being unavailable or a bug in the implementation of the observer method. When an observer method throws an exception, CDI will stop notifying listeners of the event. This means that if the first observer method notified throws an event, any observer methods that were to be notified after this method will not be notified of the event. If the event thrown by the observer method is an unchecked exception, it will be rethrown directly from the `Event.fire()` method. When the exception is a checked exception, it is not possible to rethrow the exception directly. The code firing the event would have to either catch all exceptions or declare that it could throw the base type of exception. For that case, any checked exception thrown by an observer method will be wrapped in an `uncheckedjavax.enterprise.event.ObserverException`.

Scopes and Event Delivery

When an event is fired, it is delivered to all beans that listen to that event that have a scope that is active in the current thread. Say, for example, that the current thread has an active request scope and conversation scope and the application scope is always active. If an event is fired from within this thread, it is delivered to all application-scoped beans, as well as all beans that have the same request and conversation scope as the current thread. Events will not be delivered to any dependent-scoped beans. The confusing thing here is that a dependent-scoped bean that attempts to listen to an event will not be considered a deployment problem; the CDI container will happily start if this is the case. However, the listener method will never be called when the event is fired. This could lead to confusing bugs when a dependent-scoped bean is accidentally made to listen to an event, as the listener will never be explicitly called.

Transactional Events

Many applications will use transactions to ensure the consistency of the data they store. If the transaction fails, the transaction is aborted, and all changes associated with it are undone. This poses some issues when firing an event during a transaction as there is no way to roll back the delivery of an event. Take, for example, a web shop, which may use events to notify the supply chain to start preparing the order for shipment. If payment of an order fails, the transaction should be aborted, and all changes during that transaction are undone. If the payment failed, it would be too late as the event notifying the supply chain would already have been sent and the order would still be sent. Even when not using events, there could be issues when an application has to do something that cannot be rolled back but can't be as the change doesn't support transactions.

Thankfully, CDI offers support for transactional events and transaction event observers. Transactional event observers can subscribe to be notified in certain stages of the current transaction, instead of being notified directly at the time the event is fired. Depending on which phase the observer subscribes to be notified to, the event may never be delivered. For example, an observer can subscribe to events after the transaction completes successfully. If the transaction is rolled back, the observer will never be notified for this transaction.

Firing an event for a transactional observer works in the same way as for a normal observer. If any JTA transaction is active at that point in time and there is a transactional observer, the observer will be notified once the current JTA transaction reaches the lifecycle phase the observer subscribes to. However, if no JTA transaction is available at the time of firing the event, any transactional observers will be notified immediately as if they were regular nontransactional observers.

An observer method can be made a transactional observer method using the `during` field in the `@Observes` annotation. The `during` field accepts an `enum` value from the `javax.enterprise.event.TransactionPhase` enumeration. The following `enum` values are available:

- `IN_PROGRESS`
- `BEFORE_COMPLETION`
- `AFTER_COMPLETION`
- `AFTER_SUCCESS`
- `AFTER_FAILURE`

The `IN_PROGRESS` phase is the default value for the `during` field. This means that, by default, any observer method is automatically a transactional observer. The `IN_PROGRESS` value does not denote a phase itself, but instead it describes the default behavior of an observer method, which is to notify the observer method immediately.

The `BEFORE_COMPLETION` observer methods will be notified directly before the transaction completes. This could be useful for something like a transaction log. If multiple changes are made during a single transaction, a transaction log could take the end state of the entity being changed and log the changes made during the current transaction. As this runs before the transaction completes, if there is a failure while updating the transaction log, the entire transaction will also be rolled back. This will ensure that the transaction log is always fully synchronized with the actual changes made.

Note Any exceptions that are thrown by an observer method that runs before the completion of a transaction may cause that transaction to fail.

The `AFTER_COMPLETION` observer methods will be notified directly after the transaction completes, regardless of the outcome of the transaction. This means that these observers will be notified regardless of whether the transaction completes successfully or is rolled back. This is great for observers that need to do something after the transaction, regardless of the completion status.

The `AFTER_SUCCESS` observer methods will be notified directly after the transaction completes successfully. If the transaction is rolled back, these observer methods will not be notified at all. This is great for observer methods that should be executed only once the transaction completed successfully but that make changes that cannot be rolled back. Any calls that need to be made to a nontransactional external API could be performed in an observer method that is notified after a successful transaction. Consider the earlier example of a web shop needing to notify its supply chain system. Another great example would be the back end of a mobile app that needs to send a push notification to confirm that an action has been completed successfully.

Lastly, the `AFTER_FAILURE` observer methods will be called after the transaction completes, but only if it has been rolled back. If the transaction is committed successfully, these observer methods will not be called. This could be useful for undoing some nontransactional changes that may have been made during the transaction. It could also be used to notify the user that the changes that have been made during the transaction have failed. For example, in a web shop, if the user orders something but payment fails, an after-failure observer could be used to send the user an e-mail to indicate payment failed.

Other than explicitly setting the `during` field, transactional observer methods are identical to regular observer methods. You can take a look at a quick example of writing a transactional observer. Let's assume you have a notification system that sends a notification to the user, given a user's username, but that this notification system does not support transactions. You now want to notify your user of the event that was fired during a transaction, but only if the transaction calls successfully. To do this, you can write an observer method that listens to an event that contains the username of the user.

```
public class TransactionalEventDemo {
    @Inject
    private NotificationSystem notificationSystem;

    @Inject
    private Event<NotifyUserEvent> notifyUserEvent;

    @Transactional
    public void doSomething(String username) {
        // Make changes here

        notifyUserEvent.fire(new NotifyUserEvent(username));

        // Finish making changes before transaction commits
    }

    private void notifyUser(@Observes(during = AFTER_SUCCESS)
      NotifyUserEvent event) {
        notificationSystem.notifyUser(event.getUsername());
    }
}
```

In some cases, it is no longer possible to schedule an observer method to be notified of an event at a certain point of the transaction. This can be the case if the transaction is already marked for rollback or if it is about to commit. In these cases, the transactional observer method may be executed immediately instead of at the point they should execute. Take, for example, a transactional observer that should execute after the transaction fails. If the transaction is already marked for rollback at the point an event is fired for this observer, the observer may be executed directly instead of after the transaction fails.

Asynchronous Events

By default, all observer methods are called within the same thread that originally fired the event. This means that each observer method will be called one at a time and the method that originally fired the event will be blocked until the last observer method has completed. If an observer method is long-running, the firing method may not run for a long time. In some cases, executing observer methods in a fire-and-forget method may be preferable, allowing the firing thread to do other work instead of waiting on the observers to complete.

CDI 2.0 introduces the concept of asynchronous events. When a method fires an event, the sender will no longer be blocked until all listeners complete. Instead, the sender continues, and the listeners are notified in one or more background threads. Asynchronous events are fairly similar to regular events, except for a number of restrictions. For one, both the sender and the observer must explicitly support asynchronous events. The main reason for this is that, as the observer methods are called in a different thread, the observer method may have a different set of active scopes than were active at the time of the event being fired. None of the built-in scopes is propagated to the background thread automatically, so they may not be available to the observer method. The same thing goes for transactions; they are not propagated to the background threads, so asynchronous observers do not support transactional events. For these reasons, both the sender and observer must explicitly opt in to asynchronous events.

Observing Asynchronous Events

A bean can observe asynchronous events by declaring an asynchronous observer. Declaring an asynchronous observer method is almost identical to declaring a synchronous observer method. The only difference is the annotation that is applied to the event parameter. Whereas synchronous observers use the `@Observes` annotation, asynchronous observers use `@ObservesAsync` instead. Like the `@Observes` annotation, the `@ObservesAsync` annotation supports the `notifyObserver` field to allow an observer method to be declared conditional.

Let's take the first example observer from earlier in the chapter. You can convert this into an asynchronous observer by simply replacing the `@Observes` annotation with the `@ObservesAsync` annotation, like so:

```
private void onXEvent(@ObservesAsync @X String event) {
    // Handle event here
}
```

Where beans with synchronous observer methods must always have a scope other than the dependent scope, the same does not apply to beans with asynchronous observer methods. Beans with asynchronous observer methods may in fact be (implicitly) dependent-scoped. In that case, each time the observer method is called, a new instance of the bean will be created to handle the event. Beans with asynchronous observer methods may also have any other scope, but care must be taken when explicitly declaring a scope. A non-dependent-scoped bean with asynchronous observer methods will be notified only if the scope of that bean is active in the background thread that calls the observer method. For the built-in scopes, this severely limits which scopes can be applied to an asynchronous observer method as the built-in scopes do not propagate to the background thread. The application scope can be safely used for asynchronous observer beans as it is always active in all threads.

Another scope that is suitable for use for asynchronous observer beans is the request scope, but there is one major caveat. If you'll recall from the previous chapter, the request scope is defined to be started during the execution of an observer method if no request scope is active at that time. As the request scope will also not be propagated to the background thread, this means that every asynchronous observer method will be executed with a new instance of the request scope. This instance will be active only for the duration of that observer method. This means that if the firing bean has a request scope active, all asynchronous observer methods will each execute in a different request scope. In fact, the request scope doesn't even need to be active at all in the thread that fires the event.

It's important to note that asynchronous observer methods are notified only for asynchronous events. They will not be notified of synchronous events. It's also illegal to declare the event parameter with both the `@Observes` and `@ObservesAsync` annotations at the same time. If a bean needs to be able to observe the same type of event both synchronously and asynchronously, that bean needs to declare two separate observer methods. If the code for both types of events is identical, the actual implementation could be delegated to a third private method to avoid having to duplicate any logic. The following is an example of observing both sync and async events of the same type:

```
private void onXEvent(@Observes @X String event) {
    handleEvent(event);
}

private void onXEventAsync(@ObservesAsync @X String event) {
    handleEvent(event);
}
```

```
private void handleEvent(String event) {
    // Handle event here
}
```

Firing Asynchronous Events

Just like observing asynchronous events, firing them is nearly identical to firing a synchronous event. Just like synchronous events, asynchronous events can be fired using an instance of the Event interface. Beside the synchronous fire() method, the Event interface also defines an asynchronous fireAsync() method. The fireAsync() method takes the event object as its only parameter, just like the fire() method, and will return immediately instead of waiting for the observer methods to complete.

```
public class AsynchronousEventFiringBean {
    @Inject
    @Foo
    private Event<String> event;

    public void fireEvent(String string) {
        event.fireAsync(string);
    }
}
```

Note When firing an asynchronous event, it's best to use an event object that is immutable. As multiple observer methods may be executed at the same time, any modifications they may make could cause race conditions between the different asynchronous observer methods. Even if the event object is fully thread-safe, one observer method modifying the event object may have unexpected consequences for another observer method.

One big difference between the fire() and fireAsync() methods is that the fire() method does not return a result, while fireAsync() returns a CompletionStage<U>, where U is the compile-time generic type of the event object. The CompletionStage interface is a new interface that was introduced in Java 8 that models a stage of an asynchronous computation. You can think of it as a more powerful equivalent of the `Future` interface (in fact, the main implementation of `CompletionStage` is the `CompletableFuture` class). Whereas getting a result from a `Future` needs a call that will block the current thread if the result is not yet available, `CompletionStage` allows additional asynchronous tasks to be appended to it that will execute once it completes. To put it differently, with a `Future` you need to wait until the result becomes available to be able to process it, but with a `CompletionStage` you can schedule another task that will process the result, without having to block any thread.

To summarize, `CompletionStage` is powerful for scheduling asynchronous tasks. We won't go into the full details of all the possibilities of `CompletionStage` here, but instead we'll cover two useful use cases for asynchronous events. If you want to know more about `CompletionStage` (and its main implementation, `CompletableFuture`), beyond what we discuss here, the Javadoc for the interface is a good place to start.

The `CompletionStage` returned by the `fireAsync()` method models calling all of the relevant observer methods. Once this stage completes, all the observer methods have been notified. You can use this to have the firing bean be notified of the completion of all relevant observer methods. For example, the firing bean may hold on to some resource that cannot be released until all observer methods have been notified of an event. You can achieve something like this by attaching an additional stage to the `CompletionStage`. There are a number of methods on `CompletionStage` that could be used for this, the most important of which are `thenAccept()` and `thenRun()`. The `thenAccept()` method accepts a `Consumer` function that "consumes" the result from the previous stage. In the case of the `CompletionStage` returned by `fireAsync()`, the result is the event object itself. This is useful if the event object is needed to know which resource to close. The `thenRun()` method takes a `Runnable` function instead, so it does not receive any parameters. Both these methods will execute the function passed into it directly in the thread that executes the previous stage, which should be the thread that executes the last observer method to complete. If the observer methods have already been completed when `thenAccept()` or `thenRun()` is called, the functions are called directly in the thread that calls these methods. Both methods also have an alternative equivalent, `thenAcceptAsync()` and `thenRunAsync()`, which take an additional `Executor` as a parameter. This allows both functions to be called on a certain `Executor` instance once the previous stage has completed.

Let's say you have a bean that manages multiple resources and wants to notify all observer methods of its intention to close one resource. The observer methods may want to use the resource just before it is close, so you have to wait until all observer methods complete successfully. As you need to keep track of which resource to close, you need to call `thenAccept()` on the resource to close. You can pass a lambda to this method that takes the event object and uses it to close the correct resource.

```
preResourceDisposalEvent.fireAsync(resourceId)
                        .thenAccept(id -> closeResource(id));
```

This will close the resource once all the observer methods have been called. However, one of these observer methods may also throw an exception, which would prevent the additional stage from being executed and the resource from being closed.

This brings us to the second main use case for the `CompletionStage` returned by the `fireAsync()` method: exception handling. The `CompletionStage` interface defines a method called `handle()` that can be used to handle exceptions thrown by a previous stage. This method takes a `BiFunction` that receives two parameters, the result of the previous stage and an optional exception. If no previous stage threw an exception or if it is handled by another handling stage, the exception parameter will be `null`. If an exception was thrown, the exception parameter will be set to that exception, and the result from the previous stage will be set to `null`. Keep in mind that the result from the previous stage may also be `null` under normal circumstances, if the previous stage did not produce any result. The function passed to the `handle()` method must also return a result; this will be set as the result from that stage. If there was no exception, usually the result from the previous stage should be returned directly.

If an asynchronous observer method throws an exception, the exception parameter passed to the handling function will be set. Unlike with synchronous observer methods, the processing of the event will still continue after one observer method throws an exception. This means that multiple exceptions can be thrown by different observer methods. To deal with this, once one or more observer methods throw an exception, the `CompletionStage` is marked as having completed exceptionally with an exception of type `java.util.concurrent.CompletionException`. This `CompletionException` will have all the exceptions thrown by any of the observer methods as suppressed exceptions. This means that, when implementing a function to handle the exceptions, it's possible to iterate over all the exceptions thrown by the observer methods.

You can combine this with the previous example to handle any exceptions that may be thrown to ensure your resource will be closed after all observer methods have executed. As you need the resource ID to close the correct resource, you should return the given resource ID when an exception has been thrown. The following is an example of handling exceptions with asynchronous observer methods:

```
preResourceDisposalEvent.fireAsync(resourceId)
  .handle((id, exception) -> {
    if (exception != null) {
        for (Throwable suppressed : exception.getSuppressed()) {
            logThrowable(suppressed);
        }

        return resourceId;
    } return id;

  })
  .thenAccept(id -> closeResource(id));
```

CHAPTER 6

Decorators and Interceptors

The decorator pattern is a fairly commonly used design pattern. It allows one object to be wrapped by another so that the wrapping object can either extend or completely override its functionality.

Two good examples of the decorator pattern being used within Java are the `InputStream` and `OutputStream` classes. Wrapper classes, like `BufferedOutputStream` and `FilteredOutputStream`, add functionality to the `OutputStream` they wrap.

CDI supports the decorator pattern through decorators and interceptors. Decorators are strongly tied to a bean being decorated and can be applied to a bean that the developer has no control over. Interceptors, on the other hand, are loosely coupled to the beans being decorated and can be applied only in the definition of the decorated bean itself. Because of the strong ties to the decorated bean, decorators are primarily suited to overriding specific logic on beans that you do not have control over, while interceptors are more useful for implementing more generic services.

Decorators

Decorator beans allow the logic of one or more other beans to be extended or even completely overridden. They can change any of the arguments supplied to a bean method or change the return type from a method. A decorator bean inherits from one of the types it wants to decorate. This means that when implementing a decorator, the methods to be decorated must be known at compile time. It's not possible to dynamically override methods using a decorator bean.

When a bean is decorated, CDI will inject a proxy instead of the bean directly. This proxy will delegate method calls to the decorator instead of the bean itself. This means that, much like the case for scopes, a decorator can be applied only to a proxyable type.

J. Beernink and A. Tijms, *Pro CDI 2 in Java EE 8*, https://doi.org/10.1007/978-1-4842-4363-3_6

To implement a decorator, simply create a new bean class that inherits from the type that contains the method you want to decorate. Let's say you have a FooBean that inherits a foo() method from FooInterface that you want to decorate; you could have your decorator bean either extend FooBean directly or implement FooInterface instead. The decorator bean only needs to implement the beans that will need to be decorated, and the decorator bean class may even be abstract. When using an abstract decorator bean class, the CDI container will provide an implementation of the decorator bean class that provides an implementation for all methods the decorator bean class itself does not implement.

Next, a delegate must be injected into the decorator bean. The delegate must be annotated with @Inject @Delegate and can be injected in a field, as an initializer parameter or as a constructor parameter, just like any other injected dependency. The delegate can be used to call the next decorator or, if there is no other decorator remaining, to call a method on the actual bean.

The delegate also serves another purpose in that the type of the delegate and any qualifiers defined on it will determine what type of beans will be decorated by the decorator bean. The decorator will automatically be applied to any bean that's the same type as the injected delegate or is a subtype of that type. It's important to note that the type of the delegate does not need to match the type of the decorator bean. The delegate can implement any type that the delegate type inherits from and that defines the methods the decorator bean will override. In addition to this, it is also possible to apply qualifiers to the delegate. This will restrict the application of the decorator bean to only those beans that both match the type of the delegate and have the same qualifier annotations as the injected delegate.

Let's assume you have a GreetingBean with two separate methods, getGreetingMessage() and getGoodByeMessage(), which both return a string. You want to create a GreetingDecoratorBean that appends the current time to the greeting created by the GreetingBean. The GreetingBean itself would be fairly straightforward and is shown in Listing 6-1.

Listing 6-1. The GreetingBean

```
public class GreetingBean {

    public String getGreetingMessage(String name) {
        return "Hello, " + name + "!";
    }
```

```
    public String getGoodByeMessage(String name) {
        return "Good bye, " + name + "!";
    }
}
```

Next you create your decorator bean by extending the GreetingBean class. You need to annotate the decorator bean class with @Decorator, and you need to inject the @Delegate instance so you can call the original bean. Next you simply override the getGreetingMessage() method and call the same method on the delegate to get the original greeting. Then you append the timestamp to this string before returning it. See Listing 6-2.

Listing 6-2. The GreetingDecoratorBean

```
@Decorator
public class GreetingDecoratorBean extends GreetingBean {

    private static final DateTimeFormatter FORMATTER =
      DateTimeFormatter.ofLocalizedTime(FormatStyle.FULL);

    @Inject
    @Delegate
    private GreetingBean greetingBean;

    @Override
    public String getHelloMessage(String name) {
        return greetingBean.getHelloMessage(name) + " The time is now "
           + FORMATTER.format(LocalTime.now());
    }
}
```

Now let's say you need to support multiple languages. You extract a GreetingInterface from GreetingBean and will have multiple different beans available to provide the greetings for each language. To differentiate between the beans, you add an @Language qualifier annotation, which takes the language as the value. See Listing 6-3.

Listing 6-3. Qualifier Annotation

```
@Qualifier
@Retention(RetentionPolicy.RUNTIME)
@Target(value = {FIELD, PARAMETER, METHOD, TYPE})
public @interface Language {
    String value();
}
```

You can now have your `GreetingDecoratorBean` immediately implement the `GreetingInterface`. As you care only about the `getGreetingMessage()` method, you will implement only that method. However, as you always need to implement all methods defined by an interface, you now have to declare the decorator bean class as abstract as you will not implement the `getGoodByMessage()` method. The decorator also only supports English, so you need to include the qualifier annotation on the delegate field to ensure that your decorator will not be called for other languages. See Listing 6-4.

Listing 6-4. Injecting a Qualified Delegate

```
@Decorator
@Priority(Interceptor.Priority.APPLICATION + 1)
public abstract class GreetingDecoratorBean implements GreetingInterface {

    private static final DateTimeFormatter FORMATTER =
      DateTimeFormatter.ofLocalizedTime(FormatStyle.FULL);

    @Inject
    @Delegate
    @Language("English")
    private GreetingInterface greetingBean;

    @Override
    public String getHelloMessage(String name) {
        return greetingBean.getHelloMessage(name) + " The time is now "
          + FORMATTER.format(LocalTime.now());
    }
}
```

If someday you want to expand your decorator to also decorate the bean for another language, you can simply declare another @Language annotation on the delegate field for the language you want to support. The field declaration would look like Listing 6-5.

Listing 6-5. Injecting a Delegate for Multiple Qualified Beans

```
@Inject
@Delegate
@Language("English")
@Language("Dutch")
private GreetingInterface greetingBean;
```

You can also apply your decorator to any matched bean. You can do this by applying the @Any annotation instead of explicitly listing any qualifiers. See Listing 6-6.

Listing 6-6. Applying a Decorator to Multiple Types of Bean

```
@Inject
@Delegate
@Any
private GreetingInterface greetingBean;
```

One important requirement is that a decorator bean must not have any explicit scope declared on it, other than the dependent scope. For each decorated bean instance, a new decorator bean instance is created. As this decorator bean is dependent-scoped, it will be destroyed at the same time as the bean it is decorating. As a result, multiple subsequent calls to a decorated bean will always be handled by the same decorator bean instance(s).

Once the decorator class has been written, all that's left to do is to enable the decorator so that it is actually used at runtime. To enable a decorator, the decorator needs to be activated either for the entire application or for a single bean archive. When activating a decorator for the entire application, it will automatically be applied to all matching beans, regardless of which bean archive the bean was defined in. Conversely, when activating a decorator for a single bean archive, it will be applied only to the beans defined in that bean archive. This could be useful in cases where some business logic may need to be overwritten, but only for matching beans in a single bean archive.

A decorator can be activated for the entire application by applying the @Priority annotation to the decorator class. The @Priority annotation will determine the order in which the decorators are executed when there is more than one active decorator.

This works in the same way as it does for event observers. Decorators with a lower number in the @Priority annotation are executed before decorators with a higher number. As decorators are mostly meant to extend or override the business logic declared in an existing bean, most decorators should have priorities in the range between Interceptor.Priority.APPLICATION and Interceptor.Priority.LIBRARY_AFTER. To declare a decorator to run as (one of) the first decorators to run, the priority annotation should be defined as @Priority(APPLICATION).

You can take the GreetingDecoratorBean from earlier in the chapter and activate it application-wide. Let's say that the GreetingDecoratorBean in the application should execute as one of the first decorators, if there are multiple, but not necessarily the first. To do so, you can use a priority of APPLICATION + 5. This is a fairly high priority for a decorator but still allows room for other decorators to be declared to run before your new decorator. You then apply the @Priority annotation with the new priority to your class, which makes your decorator class declaration look like the following.

```
@Decorator
@Priority(Interceptor.Priority.APPLICATION + 5)
public class GreetingDecoratorBean extends GreetingBean {
```

A decorator can be activated for only a single bean archive using the beans.xml file for that archive. To declare the decorator in the beans.xml file, a section named decorators must be added. Each decorator must be individually declared using a class tag. The contents of this tag must be the fully qualified name for the decorator. The order in which the decorators are declared determines the order in which the decorators will be executed. Decorators listed first will be executed before decorators declared later. Decorators activated at the application level will always be executed before the first decorator enabled at the archive level. This means that if the decorator should be executed between other decorators activated at the application level, this decorator must itself also be activated at the application level instead of at the bean archive level.

Note If a decorator is activated both at the application level and at the bean archive level, the application-level activation will take precedence. When the decorator is executed will be determined solely by the @Priority annotation in this case.

If you go back to your GreetingDecoratorBean, you can activate it only for a single bean archive by declaring it in the beans.xml file of that archive. You simply update your bean.xml archive to have a reference to the fully qualified class name of your decorator. If you want any decorators to be run before your decorator, you need to declare these before GreetingDecoratorBean. Likewise, any decorators that need to run after it should be declared after GreetingDecoratorBean.

```
<beans xmlns="http://java.sun.com/xml/ns/javaee">
    <decorators>
        <!--Higher priority decorators go here.-->
        <class>com.foo.bar.GreetingDecoratorBean</class>
        <!--Lower priority decorators go here. -->
    </decorators>
</beans>
```

Interceptors

Interceptors are the second way the decorator pattern can be used in CDI. Interceptors can also be seen as an implementation of aspect-oriented programming (AOP) in CDI. You may already have encountered AOP before. AOP is a way of making code more modular by separating cross-cutting concerns from business logic. Once these cross-cutting concerns are separated, they can be applied to any existing code. A good example of this would be transaction management. A lot of business logic relies on a transaction being active while that logic is being executed, but starting and aborting or completing of a transaction could be seen as a cross-cutting concern. In AOP, the transaction logic would be separated from the transaction logic in a way that allows it to be applied to any business logic when needed. Both Spring and Java EE define an @Transactional annotation that is used for exactly this. In fact, in Java EE, @Transactional is implemented through the use of interceptors. If you'd like more information about AOP or examples of how it can be used, the book *Aspect-Oriented Software Development with Use Cases* by Ivar Jacobson is highly recommended.

Interceptors share a number of similarities with decorators, but there are also a number of important differences. The main difference is that interceptors are not defined by the CDI specification itself. Instead, interceptors are defined by a separate specification and can, at least in theory, be used without using CDI. However, interceptors have an important place in the CDI ecosystem. They can be used to enable new features and services and are generally powerful, which is why we'll cover them here. The more dynamic nature of interceptors makes them suitable for things like caching method results, logging, and starting and stopping scopes dynamically. In fact, as we've covered in the scopes chapter, there is a scope to automatically start and stop the request scope when a method is invoked.

Just like decorators, interceptors are dependently scoped. Interceptors are also invoked in a chain. When there are multiple interceptors, each interceptor invokes the next one, and the last interceptor in the chain will invoke the intercepted method. An important difference between interceptors and decorators is the fact that interceptors allow for the dynamic decoration of beans. When implementing an interceptor, you don't need to know which types of beans the interceptor will be applied to. Instead, the interceptor can be applied to a large number of different bean types, some of which may not have even been written at the time the interceptor is written. This allows interceptors to be used for a much broader set of use cases than decorators, as decorators are mainly suited for extending or overriding business logic. Interceptors can be used to provide additional services to CDI beans. For example, an interceptor could be created that starts a CDI scope when an intercepted method is called and then destroys that same scope once the method call completes. Another difference between decorators is that while a decorator determines itself on which beans it will be applied, for interceptors this is reversed. It is the bean class that determines which interceptors will be invoked.

An interceptor can intercept either regular method calls, constructor calls, or timer timeouts. The latter is mainly interesting when applying an interceptor to an Enterprise JavaBean (EJB). EJB isn't that relevant when talking about CDI, so we won't cover this case in this chapter. The constructor interception is mostly useful when you want to perform some actions before or after a bean's constructor is called, or even if you want to bypass the constructor call to return a cached instance of the bean. For now, we'll only look at regular method interception, and we'll dive deeper into constructor interception later.

The actual work in an interceptor is done by an interceptor method. To implement an interceptor, you simply define a class with an interceptor method. Unlike decorators, you won't need to implement any interfaces or extend any existing classes. Instead of being defined in another class or interface, the interceptor methods follow a convention. As a result, the name of the interceptor method is irrelevant, and you can name it anything that describes what it does clearly. When declaring an interceptor method, there are a few things you must adhere to. First, the interceptor method must have `Object` as a return type. This is because, as interceptors dynamically intercept methods, you won't know what the return type of your intercepted methods is at runtime. The return type of the intercepted method could be any primitive type or object type or could even be void. The only thing that all of these types have in common is that they can all be represented by objects. All primitive types have a corresponding object wrapper type, and void can be represented by null. Using Object as a return type allows you to intercept any method, regardless of the return type.

The interceptor method must also declare that it throws Exception for this same reason. The interceptor will (indirectly) call the intercepted method, and you don't know what types of checked exception, if any, the intercepted method will throw. By default, you should propagate up any exception thrown by the intercepted method.

The interceptor method should accept a parameter of javax.interceptor.InvocationContext. The InvocationContext parameter has a proceed() method, which will cause the next interceptor in the invocation chain to be called. If there are no interceptors left in the chain after the current one, calling proceed() will cause the intercepted method itself to be called. The value returned by proceed() will be the return value from the next interceptor in the chain or from the intercepted method itself. There are a few other useful methods on the InvocationContext, but we'll dive into them a bit later.

You'll need to indicate whether your interceptor will intercept either constructors or methods. To declare that your interceptor method intercepts regular methods, you need to annotate your interceptor method with javax.interceptor.@AroundInvoke. If you were to write the simplest possible interceptor, which does nothing but call the next interceptor in the chain, it would look something like Listing 6-7.

Listing 6-7. Basic Dummy Interceptor

```
public class DoNothingInterceptor {
    @AroundInvoke
    public Object aroundInvoke(InvocationContext context) throws Exception {
        return context.proceed();
    }
}
```

The InvocationContext parameter defines a number of useful methods that can be used to get more information about the target method the interceptor is intercepting. The InvocationContext class defines the following methods:

- Object getTimer()
- Object proceed()
- Object[] getParameters()

- `void setParameters(Object[] params)`
- `Method getMethod()`
- `Constructor<?> getConstructor()`
- `Object getTarget()`
- `Map<String,Object> getContextData()`

The `getTimer()` method is used only for EJB invocations, which we won't cover here. The `proceed()` method you already saw previously. When an interceptor calls the `proceed()` method, the next interceptor in the interceptor chain will be invoked. If there is no interceptor left after the current one, the actual bean method is called. The result of calling `proceed()` depends on both the interceptors that are in the interceptor chain itself. Under normal circumstances, the result of calling `proceed()` will be the result of the method. If the method itself doesn't have a return type, the result will be `null` instead.

However, any interceptor in the chain can decide to override the result from the bean method by returning a different value. This is possible as long as the value returned by the interceptor matches the return type of the actual method. As the interceptor has a return type of `Object`, the value is cast to the correct type for the actual method once it gets back to the top of the interceptor chain. When the value returned by topmost interceptor doesn't match the return type of the actual method, a `ClassCastException` is thrown. One important thing to note is that it is not necessary for a method interceptor to call `InvocationContext.proceed()`. Instead, the interceptor could decide to completely bypass the underlying method and return a value directly. This could be useful, for example, when a method takes long to compute the result but will always return the same result for the same input. An interceptor could be written that can cache the output of any method. If the result is already present in the cache, the interceptor would not need to call the intercepted method to get the result, but could return the cached result instead.

Let's take the `GreetingBean` from earlier in the chapter. Say you want to change the exclamation marks in the returned string of this bean and in other beans but don't want to change the method itself. You could use an interceptor to change the result of the method. To do so, you should call `InvocationContext.proceed()` to get the actual value returned by the method. You can then check whether this value is a string and, if this is the case, replace any exclamation marks with periods. See Listing 6-8.

Listing 6-8. Overriding Method Result in an Interceptor

```
@AroundInvoke
public Object changeResponseString(InvocationContext context)
  throws Exception {
    Object result = context.proceed();

    if (result instanceof String) {
        return ((String) result).replace('!', '.');
    }

    // Fallback for when the result isn't a string
    return result;
}
```

The getParameters() method returns the parameters passed to a method invocation as an array. This allows an interceptor to inspect the method parameters for the current invocation and take action based on them. For example, for the previous example of a caching interceptor, the parameters could be used to cache the actual method's results using the parameters as a cache key. The order of the elements in the array is the same as the order in which the parameters are defined in the method declaration. If a method does not have any parameters, a call to getParameters() will return an array of size 0.

A simple implementation of such a caching interceptor could use a ConcurrentHashMap as a cache. As it should be impossible that the cache key would be modified over time, the cache key containing the parameters is made immutable by creating a list from the parameter array and then creating an immutable copy from the resulting list. See Listing 6-9.

Listing 6-9. Caching Interceptor

```
private final ConcurrentHashMap<List<Object>, Object> cache =
  new ConcurrentHashMap<>();

@AroundInvoke
public Object aroundInvoke(InvocationContext context) throws Exception {
    // Make an immutable copy of the parameters to use as cache key.
    List<Object> parameters = List.copyOf(Arrays.asList(context.
    getParameters()));
```

```
    if (cache.contains(parameters)){
        return cache.get(parameters);
    }

    Object result = context.proceed();

    cache.put(parameters, result);

    return result;
}
```

The setParameters() method can be used to change the actual parameters passed to the method. It takes an array of objects as a parameter. Once called, the parameters will be used in the actual method call instead of the original parameters. Interceptors that are lower in the chain will also see the new parameters if they call InvocationContext.getParameters() instead of the original parameters. Just like with getParameters(), the position in the array matches the order in which the parameters are declared in the method. The array passed to setParameters() must match the exact number of parameters, and each of the values must match with the type of the actual parameters themselves. Just like when returning a result with the wrong type from an interceptor, passing a parameter of an incorrect type will cause a ClassCastException to be thrown.

In a previous example, you took the result from a method and replaced the exclamation marks in the result with a period, if the result was a string. You can do the same thing for the input parameters using the setParameters() method. To do this, you need to check each parameter to see whether it's indeed a string. If so, you replace the exclamation marks by periods. Then you collect all parameters together in a new array and pass this new array to the setParameters() method. See Listing 6-10.

Listing 6-10. Updating the Parameters in an Interceptor

```
@AroundInvoke
public Object replaceCharsInParameters(InvocationContext context)
  throws Exception {
    Object[] parameters = context.getParameters();
    if (parameters.length > 0) {
        Object[] newParameters = Arrays.stream(parameters)
          .map(parameter -> {
```

```
                if (parameter instanceof String) {
                    return ((String) parameter).replace('!', '.');
                }

                return parameter;
            }).toArray();

        context.setParameters(newParameters);
    }

    return context.proceed();
}
```

The getMethod() method returns the method actually being invoked. This allows the interceptor to inspect the actual method being called through reflection. For example, the interceptor could use this to get the name of a method, its return type, the number and type of the parameters it expects, and any exceptions it declares. When intercepting anything other than a method, getMethod() will return null. The reflective method reference returned by getMethod() can be useful in a number of situations. For example, it can be used to log information about the method that is currently being intercepted, for example in an interceptor that measures the time that it takes to invoke a method.

In addition to getMethod(), the getTarget() method will return a reference to the bean that is actually being intercepted. This will return a proxy instance that looks up an instance of the underlying bean and delegates any calls to that instance. When combined with the result of the call to getMethod(), it's possible to perform another call to the method that is currently being intercepted. This call will restart the entire interceptor chain from the beginning, which means that the current interceptor will also be called. This could be useful in the case that an interceptor needs to force a second call to the interceptor.

Let's assume you have an interceptor that checks the first parameter for a method. If that parameter is set to true, it instead sets it to false and then restarts the entire interceptor chain. To prevent an infinite loop, the interceptor just calls InvocationContext.proceed() to continue the chain if the first parameter is already set to false. You can use the getMethod(), getTarget(), and getParameters() methods to achieve this. First you need to get the parameters for the method invocation and check the value of the first parameter. If this is indeed true, you create a copy of that array with the new value. Then you invoke the method using the reference you obtain, with the target bean (the proxy) and the new set of parameters as a value. This will restart the entire interception chain, so the current interceptor will be called again but with the new value.

```
@AroundInvoke
public Object setFirstParameterToFalse(InvocationContext context)
  throws Exception {
    Object[] parameters = context.getParameters();
    if (parameters.length > 0 && Objects.equals(parameters[0], true)) {
        Object[] newParameters = Arrays.copyOf(parameters,
        parameters.length);
        newParameters[0] = false;

        Object target = context.getTarget();
        Method method = context.getMethod();

        return method.invoke(target, newParameters);
    }

    return context.proceed();
}
```

The bean instance the proxy returned by `getTarget()` will delegate to depends on the scope of the bean and the currently active scope. For any dependent-scoped beans, the target proxy will delegate to the same bean instance as is being intercepted. For scoped beans, the interceptor could use this to replace the currently active scope with another one and then start the entire interceptor chain anew on the bean instance from the new scope.

The `getContextMetadata()` method returns a map containing metadata for the context. This metadata can be read or updated by the interceptor. This allows an interceptor to pass along information, which is then made available for an interceptor further down the interceptor chain.

To add something to the context metadata, you simply take the context metadata map and put a key-value pair in it. If a later interceptor in the chain then tries to get the data from the same key, the value of the first example will be returned. An interceptor higher up in the chain can also see the values put in the context metadata by interceptors later in the chain, by checking the values after calling `InvocationContext.proceed()`.

Let's say you want to measure the amount of time that is taken in between two interceptors in the same interceptor chain. This could be useful, for example, to measure the performance of multiple interceptors in the chain. To do so, you would take the current time and add it to the context metadata map. See Listing 6-11.

Listing 6-11. Storing Data in the Context Metadata

```
@AroundInvoke
public Object aroundInvoke(InvocationContext context) throws Exception {
    Instant startTime = Instant.now();
    context.getContextData().put("startTime", startTime);
    return context.proceed();
}
```

In your second interceptor, you need to use the same value to read from the map. Note that the map has generic type `Object` for its values. Because an interceptor in between may have accidentally used the same key, it is good to check the type of the value returned from the map before blindly casting it. However, a good approach would be to use the package name of the interceptor as a prefix for the key. This will prevent most conflicts in the name of keys in the context metadata. After you've checked the type of the value contained in the context metadata, you can safely cast it and use it. See Listing 6-12.

Listing 6-12. Reading from the Context Metadata

```
public Object aroundInvoke(InvocationContext context) throws Exception {
    Object startTime = context.getContextData().get("startTime");
    if (startTime instanceof Instant) {
        Duration duration = Duration.between((Instant) startTime,
          Instant.now());

        logger.info("Execution took " + duration.toMillis() + "ms.");
    }

    return context.proceed();
}
```

Applying an Interceptor

Now that you've written an interceptor, you need to apply that interceptor. Interceptors are typically applied by annotating a single method or an entire class with that annotation. When annotating a class, the interceptor will be invoked for each public method for that class, but only if those methods are called through a bean proxy. This means that any internal calls within a bean itself will not be intercepted.

There are two ways to apply an interceptor through an annotation. It's possible to apply an interceptor through a generic annotation or through a custom dedicated interceptor annotation. The generic approach is the simplest approach and can be achieved by applying the `javax.interceptor.Interceptors` annotation. This annotation takes as a value an array of interceptor classes. The order in which the interceptor classes are executed in the interceptor chain is determined by the order in which they are declared.

Let's imagine for a moment that you have two interceptor classes, `FooInterceptor` and `BarInterceptor`, that you would like to apply to your class. You can define the `@Interceptors` annotation on your class, listing both interceptors in the order you want them in the chain. The resulting class definition would look something like Listing 6-13.

Listing 6-13. Applying Interceptors Using @Interceptors

```
@Interceptors({FooInterceptor.class, BarInterceptor.class})
public class MyBean {

    // Implementation methods go here.
}
```

Using the `@Interceptors` annotation is fairly straightforward but has a number of downsides. For one, it's not possible to control or override the interceptors later. It also means that the class being intercepted needs to know the class that implements the interceptor. It's not possible to switch out the interceptor implementation with a different one at a later point.

The other approach is to define a custom annotation for the interceptor. This has a few advantages as it decouples the intercepted classes from the interceptor implementation. It also requires the interceptor to activated, so it's possible to have interceptors that are enabled only under certain circumstances. Think of an interceptor that tracks information for debugging, for example. You may not want to have this interceptor active under normal circumstances, but you don't want to have to recompile each bean to add the interceptor so it can be used.

You will define your custom annotation by implementing an interceptor binding annotation. This annotation must have `RUNTIME` retention and should be able to be applied to both types and methods. The annotation must also be annotated with the `javax.interceptor.@InterceptorBinding` annotation. A typical interceptor binding would look something like Listing 6-14.

Listing 6-14. An Interceptor Binding Annotation

```
@InterceptorBinding
@Retention(RUNTIME)
@Target({TYPE, METHOD})
public @interface ExampleInterceptorBindingAnnotation {
}
```

Next, the interceptor binding annotation must also be applied to the interceptor itself so that the container will link the binding annotation to your interceptor implementation at runtime. You must also annotate the interceptor class with the `javax.interceptor.@Interceptor` annotation. This last annotation marks your interceptor class as an annotation and tells CDI that you are defining your class to be the implementation of your binding annotation, instead of trying to use the annotation to apply the interceptor to the current class. Please note that the `@Interceptor` annotation may be present only when the binding annotation approach is used; in all other cases you don't need to apply it to your interceptor. It is possible to use the same interceptor binding for multiple interceptors. When reusing an interceptor binding, each interceptor that has been annotated with that binding annotation will be executed. This makes it possible to apply multiple interceptors by using only a single annotation. However, this could lead to confusion and would make it harder to apply only one of the interceptors that has that annotation. For that reason, it is preferable to use a single unique interceptor binding for each unique interceptor.

Let's create a bean called `MyInterceptor` that you want to bind to an annotation named `@MyInterceptorBinding`. You can link the binding to the interceptor simply by annotating the interceptor itself with both `@Interceptor` and `MyInterceptorBinding`, which would make the class definition look like Listing 6-15.

Listing 6-15. Linking an Interceptor Binding to an Interceptor

```
@Interceptor
@MyInterceptorBinding
public class MyInterceptor {

    // Interceptor methods here
}
```

Now you can apply your interceptor to any bean or method by annotating it with `@MyInterceptorBinding`.

Interceptor Activation

When you define an interceptor binding annotation for your interceptor, the interceptor will not be used by default. Instead, the interceptor must first be activated. Just like with decorators, an interceptor can be activated both at the level of a single bean archive as well as globally for the entire application. This gives some flexibility in how and when interceptors are used. It's possible to have an interceptor be active only during development but then have it de-activated in production, without the need to remove the annotation from all intercepted classes. The way in which this is achieved is similar to how decorators are activated.

To activate an interceptor application-wide, you need to apply the `@Priority` annotation to the interceptor class. Just like with decorators, a lower number means that the interceptor will be executed earlier in the interceptor chain, and a higher number for the priority means that the interceptor will be executed later in the interceptor chain. Let's say you take your example interceptor from earlier in the chapter and want to make it execute as an application-wide interceptor. You want it to be one of the first interceptors to run, but not necessarily the first, so you'd ideally like to leave some room for other interceptors to run before it. To do this, you'd give your interceptor a priority of `APPLICATION + 5`. The interceptor class itself would then look like the following:

```
@Interceptor
@MyInterceptorAnnotation
@Priority(Interceptor.Priority.APPLICATION + 5)
public class MyInterceptor {
```

```
    @AroundInvoke
    public Object aroundInvoke(InvocationContext context) throws Exception {
        return context.proceed();
    }
}
```

Activating an interceptor for a single bean archive is similar to activating a decorator for a single bean archive. Just like with decorators, you need to add a section to the `beans.xml` file, which will list all the interceptors to be executed in order. To do so, you need to add a section named `interceptors` to the `beans.xml` file for the archive you want to activate the interceptors for. Within this section, you add multiple `class` tags, containing the fully qualified name of the interceptor class, just like you do with decorators.

Let's say you have three interceptors, which you want to execute in a specific order for a single bean archive, named `FirstInterceptor`, `SecondInterceptor`, and `ThirdInterceptor`. To have them execute in this order, you would need to define them in that order in the `beans.xml` file for that bean archive. The `beans.xml` file would end up looking something like Listing 6-16.

Listing 6-16. Interceptors Declared in beans.xml

```
<beans xmlns="http://java.sun.com/xml/ns/javaee">
    <interceptors>
        <class>com.foo.bar.FirstInterceptor</class>
        <class>com.foo.bar.SecondInterceptor</class>
        <class>com.foo.bar.ThirdInterceptor</class>
    </interceptors>
</beans>
```

Note Interceptors that are activated application-wide will always be executed before archive-specific interceptors. If an interceptor is activated both application-wide and for a specific bean archive, the application-wide activation and priority will always take preference. In this case, the interceptor may execute before other interceptors declared in the same `beans.xml` file, even though it was declared to run after them in that same file.

Constructor Interceptors

Interceptors can also be made to intercept calls to a constructor. Intercepting a constructor invocation works in the same way as for a regular method; the only difference is the annotation that is applied to the interceptor method. By applying the `javax.interceptor.@AroundConstruct` annotation to the method instead of the `@AroundInvoke` annotation, the method can be used to intercept constructor calls instead of regular method calls. One other difference between regular method interceptors and constructor interceptors is that, for a constructor invocation, the `InvocationContext.proceed()` method will always return `null`. There's also a slight difference in method signature for constructor interceptor methods. While they may return `Object`, just like regular interceptor methods, the actual value returned is always ignored. As the return value will always be ignored, it's also allowed for constructor methods to simply return `void`. However, unlike the regular interceptor methods, constructor interceptor methods must always call `InvocationContext.proceed()` to ensure the bean is actually created. See Listing 6-17.

Listing 6-17. The Most Basic Constructor Interceptor Example

```
@AroundConstruct
public Object aroundConstruct(InvocationContext context) throws Exception {
    return context.proceed();
}
```

You are, in fact, allowed to apply the `@AroundInvoke` and `@AroundConstruct` methods to the same method. This allows a single interceptor method to be used to intercept both constructor and method invocations. This could be useful for instances where the interceptor needs to be applied to both constructors and methods with similar logic. Consider, for example, an interceptor that measures the amount of time that it took to execute a constructor or method and then logs this metric. The logic for this interceptor would be exactly the same in both cases, so to avoid having to write the same code twice or add unnecessary boilerplate, a single interceptor method could be defined for this. As the interceptor method must work for both constructors as well as regular methods, it must have `Object` as its return type. The compatibility with regular interceptor methods is also why the constructor interceptor methods are allowed to return a value, even though it will always be ignored.

```
@AroundInvoke
@AroundConstruct
Object measureInvocation(InvocationContext context) throws Exception {
    long start = System.nanoTime();
    try {
        return context.proceed();
    } finally {
        long stop = System.nanoTime();
        if (context.getConstructor() != null) {
            logger.info(context.getConstructor() + " took " +
                TimeUnit.NANOSECONDS.toMillis(stop - start) + "ms.");
        }
        else {
            logger.info(context.getMethod() + " took " +
                TimeUnit.NANOSECONDS.toMillis(stop - start) + "ms.");
        }
    }
}
```

We previously briefly covered the `getConstructor()` method on the `InvocationContext`. This method will return a reflective reference to the constructor, which can be used to get more information about the constructor that is being intercepted. However, unlike the method reference returned by `getMethod()`, it's not possible to use this constructor reference to create a new instance using reflection and return this instead. First, the result of the `@AroundConstruct` method will be ignored. Second, when the constructor interceptor calls `InvocationContext.proceed()`, the CDI container will create a fully managed instance of the bean. If you were to call the constructor manually, you would have an unmanaged instance of the bean. As the dependency injection may not have occurred, you may end up with a partially created bean instance, which could lead to errors if you were to try to use it.

Interceptors and Producer Methods

One area where it was previously impossible to apply interceptors was through beans produced by producer methods. While it is possible to annotate a producer method to indicate that an interceptor should be used, the interceptor would be applied to the producer method itself, not to the bean that was produced by the producer method. Thankfully, this issue was fixed in CDI 2.0, where an API was added to programmatically add interceptors to any unmanaged object in the form of the `InterceptionFactory` class.

The `InterceptionFactory` class either can be injected into the producer method directly or can be created through the `BeanManager`. The `InterceptionFactory` class has a generic type parameter, which denotes the type of beans that it can apply interceptors to. When injecting the `InterceptionFactory`, the generic type must be set to a type that is compatible with the type you want to return from the producer method. Note that this does not have to be the same as the return type of the producer method; it can in fact be a different method. You first need to configure the factory to apply any interceptors to the bean. This can be done through the `configure()` method on the factory. This method returns an instance of `AnnotatedTypeFactory`, which defines a method to add new annotations. When a producer wants to apply a certain interceptor, it should create an instance of the annotation and pass it to `AnnotatedTypeFactory.add()`. You can create an instance of the annotation by using the `AnnotationLiteral` helper class you used in a previous chapter. Once the annotations have been configured on the factory, the bean instance can be passed to the `createInterceptedInstance()` method on the factory so you get a proxy instance that will start the interceptor chain instead of calling the actual bean methods.

Say you have a producer method that returns a list of the first few prime numbers and you want to apply an interceptor that has an `@Foo` binding annotation. You create your list as you usually would and then you apply the `@Foo` annotation to the interception factory, before wrapping your new list in a proxy. You can now return the proxy you just created instead of the bean instance itself, so that when the list is injected somewhere, all calls will go through the interceptor you just registered. See Listing 6-18.

Listing 6-18. Applying an Interceptor in a Producer Method

```
public class FooLiteral extends AnnotationLiteral<Foo> implements Foo {
}

public List<Number> produceInterceptedList(
  InterceptionFactory<List<Number>> factory) {
    List<Number> numbers = List.of(2, 3, 5, 7);

    factory.configure().add(new FooLiteral());

    return factory.createInterceptedInstance(numbers);
}
```

It's also possible to get the InterceptionFactory through the BeanManager. To do so, you need to have a CreationalContext for the type of bean you need to inject. When you have this context, you need to call the createInterceptionFactory() method of the BeanManager and pass the context and the class of the type of bean you want to apply an interceptor to. The result of this is the same InterceptionFactory as you have in the previous example. Let's say you take your previous @Foo annotation and want to apply it to a GreetingBean instance that you create in a producer method; you can inject both the BeanManager and CreationalContext. After creating the factory, everything works pretty much the same as in the previous example.

```
public GreetingBean produceInterceptedListThroughBeanManager(
  BeanManager beanManager, CreationalContext<GreetingBean> context) {
    InterceptionFactory<GreetingBean> factory =
      beanManager.createInterceptionFactory(context, GreetingBean.class);

    factory.configure().add(new FooLiteral());

    return factory.createInterceptedInstance(new GreetingBean());
}
```

In some cases, the producer method may produce a result that is a nonproxyable type because it has final methods. Normally, it wouldn't be possible to apply interceptors to objects of a nonproxyable type, but it is possible to do so using the InterceptionFactory. The InterceptionFactory defines a method called ignoreFinalMethods(). Calling this method will cause the generated proxy to ignore any final methods defined on the proxied object. When using this to ignore the final methods, the final methods must never be invoked on the proxy. As these methods cannot be delegated to the actual bean instance, they are invoked upon the proxy instance, which could lead to unpredictable results.

CHAPTER 7

Dynamic Beans

As mentioned in the previous chapters, specifically in Chapter 3, a bean in CDI is everything for which a `Bean<T>` instance can be created. CDI internally creates such instances automatically from suitable classes and producers, but you can create them directly (programmatically) as well. Because you can create them on the fly, even many of them within loops, they are called *dynamic beans*. This chapter is about how to create and work with such beans.

Why Dynamic Beans?

Creating beans dynamically (that is, adding `Bean<T>` instances directly to the runtime) is an advanced topic. Many business applications will rarely, if ever, find a strong need to do this. For those applications, the beans that are generated by CDI from managed beans and from producers cover basically all aspects of business functionality.

However, in some cases, more flexibility is needed, and this flexibility is primarily needed by third-party libraries or by libraries that integrate other bean-like systems with CDI (often called *connectors* or *bridges*).

Dynamically creating `Bean<T>`s would allow you, for instance, to create the often discussed but never realized concept of defining CDI beans in XML (or, as it is 2019 at the time of writing, in JSON or perhaps YAML). This could also work for a small, custom domain-specific language (DSL), where only a few bits of data are provided by the user, and the library generates larger (sets of) beans from that. A practical example that you'll be looking at later in this chapter is simulating generic producers to some degree; that is, you'll be adding `Bean<T>` instances for each injection point type that you'll encounter. This type of functionality can't be achieved with regular managed beans (apart from code-generating techniques, which however opens another can of worms).

J. Beernink and A. Tijms, *Pro CDI 2 in Java EE 8*, https://doi.org/10.1007/978-1-4842-4363-3_7

Creating Dynamic Beans

`Bean<T>` instances can be created in two main ways. The first is by creating a direct implementation of the interface `javax.enterprise.inject.spi.Bean<T>`; the second is by using a builder that's provided by the CDI API to make this task easier and take away some of the guesswork inherent in implementing the somewhat large interface of a `Bean<T>`.

Manually Implementing a Bean<T>

A `Bean<T>` essentially bundles a factory type with metadata. The pure factory methods are in the `Contextual<T>`, a type already discussed in Chapter 4. In that chapter, you looked at it from the point of view of a bean type that was already created in some way or another. Here you'll be looking at it from the point of view of creating a type.

Part 1: The Contextual

The core interface of the factory part of a `Bean<T>` is relatively simple, as shown here:

```
public interface Contextual<T> {
   T create(CreationalContext<T> creationalContext);
   void destroy(T instance, CreationalContext<T> creationalContext);
}
```

For simple types, which are types not otherwise managed and/or injected by CDI, all you have to do is return an instance from the `create()` method. For instance, for a `String` type, you'd have to do the following:

```
@Override
public String create(CreationalContext<String> creationalContext) {
   return "Our own bean";
}

@Override
public void destroy(Integer instance, CreationalContext<Integer>
creationalContext) {
   // Nothing to do here
}
```

Part 2: The Core Attributes

As mentioned, a Bean<T> is a combination of a factory part and a metadata part. The metadata concerns the core bean attributes first discussed in Chapter 3. We'll repeat them here for convenience:

- Types
- Qualifiers
- Name
- Scope
- Stereotypes
- Alternative (a Boolean indicating the bean is an alternative or not)

From the point of creating a bean, these attributes largely determine how the bean returned from the create() method is indexed (under which identifiers it is stored in the internal bean store and in which contextual "cache" the instance is stored).

For the metadata, the core interface consists of read-only attributes that directly correspond to the previous list.

```
public interface BeanAttributes<T> {
    Set<Type> getTypes();
    Set<Annotation> getQualifiers();
    Class<? extends Annotation> getScope();
    String getName();
    Set<Class<? extends Annotation>> getStereotypes();
    boolean isAlternative();
}
```

When implementing this interface, you have to take the required defaults into account. Unfortunately, the interface provides no guidance to what these defaults are, not in Javadoc and not by means of default methods. The CDI specification does, however, provide some guidance, which interestingly means that whenever you implement a Bean<T> yourself, you have to implement some requirements of the specification. Or in other words, parts of the specification's rules and behavior actually live within the artifacts you implement and not so much in the core runtime code. CDI is not an exception in Java EE with this, as in JSF, for instance, much of what seems to be the core framework behavior actually lives within the user-provided `UIComponents`.

The following shows a minimal implementation for the `String` bean you returned earlier from the `create()` method:

```
@Override
public Set<Type> getTypes() {
   return new HashSet<Type>(asList(String.class, Object.class));
}

@Override
public Set<Annotation> getQualifiers() {
   return singleton((Annotation) Default.Literal.INSTANCE );
}

@Override
public Class<? extends Annotation> getScope() {
   return Dependent.class;
}

@Override
public String getName() {
   return null;
}

@Override
public Set<Class<? extends Annotation>> getStereotypes() {
      return emptySet();
}

@Override
public boolean isAlternative() {
   return false;
}
```

To elaborate a little on the return values here, let's take a look at `getTypes()` first. You have to provide all the (Java) types you want to have your bean known as explicitly. At this level, the CDI runtime does not scan any of the types of the `T` in the `Bean<T>` or that of the instance that you return from `create()`.

For the getQualifiers() method, you must return a set with the Default annotation literal instance inside it in absence of any other specific qualifiers. Again, at this level, the CDI runtime provides no defaults for you, and you can't return a null or an empty set here without running into undefined behavior (likely an exception of some sort, as the CDI runtime would not expect such value).

For the getScope() method, a similar reasoning holds as for the getQualifiers() method; you must explicitly return the Dependent scope here in absence of any other scope. The CDI specification mandates any bean not having an explicit scope to be dependent-scoped, and once again at this level the CDI runtime is not going to default things for you.

The getName() method is the only method in the BeanAttributes interface where you can return a null if you're not using a name. Remember that a bean name is fully optional in CDI and there's no default name of any kind, so you don't have to provide anything here.

Stereotypes are fully optional as well, but for getStereotypes() you can't return a null in practice; you have to return an empty set instead. Finally, for isAlternative(), there's little ambiguity in being a method that returns a primitive Boolean, and you can simply return false here when the bean is not an alternative.

Part 3: The Bean

Up until now you have seen interfaces representing the factory (Contextual) and the metadata (BeanAttributes) but not yet how they are combined. Neither have you seen what the Bean<T> interface that we started the discussion with looks like.

You'll now take a look at the Bean<T> interface itself, as that happens to be the exact thing that combines the factory and metadata. In addition, it contains a small amount of extra data regarding the bean itself.

```
public interface Bean<T> extends Contextual<T>, BeanAttributes<T> {
   Class<?> getBeanClass();
   Set<InjectionPoint> getInjectionPoints();
}
```

The most important part of the Bean<T> interface is the extends part, where it actually combines Contextual and BeanAttributes. It contains two methods of its own (three actually, but the third one is deprecated, so we have omitted it here).

Of the two methods in the Bean<T> interface, getBeanClass() is somewhat peculiar. It is documented as follows:

> *"The bean of the managed bean or session bean or of the bean that declares the producer method or field."*

In other words, if you have the following managed bean:

```
@RequestScoped
public class SomeBean extends SomeOtherBean implements SomeInterface {

}
```

then the bean class will be SomeBean. Whereas if you have the following producer:

```
public class SomeBean extends SomeOtherBean implements SomeInterface {
   @Produces @RequestScoped
    public MyBean doProduce() {
        return new MyBean();
    }
}
```

then the bean class will be SomeBean again and not MyBean. The bean class is thus not necessarily related to the type that can be injected or obtained. For this you already have the getTypes() method after all.

The documentation of getBeanClass() is not fully complete, as of course not all Bean<T>s are generated from a managed bean or a producer (otherwise we wouldn't be having the discussion about Bean<T> in this chapter now).

This does beg the question, what is the bean class used for, and what should it be in the case of implementations that are not generated from managed beans or producers?

To start with the first question, a bean class is used to determine class visibility in the face of a modular/multiclassloader environment. In Java EE, the prime example of this is an EAR module with several WAR modules. Classes can be defined at, for example, the EAR level, making them visible to all WARs, or at the WAR level, making them not visible (isolated from) the other WARs.

In the CDI specification, this is expressed by the following statement:

> *"A bean is available for injection in a certain module if the bean class is required to be accessible to classes in the module, according to the class accessibility requirements of the module architecture."*

Though this statement can be a tiny bit difficult to parse, it basically means that CDI follows the classloader visibility rules of whatever environment it's being used in. To determine class loader visibility, you need a class that represents that classloader (i.e., is loaded by that classloader). As mentioned, this is not necessarily the bean type. In the case of the producer you saw earlier, MyBean could well be defined at the EAR level, while SomeBean resides within one of the WAR modules. Since it's SomeBean that fully defines the bean (it optionally adds the scope and qualifiers to the bare class type), it's the visibility of SomeBean we'll show here.

For example, assume that you have the following in WAR 1:

```
public class SomeBean1 extends SomeOtherBean implements SomeInterface {
    @Produces @RequestScoped
    public MyBean doProduce() {
        return new MyBean("war1");
    }
}
```

And assume you have the following in WAR 2:

```
public class SomeBean2 extends SomeOtherBean implements SomeInterface {
    @Produces @ApplicationScoped
    public MyBean doProduce() {
        return new MyBean("war2");
    }
}
```

Furthermore, assume MyBean is defined at the EAR level.

If injection of a MyBean is now requested from WAR 1, you need to look at SomeBean1 and not at SomeBean2. Since SomeBean2 is not visible to WAR 1, as determined by its classloader visibility, SomeBean2 is not being considered, and only SomeBean1 is. Had you looked only at the bean type (the return type), MyBean, then both producers would have been visible, and an ambiguity would have existed. As explained elsewhere in this book, if the CDI runtime encounters an ambiguity, it aborts the startup of an application with an exception.

Moving on to the second question of what the bean class should be in the case of implementations of Bean, which are not generated from managed beans or producers but are instead implemented directly. Unfortunately, there's no direct guidance for this in either the CDI specification or the Javadoc, but it's essentially implied as explained earlier that it should be the class that "provides" (creates) the bean instance, so in the case of your Bean<T> implementation, that would simply be the Bean<T>'s class.

Finally, you have the `getInjectionPoints()` method. Whereas scope and qualifiers can be seen as the external metadata (the attributes with which the bean is seen by the outer world), the injection points are in a way part of the internal metadata (the outside world doesn't see these; only the CDI runtime does). This method is special, though. It doesn't provide the primary injection point metadata, but instead just a declaration of them. The CDI runtime merely uses them for checking whether dependencies are available. More concretely, it uses each returned injection point to form the key `{type + qualifiers}` and does a lookup for that (e.g., using `beanManager.getBeans()`). If the result is empty or ambiguous, an exception is thrown; otherwise, it means the dependencies are available, and everything is fine. Specifically, the injection points returned by `Bean<T>#getInjectionPoints()` are thus *not* used for the actual injection. The reason there's a separate set of injection points in the Bean<T> interface is to make sure the CDI runtime can do its validation at runtime, and when doing so, it does not have to call the potentially expensive `create()` method to actually create an instance, scan it, and then validate. There are a few potential other use cases for `getInjectionPoints()`, such as for deserializing, but the main case is validation.

Part 4: Serialization Support

There are a few additional interfaces that dynamic beans can implement. One of those is the `javax.enterprise.inject.spi.PassivationCapable` interface, which is almost mandatory to be implemented, as it's required for a bean to be injected into any other bean that has a passivating scope (`@NormalScope` with the `passivating` attribute set to `true`). As you don't control in which other beans users want to inject your bean, not implementing `PassivationCapable` typically leads to much annoyance when your bean is attempted to be used in, for instance, beans that use the well-known `@SessionScoped` scope. This is why it's practically an interface that a Bean<T> implementation should always implement as well; only omit this if there are very specific reasons to. It's very well possible that a future version of CDI will indeed mandate this interface to be implemented, so if nothing else, it's good to implement this now just to be future proof.

What the `javax.enterprise.inject.spi.PassivationCapable` interface brings to the table is giving the bean another unique `String`-based ID. This ID is used for serialization purposes, specifically for those cases that the Bean<T> instance is not (also) serializable.

The observant reader might ask why yet another ID is needed, since a bean already has two (type + qualifiers and EL name). The answer might be a bit of a mixed bag. An EL name for starters is not really suited. It is a string already, but since it's an optional name and typically a shorter (alias-like) human-friendly one, it may quickly (and unintentionally) clash if all beans were to have such name. Next, type + qualifiers are obviously not a string to begin with. You could formalize a format to turn them into a string, but then you hit the next issue: these identifiers don't necessarily identify a single bean but in fact a set of beans. And, interestingly, they are in practice more akin to a query into the bean repository, which may yield different results at different times. For the stability of our system, we do like to limit getting different results as much as possible, but it's simply something that can happen and therefore has to be taken into account.

For an identifier that's used for serialization, you need something that is fully unique and hence identifies a single bean only. This is where the getId() method of the PassivationCapable interface comes in, as it does indeed exactly that.

For Bean<T> instances that are generated from managed beans or producers, the string returned by getId() is often based on the types, qualifiers, and other attributes of the bean. For instance, Weld, the CDI reference implementation, uses approximately the following for this string:

```
new StringBuilder("WELD%AbstractSyntheticBean%")
   .append(beanClass.getName()).append("%")
   .append(attributes.getName()).append(",")
   .append(attributes.getScope().getName()).append(",")
   .append(attributes.isAlternative())
   .append(createCollectionId(attributes.getQualifiers()))
   .append(createCollectionId(attributes.getStereotypes()))
   .append(createCollectionId(attributes.getTypes()))
   .toString();
```

As you can see, the unique identifier here is a combination of a Weld prolog string + {beanClass, name, scope, alternative, qualifiers, stereotypes, types}. It's a little more than just {types, qualifiers}, but otherwise it's all the public data contained in a Bean<T>.

For Bean<T> instances that you create yourself and for which there is only a single instance created, just the fully qualified class name is typically enough to function as unique identifier. If you create and subsequently add multiple instances of a Bean<T> class, you need something to distinguish these.

For instance, suppose you have a `com.example.MyBean<T>` for which you create and add two instances: one returning an `Integer` from the `create()` method and one returning a `String`. A potential identifier to be returned from `getId()` could then be `com.example.MyBean-Integer` for the first instance and `com.example.MyBean-String` for the second one.

Until now we have mentioned in passing that the string identifier returned by `getId()` is used for serialization purposes but haven't explained how and why it's exactly used for that. You'll take a look at that now.

When a bean in CDI is serialized, all normal scoped bean dependencies it has (and their transitive dependencies) are not serialized themselves, but instead the `Bean<T>` that generated them is. Think of this as backing up your iPhone to iCloud. The apps you have installed on it, the media you downloaded from iTunes, and so on, are not included in the backup itself; only a pointer to their original location in the Apple Store and iTunes is. According to the Apple website:

> ***"Your iCloud Backup includes information about the content you buy, but not the content itself. When you restore from an iCloud backup, your purchased content is automatically redownloaded from the iTunes Store, App Store, or Books Store."***

When a bean is serialized (*passivated* in CDI terms), what is actually serialized in terms of its normal scoped dependencies are the proxies with a reference to a `Bean<T>`, not the actual bean instance. There's generally speaking a number of different options for this reference in serialized form. In the simplest case, the `Bean<T>` is directly serializable, and CDI runtimes can use that. With this approach, there is no need to also call the `getId()` method, and the serialized proxy will contain the serialized `Bean<T>` instance in this case. When the `Bean<T>` is, however, not serializable, a CDI runtime can use the `getId()` method to obtain the string identifier, and then this string, and only this string, is serialized as a representative reference for the `Bean<T>` instance in question.

Whenever a bean is deserialized (*activated* in CDI terms), the proxies of its normal scoped dependencies are deserialized as well, and with them either directly the `Bean<T>` or the string identifier representing it. In the latter case, the CDI runtime has to perform one additional step, and that's to look up the original `Bean<T>` using its string identifier (this can be done lazily whenever the dependency is actually being accessed). This lookup can be done using the public `getPassivationCapableBean()` method of the `BeanManager`.

Whatever the approach used to deserialize the `Bean<T>`, the CDI runtime must at some point retrieve the actual bean instance. There are again two options here. Remember that deserialization can take place a long time after the initial serialization, and by that time the bean instance may no longer exist in its given scope, or it may have never existed in the first place if the dependency wasn't used before. If that's the case, the instance is created on the spot by calling the `create()` method of the `Bean<T>`. Otherwise, the instance from the scope is used.

Besides potentially saving both time and space (a rarity in IT, where you often optimize for one of those at the expense of the other), the crucial reason for serialization to be done like described earlier is to maintain consistency of the various scopes. Suppose you actually fully serialized each normal scoped bean. Then upon deserialization you would have in fact created a copy of the bean. This breaks the rules of scoping, which ensures that there's only a single instance of a bean in a given scope, which is shared by all users of that scope.

For instance, consider an application-scoped bean, of which it should be clear there should be only one instance. If a serialized and subsequently deserialized bean contains its own copy of such a bean, it would not see any changes to the original bean, and neither would any other users of that bean see the changes made to the copy. This would obviously not be correct. Effectively re-injecting the dependency upon deserialization prevents this problem completely.

Part 5: Activating Alternatives

As shown in part 2 of this section, a `Bean<T>` implementation can declare itself to be an "alternative" by returning `true` from the `isAlternative()` method. By default any `Bean<T>` that is an alternative exists in a kind of limbo state. It exists, but it's not being used for any kind of resolution. To escape from this limbo, it needs to be "activated" (not to be confused with the similarly named "activation" when deserializing). Activation can be done by the user, per bean archive, by listing the bean class under the `<beans>`, `<alternatives>`, `<class>` element in a `beans.xml` file in that archive. Alternatively, you can add a bean in a globally activated state by having its `Bean<T>` implement the `javax.enterprise.inject.spi.Prioritized` interface. This interface has one method to implement: `getPriority()`. The integer return value of this is used to select which `Bean<T>` instance is used to provide a bean, if several alternatives provide the same bean type. The highest priority wins. So, typically a system-level alternative bean would use a low priority, say, in the range from 0 to 100, meaning that a library-provided alternative (which a user is free to add) can override it at a priority of say 101 to 200. Applications, which ultimately want to decide which bean is being used, should use a high priority, say 1000 or higher in this example.

The CDI specification does not specify what happens if two or more Bean<T>s have the same priority. In that case, the result is undefined between CDI implementations (e.g., between Weld and OWB). However, a given implementation may still have its own rules to break the tie. Weld, for instance, uses lexicographic ordering of the bean class (as returned by getBeanClass) in that case. This means, for example, that when using Weld, a Bean<T> instance with a bean class of com.example.zzz with priority 10 will be selected over a Bean<T> instance with a bean class of com.example.aaa with priority 10, with all other things considered equal.

For completeness, we'll now show the full Bean<T> implementation, combining all the parts explained earlier for a non-named nonalternative bean.

```
public class MyBean implements Bean<String>, PassivationCapable {
  @Override
  public String create(CreationalContext<String> creationalContext) {
      return "Our own bean";
  }
   @Override
  public void destroy(Integer instance, CreationalContext<Integer>
  creationalContext) {
      // Nothing to do here
  }
  @Override
  public Set<Type> getTypes() {
      return new HashSet<Type>(asList(String.class, Object.class));
  }
  @Override
  public Set<Annotation> getQualifiers() {
      return singleton((Annotation) Default.Literal.INSTANCE );
  }
  @Override
  public Class<? extends Annotation> getScope() {
      return Dependent.class;
  }
```

```
    @Override
    public String getName() {
        return null;
    }
    @Override
    public Set<Class<? extends Annotation>> getStereotypes() {
        return emptySet();
    }
    @Override
    public boolean isAlternative() {
        return false;
    }
    @Override
    public Class<?> getBeanClass() {
         return getClass();
    }
    @Override
    public Set<InjectionPoint> getInjectionPoints() {
        return emptySet();
    }
    @Override
    public String getId() {
        return getClass().getName();
    }

    @Override
    public boolean isNullable() { return false; }
}
```

Adding Dynamic Beans: Using Extensions

Dynamic beans like shown in the previous section have to be added via a CDI extension.

CDI extensions are a large topic that we won't be covering fully in this book, but nevertheless we will give a quick overview about them before explaining how exactly to add a bean via such extension.

An *extension* in CDI is a special type of CDI class that implements the `javax.enterprise.inject.spi.Extension` marker interface and has to be registered by putting its fully qualified class name in the file `META-INF/services/javax.enterprise.inject.spi.Extension` on the classpath (of a JAR).

Somewhat like a `ServletContainerInitializer` in the Servlet specification, an extension can listen to lifecycle events that are fired when the CDI runtime starts up and use them to, among other things, programmatically add, modify, or remove beans from the internal CDI bean repository.

The lifecycle events are extraordinarily fine-grained and allow applications, but in practice mostly libraries, to greatly influence CDI itself. In a way, this makes CDI look a little like a Smalltalk environment, which has been described as "a living system, carrying around the ability to extend itself at runtime."

Like listeners for several other frameworks, CDI lifecycle events can be broadly categorized into two main groups.

- Events fired when starting up
- Events fired when shutting down

The most interesting bit is in the "Events fired when starting up," which can be subdivided into two logical groups.

- Discovering plain Java types
- Discovering CDI beans

We'll briefly go through both of these next.

Discovering Plain Java Types

This group of events consists of three events.

- `javax.enterprise.inject.spi.BeforeBeanDiscovery`
- `javax.enterprise.inject.spi.ProcessAnnotatedType<X>`
- `javax.enterprise.inject.spi.AfterTypeDiscovery`

The `BeforeBeanDiscovery` event is fired before the type scanning starts. For consistency sake, maybe this event should have been called `BeforeTypeDiscovery`, but alas. Observing this event you can add completely new types to the list of types CDI will consider for its next phases. This is, for instance, useful when you're in a bean archive where CDI scanning is severely limited, such as the bean archives representing the Java EE internal libraries such as JSF and EE Security. The types in these JARs are not scanned by CDI, and any type that you do want to add you can do here manually. For instance, Soteria, the EE Security reference implementation, does the following:

```
public void register(@Observes BeforeBeanDiscovery beforeBean, BeanManager
beanManager) {
        addAnnotatedTypes(beforeBean, beanManager,
            AutoApplySessionInterceptor.class,
            RememberMeInterceptor.class,
            LoginToContinueInterceptor.class,
            FormAuthenticationMechanism.class,
            CustomFormAuthenticationMechanism.class,
            SecurityContextImpl.class,
            IdentityStoreHandler.class,
            Pbkdf2PasswordHashImpl.class
        );
    }
```

addAnnotatedTypes is defined as follows:

```
public static void addAnnotatedTypes(BeforeBeanDiscovery beforeBean,
BeanManager beanManager,
    Class<?>... types) {
        for (Class<?> type : types) {
            beforeBean.addAnnotatedType(type, "Soteria " + type.getName());
        }
    }
```

Note that an identifier is required when adding types manually, which the CDI runtime can use to determine where types have been added and distinguish between the same types being added multiple times.

Observing the ProcessAnnotatedType event, you get called for each and every plain Java type (class or interface) that the CDI runtime finds in a bean archive. You can use this to look at the type (and, for instance, log it), modify the type (replace it fully, or replace it with a type based on the encountered type), or remove the type fully so CDI will no longer "see" it. There's a convenience builder available via configureAnnotatedType to easily add or remove annotations at the class, field, or method level of the type that was found.

Observing the AfterTypeDiscovery event, we get called after the CDI runtime has done all the scanning for types it was supposed to be doing. Here too you can add completely new types to the list of types CDI will consider for its next phases.

Discovering CDI Beans

After the CDI runtime has discovered the raw types, the next phase is to analyze these types and create, among others, Bean<T> instances out of them.

- ProcessInjectionPoint
- ProcessInjectionTarget
- ProcessProducer
- ProcessBeanAttributes
- ProcessBean
    - ProcessManagedBean
    - ProcessSessionBean
    - ProcessProducerMethod
    - ProcessProducerField
    - ProcessSyntheticBean
- ProcessObserverMethod
    - ProcessSyntheticObserverMethod
- AfterBeanDiscovery
- AfterDeploymentValidation

Figure 7-1 shows an overview of this.

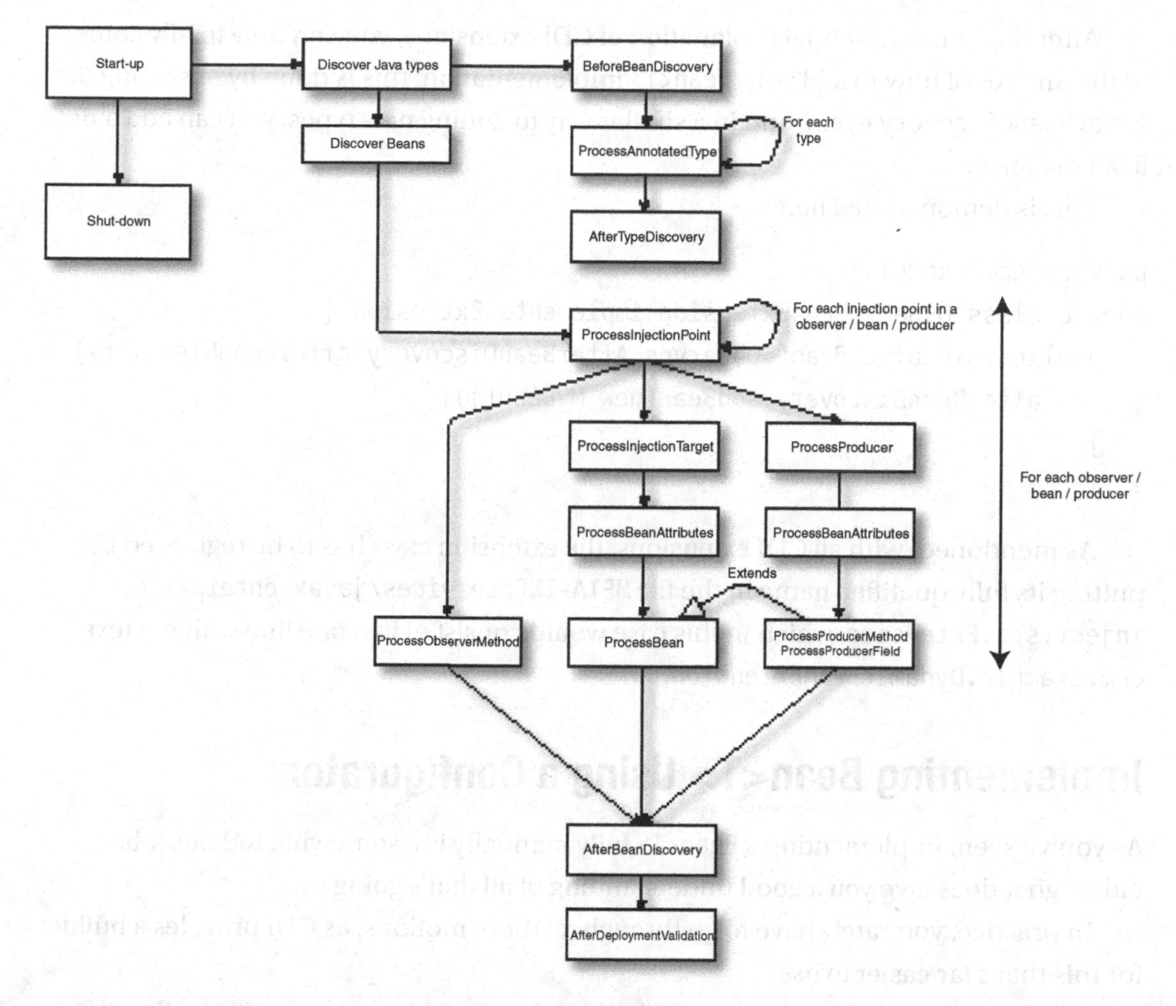

***Figure 7-1.** CDI events and their organization*

There are eight main events, and there are a couple of subevents that specialize their superevent. In those cases, observing the superevent includes getting notified of all the subevents. For instance, when observing `ProcessBean`, you get notified of all `Bean<T>`s that are processed, while if you observe `ProcessSyntheticBean`, you only get notified of `Bean<T>`s that you add manually. Note the somewhat remarkable use of the term *synthetic* for the type of `Bean<T>`s that you called *dynamic* beans in this chapter. This is remarkable since despite "synthetic" being used in various other API methods for similar cases, it's otherwise not used in the CDI specification text or in the CDI community.

After this somewhat brief explanation of CDI extensions, you can now finally come to the answer of how to add your Bean<T> implementation: this is done by observing the AfterBeanDiscovery event, and in a similar way to adding new types, you can add a new Bean instance.

This is demonstrated here:

```
package com.example;
public class DynamicBeanExtension implements Extension {
   public void afterBean(@Observes AfterBeanDiscovery afterBeanDiscovery) {
       afterBeanDiscovery.addBean(new MyBean());
   }
}
```

As mentioned, with all CDI extensions, the extension class has to be registered by putting its fully qualified name in the file META-INF/services/javax.enterprise.inject.spi.Extension, which in this case would consist of just one line with the text com.example.DynamicBeanExtension.

Implementing Bean<T> Using a Configurator

As you've seen, implementing a Bean<T> fully manually is a somewhat tedious job, although it does give you a good understanding of all that's going on.

In practice, you rarely have to go through all these motions, as CDI provides a builder for this that's far easier to use.

CDI features provides a convenient builder that not only makes creating a Bean<T> instance far less verbose but also takes away most of the guesswork. The following shows an example:

```
public class DynamicBeanExtension implements Extension {
    public void afterBean(@Observes AfterBeanDiscovery afterBeanDiscovery) {
        AfterBeanDiscovery
            .addBean()
            .createWith(e -> "Our own bean")
            .types(String.class, Object.class)
            .id(DynamicBeanExtension.class.getName() + " String")
    }
}
```

The previous way only lets you specify what differs from the defaults, making the definition much more compact.

Note specifically how `id` blends into the `Bean<T>` builder, barely making it obvious that this one actually is part of another interface and further giving evidence that `getId()` should perhaps have been part of the `Bean<T>` interface to begin with. Also note that the CDI specification is not entirely clear on whether the `Bean<T>` is by default passivation capable when no explicit ID is provided. The instances generated by both Weld and OWB do always implement the `PassivationCapable` interface, but they somewhat differ in their behavior. Weld always generates an ID if there's not one provided. Weld generates this ID in the same way that the ID is generated for managed beans or producers. OWB, however, generates an ID only if the `Bean<T>` has itself a passivating scope. Seemingly the only sure way to have the ID is to manually add it yourself.

Besides being just a plain builder that collects the data returned by the getters in the `Bean<T>` with defaults for data not provided, the builder gives access to higher-level functionality that would not otherwise be available. One example of this is the `addTransitiveTypeClosure()` method, which is backed by quite elaborate functionality to discover all the types that a given bean has (superclasses and their superclasses, the interfaces any of these implements and their superinterfaces, etc.). Using that method in the builder, you don't have to list all types explicitly (if you want the bean to be available for all the types it has). This is essentially the same thing that the CDI runtime does when it generates `Bean<T>` instances from managed beans or producers. The following shows an example:

```
public class DynamicBeanExtension implements Extension {
    public void afterBean(@Observes AfterBeanDiscovery afterBeanDiscovery) {
        afterBeanDiscovery
            .addBean()
            .createWith(e -> "Our own bean")
            . addTransitiveTypeClosure(String.class)
            .id(DynamicBeanExtension.class.getName() + " String");
    }
}
```

Note that you didn't have to supply the `Object.class` argument here, as that will be autodiscovered by the type closure algorithm. Of course, for such a simple case, the difference is minimal, but in more deep-type hierarchies, this can make a big difference.

Yet another convenience feature that the builder provides is instead of giving you only a `CreationalContext`, the builder can optionally give you an `Instance` instead. This `Instance` is bound to the bean manager and creational context associated with the `Bean<T>` context. It can be used to select dependencies that the method might need. For getting that `Instance` passed in, the `produceWith()` method instead of the `createWith()` method is used. Here's an example:

```
public class DynamicBeanExtension implements Extension {
    public void afterBean(@Observes AfterBeanDiscovery afterBeanDiscovery)
{
        afterBeanDiscovery
            .addBean()
            .produceWith(instance -> {
                MyBean myBean = instance.select(MyBean.class).get();
                return "MyBean says " + myBean.hi();
            })
            . addTransitiveTypeClosure(String.class)
            .id(DynamicBeanExtension.class.getName() + " String");
    }
}
```

As somewhat of an alternative to the previous, a `createWith()` method can use the global `CDI.current()` instance instead. This is, however, not fully equal, as the global instance does not necessarily allow you to obtain, for instance, the current `InjectionPoint`, while the instance passed in does allow this. The following shows an example:

```
public class DynamicBeanExtension implements Extension {
    public void afterBean(@Observes AfterBeanDiscovery afterBeanDiscovery) {
        afterBeanDiscovery
            .addBean()
            .produceWith(instance -> {
                InjectionPoint point = instance.select(InjectionPoint.
                class).get();
                return "Injected in bean: " + point.getBean();
            })
```

```
            . addTransitiveTypeClosure(String.class)
            .id(DynamicBeanExtension.class.getName() + " String");
    }
}
```

In a createWith() method or a create() method in a Bean<T>, the following trick can be used to obtain the current InjectionPoint.

First define the following bean:

```
@Dependent
public class InjectionPointGenerator {
    @Inject
    private InjectionPoint injectionPoint;
    public InjectionPoint getInjectionPoint() {
        return injectionPoint;
    }
}
```

Then define the following utility methods:

```
public static InjectionPoint getCurrentInjectionPoint(
    BeanManager beanManager,
    CreationalContext<?> creationalContext) {
    Bean<InjectionPointGenerator> bean =
        resolve(beanManager, InjectionPointGenerator.class);
    return
        bean != null ? (InjectionPoint)
            beanManager.getInjectableReference(
                bean.getInjectionPoints().iterator().next(),
                creationalContext)
        :
        null;
}
public static <T> Bean<T> resolve(
    BeanManager beanManager,
    Class<T> beanClass, Annotation... qualifiers) {
    Set<Bean<?>> beans = beanManager.getBeans(beanClass, qualifiers);
```

```
    for (Bean<?> bean : beans) {
        if (bean.getBeanClass() == beanClass) {
            return (Bean<T>)
                beanManager.resolve(
                    Collections.<Bean<?>>singleton(bean));
        }
    }
    return (Bean<T>) beanManager.resolve(beans);
}
```

The current `InjectionPoint` can then be obtained by calling `getCurrentInjectionPoint()`. Obtaining this from the `createWith()` or `create()` method in an easier way is targeted to be added in CDI 2.1 (but of course there's no guarantee it indeed will be added).

Unfortunately, there is one key element missing from the builder, and that's the ability to set a priority and thus globally enable an alternative. Using the standard CDI APIs, there is not really any convenient way of adding this, short of listening for the `ProcessSyntheticBean` event (which will be fired after you add the bean via the builder here), taking the `Bean<T>` from that event using the `getBean()` method, and wrapping that in a new `Bean<T>` that does implement the `Prioritized` interface. At that point, you could just as well start out with your own `Bean<T>` implementation and not bother going through the builder at all.

This painful omission in the API is a known problem, and an implementation like Weld provides a custom solution for this. The `BeanConfigurator` returned by `AfterBeanDiscovery.addBean()` can be cast to an `org.jboss.weld.bootstrap.event.WeldBeanConfigurator<T>`, which as its single extra method has the missing `priority()` method. Needless to say, the code won't be portable anymore when using this, and a Weld-specific dependency would be needed, which are both things one generally tries to avoid.

Simulating Generic Producers with Dynamically Created Beans

A cornerstone of CDI's design philosophy is type safety above all. For most cases, this works very well, and there's nothing to complain about. However, occasionally you do need a "generic producer," with which we mean a producer that has a generic return method, based on the type of the `InjectionPoint`.

Hypothetically, it would look like this:

```
@Produces @SomeQualifier
public <T> T thisDoesNotWork(InjectionPoint<T> injectionPoint) {
    return convert(doStuff(), injectionPoint);
}
```

so that you could do the following:

```
@Inject
@SomeQualifier
Foo foo;
@Inject
@SomeQualifier
Bar bar;
```

You can, however, to a degree, simulate this with dynamically creating `Bean<T>` instances. The approach is to first scan all injection points that the application is using and then record the types of those injection targets. Then for each type that you encounter, you add a new `Bean<T>` instance. This scanning is trivial to do in CDI, as you only have to listen to a `Process*Bean` event and then check its fields and constructors. We'll show an example where you listen to the `ProcessManagedBean` event and check for the qualifier annotation.

```
public class GenericProducerSim implements Extension {
    private Set<Type> types = new HashSet<>();
    public <T> void collect(@Observes ProcessManagedBean<T> event) {
      for (AnnotatedField<?> field : event.getAnnotatedBeanClass().
      getFields()) {
          addAnnotatedTypeIfNecessary(field);
      }
      for (AnnotatedConstructor<?> ctr: event.getAnnotatedBeanClass().
      getConstructors()) {
          for (AnnotatedParameter<?> parameter : ctr.getParameters()) {
              addAnnotatedTypeIfNecessary(parameter);
          }
      }
    }
```

```
    private void addAnnotatedTypeIfNecessary(Annotated annotated) {
        if (annotated.isAnnotationPresent(SomeQualifier.class)) {
            types.add(type);
        }
    }
}
```

What happens in the previous code is that for every `Bean<T>` that originates from a managed bean, you iterate through its fields and collect all types that have the `SomeQualifier` annotation. Given this example, you would end up with the set `{Foo.class, Bar.class}`.

In the same extension, you can now also listen to the `AfterBeanDiscovery` event and for each type that you encountered add a `Bean<T>`:

```
public void afterBean(@Observes AfterBeanDiscovery afterBeanDiscovery) {
    for (Type type : types) {
        afterBeanDiscovery.addBean(new GenericProducer(type));
    }
}
```

The `GenericProducer` here could use the passed-in `type` to return from its `getTypes()` method so it would get selected when CDI encounters the previous injection points and uses that type to base conversion on. Alternatively, you could add a single `Bean<T>` that returns for `getTypes()` all the types you encountered.

Note that this solution isn't entirely perfect, as it would obviously not see the types that are requested only programmatically, e.g., using `CDI.current().select()`. Sometimes this happens when you don't even realize it, for instance when `@Inject` is used in a servlet. A servlet is not directly managed by CDI, but often the servlet container (runtime) uses the CDI API programmatically to fetch the dependencies it needs and then manually assigns them to the `@Inject` annotated fields. Such usage is largely hidden for the CDI runtime when the application starts up, and therefore you can't collect the types.

CHAPTER 8

CDI in Java SE

It is probably evident by now that CDI provides many benefits for any nontrivial application, including applications that aren't web-based. It may be surprising to find out that the CDI specification prior to version 2.0 officially only supported Java EE. Although Java SE was not officially supported, many CDI implementations did offer support for Java SE environments prior to the 2.0 specification. For example, both Weld and Apache OpenWebBeans offered support for Java SE. As the specification didn't officially support Java SE, this meant that each container would need to provide their own nonstandardized API to allow the application to bootstrap and run the container. A major downside of having such nonstandardized APIs is that it makes it slightly harder for application developers to switch to another CDI container, as the code for bootstrapping the container in a Java SE environment would need to be rewritten. Libraries and frameworks such as Arquillian and Apache DeltaSpike Container Control do offer APIs that allow developers to bootstrap the CDI container, regardless of which container is actually in use. However, the primary focus of Arquillian is to be able to run unit and integration tests in different environments and is not as well suited to launching a CDI container within an application. Containers also need to be explicitly supported by Apache DeltaSpike Container Control. If a new container is introduced or a container changes its proprietary API in a noncompatible way, users of DeltaSpike Container Control need to wait for a new version to be released to support them.

Fortunately, official support for Java SE environments was added in CDI 2.0. As part of adding this support, the CDI specification was split into three separate parts. The first part, Core CDI, covers the core functionality common to both Java SE and Java EE. The next part, CDI in Java EE, covers additional rules and features on top of Core CDI when using CDI in a Java EE environment. The last part is CDI in Java SE, which covers the additional rules and functionality for Java SE.

J. Beernink and A. Tijms, *Pro CDI 2 in Java EE 8*, https://doi.org/10.1007/978-1-4842-4363-3_8

Bootstrap API

CDI 2.0 introduces a bootstrap API that allows Java SE containers to manage and start a CDI container instance. CDI containers must provide implementations for a number of interfaces defined by the bootstrap API in order to provide support for Java SE environments. The bootstrap API can dynamically detect and instantiate any container that is available on the classpath or module path using the `ServiceLoader` mechanism. If you are unfamiliar with the `ServiceLoader` mechanism in Java, it allows for the registration of classes that implement a specific class or interface and then dynamically loads these registered classes at runtime.

To use the bootstrap API, the CDI container and the corresponding bootstrap API implementation must be made available on the classpath. As most containers will consist of a number of separate JAR files, the easiest way to add a CDI container to a Java SE application is through the use of a dependency management tool like Maven, Gradle, or Ivy. To use Apache OpenWebBeans as CDI container, a dependency must be declared on both the container implementation and on the CDI API as provided by OpenWebBeans. For example, for Maven, the following dependencies need to be added to the `pom.xml` file to use OpenWebBeans:

```
<dependency>
    <groupId>org.apache.openwebbeans</groupId>
    <artifactId>openwebbeans-spi</artifactId>
    <version>2.0.3</version>
</dependency>

<dependency>
    <groupId>org.apache.openwebbeans</groupId>
    <artifactId>openwebbeans-impl</artifactId>
    <version>2.0.3</version>
</dependency>
```

Other CDI containers may include a transitive dependency on the API itself, without the need to explicitly declare a dependency on it. For example, for Weld it's enough to depend only on the bootstrap API implementation. The bootstrap API implementation itself depends on both the CDI API and the container implementation itself, so these are automatically included as transitive dependencies. To use Weld in a Java SE application, only the following dependency needs to be declared in the project's `pom.xml` file:

```
<dependency>
    <groupId>org.jboss.weld.se</groupId>
    <artifactId>weld-se-core</artifactId>
    <version>3.0.3.Final</version>
</dependency>
```

Note Only one CDI container implementation must be on the classpath or module path at runtime. If more than one container implementation is found by the bootstrap API, an `IllegalStateException` will be thrown when attempting to load the implementation.

The main point of entry to the bootstrap API is the `SeContainerInitializer` interface. This interface contains a number of methods that can be used to configure and finally launch a CDI container instance. The configuration methods follow the builder pattern, allowing several calls to be chained together. An instance of `SeContainerInitializer` for the correct container can be obtained by calling the static `newInstance()` method on the `SeContainerInitializer` class. The following snippet illustrates how to initialize the container in Java SE:

```
try (SeContainer container = SeContainerInitializer.newInstance()
  .initialize()) {
    // Initialize application here
}
```

Before initializing the container instance, properties can be configured using the `SeContainerInitializer`. These properties can be either standardized properties or container-specific properties. To configure a property, the `setProperty()` method can be called. This method takes a key and a value of type `String` as arguments and will add this pair to the current set of configured properties. There's also a `setProperties()` method, which takes a `Map<String, String>` as an argument. Calling this method will overwrite the current set of configured properties with the contents of the map.

Once the `SeContainerInitializer` instance has been obtained and configured, it can be used to create a CDI container by calling its `initialize()` method. Please note that the `initialize()` method should be the last method called on the `SeContainerInitializer` instance; any configuration that is required should be performed first. It's also not possible to call the `initialize()` method when a CDI container is already running. Doing so would cause an IllegalStateException to be thrown.

When the initialize() method completes successfully, it will return an instance of SeContainer. The SeContainer interface implements the Instance interface, which allows for obtaining beans with a specific combination of (generic) type and qualifier annotations. To do this, one of the overloads of the select() method can be called on SeContainer. SeContainer has overloads for obtaining a bean by only annotations, by type and a set of zero or more annotations, and by type literal and zero or more annotations. The select() method returns another Instance (where T is the type of the bean, if the overload with type or type literal is used), which can be used to obtain a bean instance by calling the get method on the instance. It's also possible to get a BeanManager instance through the SeContainer interface, which can also be used to get bean instances. However, it is recommended that you use the select() methods provided by the SeContainer instance instead.

The SeContainer interface should also be used to shut down the CDI container once the application exits. The SeContainer has a close() method, which will perform the necessary shutdown of the container. Calling this method will cause all beans managed by the container to be destroyed. Any applicable @PreDestroy method will be called before each bean is destroyed, allowing for any required cleanup operations to be performed before the container itself is destroyed. The SeContainer interface also extends the AutoCloseable interface, which makes it possible to create and automatically destroy the container in a try-with-resources statement. The close() method must be called only once. Calling it a second time will cause an IllegalStateException to be thrown.

Once the application is up and running, it may be necessary to obtain a reference to the running container, without having access to the SeContainer instance. The CDI class has a current() method. This will return an instance of the CDI class that can be used to access the current CDI container. It provides all the same functionality as SeContainer, except for the ability to shut down the CDI container.

Let's say you want to write a simple "Hello World" application using CDI. This application shall consist of two classes. The first class is a fairly trivial GreetingService, which has a single method with a greeting as a string. The second class contains the main method that is used to start the application. This main method will bootstrap the CDI instance and call the GreetingService. The instance of the GreetingService in this example is retrieved from the container by calling container.select(GreetingService.class).get(). You may notice that no cast is performed to assign the instance of the

GreetingService to the variable. Because of the generic signatures of the API, the return type in this case is inferred to be GreetingService.

```
package helloworld;

public class GreetingService {

    public String generateGreeting(String name) {
        return "Hello, " + name + "!";
    }
}
```

The following listing shows the bootstrapping of a CDI container in a Java SE application:

```
package helloworld;

import javax.enterprise.inject.se.SeContainer;
import javax.enterprise.inject.se.SeContainerInitializer;

public class HelloWorldExample {

    public static void main(String[] args) {
        try (SeContainer container = SeContainerInitializer.newInstance()
             .initialize()) {
                GreetingService greetingService = container
                    .select(GreetingService.class).get();

                String greeting = greetingService.generateGreeting("world");
                System.out.println(greeting);
        }
    }
}
```

One thing to keep in mind is the lifecycle of beans created through the bootstrap API. When a dependent-scoped bean instance is created using this API, the container keeps a reference to that instance. This reference will prevent the bean instance from being cleaned up by the garbage collector. The dependent-scoped bean instance in a way becomes linked to the lifecycle of the container that created it. When an application creates many dependent-scoped beans using the bootstrap API, the application may at some point run out of memory. To prevent this kind of memory leak from happening, the application should explicitly destroy these bean instances when they are no longer needed.

Bean Archive Scanning

When a CDI container is initialized in a Java SE environment, by default it performs bean discovery by scanning any available bean archives on the classpath. Just like in Java EE, CDI in Java SE supports both implicit and explicit bean archives. By default, the container will only detect beans in an explicit bean archive; any beans in an implicit bean archive will be ignored.

For Java SE containers, the `javax.enterprise.inject.scan.implicit` property controls whether implicit bean archives are automatically detected. There are two ways to set this property. The first is to set it as a system property, before the CDI container is initialized. This can be done by specifying `-Djavax.enterprise.inject.scan.implicit=true` on the command line when starting the application. Alternatively, it is also possible to set the system property programmatically by calling this:

```
System.setProperty("javax.enterprise.inject.scan.implicit", "true");
```

The second way to enable support for implicit bean archives is by using either the `addProperty()` or `setProperties()` method to set this property on the `SeContainerInitializer` instance before initializing the container. To configure the property, the property name must be specified as the key, and the value must be `Boolean.TRUE`.

```
SeContainerInitializer.newInstance()
  .addProperty("javax.enterprise.inject.scan.implicit", Boolean.TRUE);
```

Synthetic Bean Archive

In addition to automatically scanning bean archives, it is possible to register beans with an `SeContainer` programmatically. Each `SeContainer` has a single synthetic bean archive that can be configured only before the container is fully initialized through the `SeContainerInitializer` instance. The following methods are available to manage the synthetic bean archive:

- `addBeanClasses()`
- `addPackages()`

- addExtensions()
- enableInterceptors()
- enableDecorators()
- selectAlternatives()
- selectAlternativeStereotypes()
- disableDiscovery()

The addBeanClasses() method adds one or more bean classes to the synthetic bean archive. These beans will be fully managed by the container, exactly as if they were present in a regular bean archive. It is important that no beans are added to the synthetic bean archive that are already present in another bean archive. When this happens, the CDI container will fail to start because of encountering the same bean in more than one bean archive.

In addition to adding individual classes to the synthetic bean archive, it is also possible to add entire packages instead using the addPackages() methods. There are four forms of this method. The two main versions accept either one or more classes or packages. When using the overload that accepts classes, all beans from the package that contains these classes will be added to the synthetic bean archive. By default, only beans from the specified packages will be added, but there's an overload for both versions that allows you to recursively add beans from a package. When adding a bean package with the recursive option enabled, all beans from that package and its subpackages are added to the synthetic bean archive. Some care needs to be taken with this option as subpackages may be specified in a different archive. A parent package may not be contained in a bean archive, but one of its subpackages may be. If this is the case and the parent package is added recursively, the subpackage will also be added to the synthetic bean archive. This will cause the same situation as with the addBeanClasses() method where bean classes are specified in two different bean archives, which will prevent the container from initializing.

The enableInterceptors() and enableDecorators() methods can be used to enable an interceptor or decorator for the synthetic bean archive. These methods allow for conditionally enabling interceptors or decorators. If an interceptor or decorator is not contained in another bean archive and it is not enabled for the synthetic bean archive, the interceptor or decorator will be silently ignored at runtime. This makes it possible, for example, to enable an interceptor only if a certain command-line flag is specified or if the application is running in a certain environment.

CDI extensions can be added to the synthetic bean archive through the addExtensions() method. There are two overloads of this method, one that takes extension classes as its argument and another that takes extension instances. The latter is particularly interesting as this would allow the use of an anonymous inner class as an extension. Classes registered in this way also no longer need to be registered using a services configuration file. Like the enableInterceptors() and enableDecorators() methods, this method can be used to conditionally activate extensions for any extension that is not already defined in a service loader configuration file.

The selectAlternatives() method is used to select alternative beans in the synthetic bean archive. This method takes one or more arguments of type Class. This class must either be a bean class annotated with @Alternative or be a class containing a producer method annotated with @Alternative. The selectAlternativeStereotypes() method is similar. It takes as an argument one or more stereotype annotation classes, annotated with @Alternative. Neither the selectAlternatives() method nor the selectAlternativeStereotypes() method will add any classes to the synthetic bean archive. All required bean classes must be added separately. Both these methods will also only select these alternatives for the synthetic bean archive; other bean archives will still use the default beans unless they have alternatives specified in their respective beans.xml files.

The ClassLoader to use to scan for bean archives can be set using the setClassLoader() method. Calling this method will limit bean archive scanning only to the bean archives that are available to the given ClassLoader. One use for this would be to load bean archives and the beans they contain from outside the classpath. Consider an application server that needs to load bean archives from a predefined directory instead of the classpath. This could be achieved by specifying a custom class loader for this alternate directory.

Lastly, the disableDiscovery() method will disable bean archive scanning completely for the container. Any bean archives that may be on the classpath are ignored. All bean classes or packages, interceptor classes, and decorator classes must be explicitly registered with the synthetic bean archive. This gives more control over which classes are made available through CDI than automatic bean archive scanning does. One use case could be to select the alternatives for all bean archives in an application. Normally, all the bean archives need to be updated with a beans.xml file that declares the alternative bean selected. However, updating an existing bean archive may not always be feasible. For example, a bean archive could be shared between multiple applications, where the other applications still require the default bean to be used. In this case, using the synthetic bean archive in combination with disabling discovery allows the alternative bean to be set for all classes, without having to update any `beans.xml` files.

Having to declare all classes or packages required for the application can be a major downside. For a larger application, the list of dependencies to explicitly register can become extremely long and hard to maintain.

Testing

One area where the bootstrap API and synthetic bean archive scanning can be useful is testing. Unit and integration tests are an important part of any software development process. They can help prevent new bugs from being introduced into the codebase. This is just as valid for applications using CDI as it is for any other application. However, dependency injection can make it more complicated to test code in isolation. Complex hierarchies of beans can be difficult to manage programmatically. This can be made even more difficult when considering hierarchies of beans that use different scopes. It would be much better to run the testing code in a CDI container as well so that the primary focus of the testing code are the actual tests and not setting up bean classes and their dependencies. Arquillian already provided a framework for starting and stopping a container, but now it's also possible to do this without the need for an external dependency. The following code listing shows a simple Junit 5 test for the `GreetingService` from earlier in the chapter:

```
package helloworld;

import static org.junit.jupiter.api.Assertions.assertEquals;

import javax.enterprise.inject.se.SeContainer;
import javax.enterprise.inject.se.SeContainerInitializer;

import org.junit.jupiter.api.AfterEach;
import org.junit.jupiter.api.BeforeEach;
import org.junit.jupiter.api.Test;

class GreetingServiceTest {

    private SeContainer container;

    @BeforeEach
    void setUp() {
```

```
        container = SeContainerInitializer.newInstance().initialize();
    }

    @AfterEach
    void tearDown() {
        container.close();
    }

    @Test
    void generateGreeting() {
        GreetingService greetingService = container
            .select(GreetingService.class).get();

        assertEquals("Hello, world!",
            greetingService.generateGreeting("world"));
    }
}
```

In this example, the container is started and stopped before and after each test method using methods annotated with `@BeforeEach` and `@AfterEach`. This will ensure that each individual test method will run with a separate container instance. This can be a useful way to reset the container state between tests. For example, there may be a number of `@ApplicationScoped` beans that keep track of state that is updated during the test. By starting and stopping the container each time, each test will essentially be running in a fresh environment. If lingering state is not an issue, the CDI container could also be started and stopped from within static methods annotated with `@BeforeAll` and `@AfterAll`. The `@BeforeAll` method will be called once before any of the test methods from the test class are called, and `@AfterAll` will be called once afterward. If it's necessary to get a reference to the container during a test, it can either be stored in a static field by the `@BeforeAll` method or be retrieved by calling `CDI.current()`.

One issue that could arise is when a bean that is injected needs to be mocked or faked. Mocking or faking should be used sparingly but can sometimes be unavoidable, for example when a bean calls a remote API. A simple solution would be to mark the mock or fake bean with `@Alternative` and to register the alternative using a test-specific `beans.xml`. However, this approach will not work for most cases. The reason for this is that testing code is usually compiled to a different target folder than the code being tested. As a result, the testing code would be in a different bean archive, and as alternatives are registered only for the current bean archive, the code being tested would still use the regular bean instead of the alternative.

The synthetic bean archive can provide a solution to this problem when combined with disabling automatic bean archive scanning. By disabling archive scanning, all beans required for the test must be explicitly registered with the synthetic bean archive. The alternative beans can then be registered with the synthetic bean archive using the `selectAlternatives()` method. As all beans now live in the same archive, this will also register the alternatives for all beans covered that are part of the test. This solution also introduces a new problem as this means that the list of beans registered for the test needs to be continually updated as the code (indirectly) being tested evolves over time. As such, it may be best to avoid this approach if it's not strictly needed to use mocks or fakes.

For example, if you update the `GreetingService` to call a remote `LocalizedGreetingMessageService` to get a localized greeting message, you will need to replace the implementation of `LocalizedGreetingMessageService` during test. You can solve this by providing a `FakeLocalizedGreetingMessageService` implementation, which doesn't perform any remote calls but still provides the required outputs you need for the test. You can use the `selectAlternatives()` method to select your fake service, but if you don't disable automatic archive scanning, the updated `GreetingService` will still perform the remote call during the test run. However, if you call the `disableDiscovery()` method on the `SeContainerInitializer`, the test will call your fake service instead. Example XYZ will show what the `RemoteGreetingServiceTest` would look like:

```
package helloworld;

import javax.enterprise.inject.se.SeContainer;
import javax.enterprise.inject.se.SeContainerInitializer;

import org.junit.jupiter.api.AfterEach;
import org.junit.jupiter.api.BeforeEach;
import org.junit.jupiter.api.Test;

public class RemoteGreetingServiceTest {

    private SeContainer container;

    @BeforeEach
    void setUp() {
        container = SeContainerInitializer.newInstance()
```

```
            .disableDiscovery()
            .addPackages(RemoteGreetingService.class.getPackage())
            .selectAlternatives(FakeLocalizedGreetingMessageService.class)
            .initialize();
    }
    @AfterEach
    void tearDown() {
        container.close();
    }

    @Test
    public void testGenerateGreeting() {
        // TODO implement test here.
    }
}
```

Scopes

Scopes and contexts are one of the most important parts of CDI. They manage the lifecycle of beans managed by the container. Scopes also determine which beans events are delivered to. Scopes are fully supported by CDI in Java SE. All built-in scopes are supported, but there are a number of key differences in when some of the scopes are active. For example, as Java EE has the Servlet API, it's fairly easy to define how the request scope should work. The same cannot be said for Java SE; a Java SE application may not handle requests at all or simply use low-level server sockets to handle incoming requests. As such, it's not always possible to provide a clear definition of how scopes should function in Java SE. As a result, the request scope definition is much more limited in Java SE than it is in Java EE. As in Java EE, applications can still provide a custom scope context.

The following definitions are used for each of the built-in scopes:

- The application scope context, which is defined to be active at all times
- The request scope context, which is active during all `@PostConstruct` callback methods and all asynchronous observer methods

- The session scope context, for which no lifecycle is predefined
- The conversation scope context, which is controlled by the active application itself

Java SE applications can still override the definition of each of these by providing a custom scope context. The request scope is one example of how this could be useful. If a Java SE application handles incoming requests, the request scope can be redefined to be active during the handling of these requests. More information about overriding the built-in scopes can be found in Chapter 4.

In addition to the built-in scopes, CDI in Java SE also supports the dependent pseudoscope. Like in Java EE, dependent-scoped beans adopt the lifecycle of the bean they are injected into or created from. So if, for example, a dependent bean is injected into an application-scoped bean, the dependent bean will also adopt the application scope as its lifecycle. Note that dependent scope beans are never shared; if a bean of a certain type is injected into two other beans that have the same scope, both of these beans will get a different instance of the dependent bean.

Java FX

JavaFX was made part of the JRE and JDK starting with Java 8 and is the new UI toolkit for Java. It offers many benefits over the existing UI toolkits (AWT, Swing, and SWT) by offering a scene graph–based approach toward building a UI, with support for effects, animations, and even 3D. It's designed to support a wide variety of devices, from desktop applications to mobile apps.

The `Application` class in JavaFX can be extended to provide an entry point for a JavaFX application. When extending the `Application` class, the JVM will automatically detect the use of JavaFX and ensure the application is initialized and started on the correct thread. The `Application` class provides a simple application lifecycle through three methods. The `init()` method is called to initialize the application, the `start()` method is called to launch the application, and the `stop()` method is called to stop the application as the JavaFX framework is about to shut down. A naïve approach to integrating CDI in a JavaFX application would be to initialize the container in a `try-with-resources` statement in the `start()` method. This will not work, as the start method completes when the application starts running, not when the application is shut down, which would result in the CDI container shutting down prematurely. A better approach would be to override the `init()` method to initialize the CDI container and to assign the resulting SeContainer instance to a field in the Application subclass. To shut down the active container, the stop() method can be overridden to call the close() method on the SeContainer instance.

An alternative approach would be initialize the CDI container in a main() method before initializing JavaFX. JavaFX provides a number of static utility methods that can be used to initialize the JavaFX framework and initialize and start a JavaFX application. These methods do not complete until after the application has stopped. As a result, these methods are suitable to call in a try-with-resources block that manages the CDI container as a resource. The most straightforward method to use is Application.launch(String... args). This method can be called only from a method in a class that extends the Application class. The reason for this is that the application class is determined by looking at the stack. This snippet shows an example of initializing CDI and JavaFX in a main method:

```
public static void main(String[] args) {
    try (SeContainer container = SeContainerInitializer.newInstance()
       .initialize()) {
          Application.launch(args);
    }
}
```

A common way to create user interfaces in JavaFX is through the use of FXML. FXML is an XML-based language that is used to define all UI components and their layout within the view. The FXML language also allows a controller class to be defined for the view. FXML views are loaded from files through the FXMLLoader class. An FXMLLoader instance will parse the FXML configuration and create an instance of the view and the corresponding controller. As the controller is where input from the UI is converted to calls to the business logic, it would be great to be able to inject the controller's dependencies using CDI. The FXMLLoader class offers support for this by allowing you to define the factory that is used to create all controller instances. The factory must implement the javafx.util.Callback interface and with the class of the controller as the only argument. As the CDI container provides a way to get an instance of a bean through the class of the bean, you can use it as the controller factory. As the Callback interface is a functional interface, you can just provide a lambda expression that uses the CDI container to get an instance of the given class, either by using an available reference to the SeContainer instance or by calling CDI.current() to get it. As the controller class is now a CDI managed bean, you are able to inject any dependencies you may need directly into the controller. The following listing illustrates a simple JavaFX application that loads an FXML view:

```
package helloworld;

import javax.enterprise.inject.se.SeContainer;
import javax.enterprise.inject.se.SeContainerInitializer;
import javax.enterprise.inject.spi.CDI;

import javafx.application.Application;
import javafx.fxml.FXMLLoader;
import javafx.scene.Parent;
import javafx.scene.Scene;
import javafx.stage.Stage;

public class HelloWorldFxExample extends Application {

   private SeContainer seContainer;

   @Override
   public void init() {
       seContainer = SeContainerInitializer.newInstance().initialize();
   }

   @Override
   public void start(Stage stage) throws Exception {
       FXMLLoader fxmlLoader = new FXMLLoader();
       fxmlLoader.setControllerFactory(clazz
          -> CDI.current().select(clazz).get());
       fxmlLoader.setLocation(HelloWorldFxExample.class
          .getResource("/helloworld/hello.fxml"));
       Parent root = fxmlLoader.load();

       stage.setScene(new Scene(root));
       stage.show();
   }
```

```
    @Override
    public void stop() {
        seContainer.close();
    }
}
```

There are some caveats to using the CDI container as the factory for the controller instances. JavaFX provides a limited form of dependency injection using the `@FXML` annotation to inject components from the FXML view in the controller. It's not possible to use this injection provided by JavaFX in combination with a controller that has a CDI scope other than the dependent pseudoscope or that has any interceptors registered on it. Doing so would result in the fields marked with `@FXML` being left uninitialized after the bean has been constructed. This is a result of how CDI containers implement scopes and interceptors. When trying to obtain or inject an instance of a bean with a scope or interceptor, the container will use a proxy instead of an actual instance of the bean. When calling any method on this proxy, the proxy will first call any applicable interceptors, before delegating to the actual instance as defined by the scope of the bean. As the proxy must be assignable to any field, variable, or parameter of the type of the original bean, the proxy must be a subclass of the original bean class. This results in the proxy also inheriting any fields that were defined in the original class. If the original class contained any fields annotated with `@FXML`, the proxy's class will also have these same fields with the same annotations. As the `FXMLLoader` will get a proxy back from the controller factory you defined, it will try to inject the corresponding components from the view into this proxy. The `FXMLLoader` never "sees" the original controller bean instance, and any fields annotated with `@FXML` are left uninitialized. Any attempt to call any method on the controller that uses these components could potentially lead to a `NullPointerException` being thrown.

The easiest way to avoid this issue is to avoid the combination of interceptors and scopes with the injection of components by the `FXMLLoader`, leaving each controller class to be dependent-scoped instead. This is not an ideal solution as it means that the lifecycle of each controller instance may be tied to the lifecycle of the CDI container. If a certain view is created multiple times within an application, the controller instances must be explicitly destroyed. If these controller instances aren't explicitly destroyed, they may cause a memory leak as they may not be eligible for garbage collection until the container shuts down.

Replacing JavaFX Injection

As dependency injection is a core feature of CDI, it would be much nicer to have the CDI container inject the components rather than CDI. This would allow the controller instances to use the full features of CDI, including scopes and interceptors, as well as allowing CDI components to be injected into noncontroller classes as well. To achieve this, you need to implement a producer, which is able to provide the components based on their component ID. Ideally, the components produced by this producer will also be scoped to the current view so that if there are multiple active views in the application, the components will still be injected into the correct controller in the case of two components having the same ID.

The first thing you need to do is to define your view scope. Fortunately, you can use the MicroScoped library (which can be found at `https://github.com/tomitribe/microscoped`) to avoid much of the boilerplate of creating a scope implementation. You only need to define the scope annotation and register the scope context. For your view scope, you'll create a parameterless `@ViewScoped` annotation and use the MicroScoped `ScopeContext` with a `String` argument. Any key here would really do, but we'll use a UUID converted to a `String`.

Next, define the qualifier annotation to use for injecting the components. The component injection performed by JavaFX works based on the name of the field. You can replicate this by adding a `String` parameter for the component ID to your qualifier annotation. Normally, a `String` parameter like this would be annotated as `@Nonbinding`. This would allow a single producer method to deal with all instances of the qualifier annotation, regardless of the value of the parameter. In this case, however, you will not annotate the value parameter as `@Nonbinding`, for reasons that will become clear later.

```
import static java.lang.annotation.ElementType.FIELD;
import static java.lang.annotation.ElementType.METHOD;
import static java.lang.annotation.ElementType.PARAMETER;
import static java.lang.annotation.ElementType.TYPE;
import static java.lang.annotation.RetentionPolicy.RUNTIME;

import java.lang.annotation.Retention;
import java.lang.annotation.Target;

import javax.inject.Qualifier;
```

```
@Qualifier
@Retention(RUNTIME)
@Target({METHOD, PARAMETER, TYPE, FIELD})
public @interface Component {
    String value();
}
```

Now that you have the scope and qualifier annotation defined, you need to figure out how to make components from the view available to CDI. Since Java 9, the `FxmlLoader` offers a way to inspect the components from an FXML file as they are being loaded. Each `FxmlLoader` can have a single `LoadListener` that is called for events that happen during the parsing of the FXML file. The `LoadListener` interface defines a number of callback methods, each of which is called for a specific event. The most interesting callback method for this use case is the `endElement()` method. This method is called when the end tag for an XML element from the FXML file is read, with the element itself as a value. For example, when the end of a `Button` tag is read, the new `Button` instance created from the tag is passed to the `endElement()` method as a value. As an application may have multiple instances of the same view or have different views with the same component IDs, you'd ideally like to be able to keep the components for different views separate. For this reason, you will create an `@ViewScoped ComponentManager`, which will keep track of the components in the view and their IDs. The `ComponentManager` will be a fairly trivial class, with two methods: a `registerComponent()` method to register a component and the corresponding ID, and a `getComponent()` method that returns a component by its ID. For the implementation of these methods, storing and retrieving the components from a map should be sufficient. As the ID property of a component is optional, you should only register components that have an ID specified.

It is possible to specify callback methods on the controller for certain UI events in the FXML file. For example, a controller method can be specified for a button that is called when that button is clicked. While loading the FXML file, event handlers are registered on the components from the view being loaded that call these callback methods on the controller. As the controller itself or a bean it depends on may also be view scoped, you need to make sure that the view scope is active any time a UI event is fired for any of the components in your view. If the view scope is not active at the time an event is fired, any calls to a view-scoped bean would lead to a `ContextNotActiveException` being thrown. Each JavaFX component has a mutable `EventDispatcher` property, which is responsible for dispatching all events to the correct event handlers. Using the provided setter, the EventDispatcher can be replaced by a custom implementation, which can activate the scene scope before dispatching the event and disable it after. To allow for the correct dispatching of events, this custom event dispatcher must also wrap the original event dispatcher. As the EventDispatcher interface has only a single abstract method, it's possible to use a fairly simple lambda expression as the implementation. Events can be handled by the EventDispatcher of multiple components. This can be a problem if a scene is included in another scene. By making the scope stackable, every component's EventDispatcher starts an instance of the scene scope for its own scene, so the correct scene scope will always be active. You can register your custom EventDispatcher implementation with each component from within your LoadListener implementation. The code for loading an FXML view would then look something like in the following example:

```
// Generate a unique ID for the current view scope
String viewId = UUID.randomUUID().toString();

// Start the view scope
ScopeContext<String> viewScopeContext = (ScopeContext<String>)
  beanManager.getContext(ViewScoped.class);
viewScopeContext.enter(viewId);
try {
    FXMLLoader fxmlLoader = new FXMLLoader();
    fxmlLoader.setLoadListener(new LoadListener() {

        // Skipping the remaining methods from LoadListener
        @Override
        public void endElement(Object value) {
            if (value instanceof Node) {
                Node node = (Node) value;
                if (node.getId() != null) {
                    componentManager.registerComponent(node.getId(), node);
                }

                // Register our custom event dispatcher
                EventDispatcher eventDispatcher =
                    node.getEventDispatcher();
```

```
                node.setEventDispatcher((event, eventDispatcherChain) -> {
                    viewScopeContext.enter(viewId);
                    try {
                        return eventDispatcher.dispatchEvent(event,
                            eventDispatcherChain);
                    } finally {
                        viewScopeContext.exit(viewId);
                    }
                });
            }
        }
    });
} finally {
    viewScopeContext.exit(viewId);
}
```

Once you want to write the producer method that produces your UI components, you run into two issues. The first is that the type and qualifier annotation of an injection point need to match exactly with the producer method. Unfortunately, there are many built-in component types provided by JavaFX, and applications and libraries can define their own custom components. In a large application, it would be fairly prohibitive to provide a producer method for each unique type. If you miss a producer method for one type, you will also only find out about this problem after the application is started.

Another issue is that you need to add a scope to the JavaFX components to have them injected into the correct controllers. All JavaFX components inherit from the `javafx.scene.Node` class. The `Node` class contains a number of final methods, making proxying JavaFX components impossible. Recall that a proxy needs to be of the same type as the type that is being injected. This means that the proxy must extend the component type itself in order to proxy it and override any methods to delegate to the actual instance. As final methods cannot be overridden, it is impossible to delegate calls to these methods to the actual instance, and these methods will be executed only on the proxy instead.

Fortunately, you can solve both issues at the same time using the dynamic bean feature in CDI 2.0. You can implement a CDI extension that listens to the `ProcessManagedBeanType` event. When a new bean is discovered, you will scan the fields that the bean has, check for any fields that are annotated with your component qualifier annotation, and keep the combination of the type of the field and the qualifier annotation of these fields in a `Set`. When the `AfterBeanDiscovery` callback on the extension is called, you can use the `BeanConfigurator` to register a dynamic producer for each combination of type and qualifier annotation you need. When configuring your producer, you can also specify the scope annotation to apply to the beans produced by it. The actual implementation of the dynamic producer consists of a callback method that is passed an `Instance`. You can use this `Instance` in your dynamic producer to perform a lookup for the component manager you defined earlier. Once you have the component manager, you can get do a simple lookup for the component you want. However, the producer cannot read the qualifier annotation specified on the injection point. This is where making the component ID a nonbinding parameter in your qualifier annotation will become useful, as you can now simply hard-code it in the dynamic producer. For each separate value of the component ID, you will create a new dynamic producer.

To solve the problem with proxying your component because of the final methods on the `Node` class, you will need to make your producer return a different type that is proxyable. This means you will need to wrap the component returned in another type. Unfortunately, this does mean it won't be possible to inject the components directly, but a method call will be needed to get the component itself. The only requirements for this wrapper type are that it is nonfinal, has only nonfinal methods, and has a method to get the wrapped component with a generic return type. The `java.util.function.Supplier` type is a good fit for this. It is an interface, so it can easily be proxied, and it has a single generic method. After you look up the component in your producer, you can then return a `Supplier<?>` that will always return the component you retrieved from the `ComponentManager`.

```
import java.lang.reflect.Type;
import java.util.AbstractMap;
import java.util.HashSet;
import java.util.Map.Entry;
import java.util.Set;
import java.util.function.Supplier;

import javax.enterprise.event.Observes;
import javax.enterprise.inject.spi.AfterBeanDiscovery;
import javax.enterprise.inject.spi.AnnotatedField;
import javax.enterprise.inject.spi.Extension;
import javax.enterprise.inject.spi.ProcessManagedBean;
```

```
import javafx.scene.Node;

public class FxmlComponentProducerExtension implements Extension {

  private static final Set<Entry<Component, Type>> types = new HashSet<>();

  public <T> void collect(@Observes ProcessManagedBean<T> event) {
    for (AnnotatedField<?> field : event.getAnnotatedBeanClass()
      .getFields()) {
        if (field.isAnnotationPresent(Component.class)) {
          Component component = field.getAnnotations(Component.class)
            .stream().findFirst().get();

          types.add(new AbstractMap.SimpleEntry<>(component,
            field.getBaseType()));
        }
    }
  }

  public void afterBean(
    @Observes AfterBeanDiscovery afterBeanDiscovery) {
      types.forEach(entry -> {
        afterBeanDiscovery
          .addBean()
          .scope(ViewScoped.class)
          .types(entry.getValue())
          .addQualifier(entry.getKey())
          .produceWith(f -> {
            ComponentManager componentManager =
             f.select(ComponentManager.class).get();

            Node component = componentManager
             .getComponent(entry.getKey().value());

                    return (Supplier<?>) () -> component;
          });
      });
  }
}
```

Now that you are able to inject the components into the controller, you may need to perform some logic using them after the view is loaded. For example, in an application that shows the current date, a text field may be updated by the controller after loading to show the date. There are two ways of performing such logic in the controller; which option is preferable depends on when the initialization logic should be executed. The first option is to use an `@PostConstruct` method, like any regular CDI bean. One problem with putting this logic in an `@PostConstruct` method is that any scoped CDI bean is lazily initialized. That means that the bean is not created until one of its methods is called, for example in the case of a callback after a UI event. This can lead to an odd user experience, where the user interface may only be properly initialized after the user does something that causes a method on the controller to be called.

The `FXMLLoader` mechanism itself provides a solution for this issue. After loading the view and creating all view components and the controller, the `FXMLLoader` will scan the controller class for any instance method named `initialize()` and then call this method, if found. Calling this method has a side effect of causing the initialization of the controller instance before the `FXMLLoader` returns the loaded view; any initialization logic put in this method will be executed before the view is displayed. As you've already made sure that the view scope is active, it is safe to interact with any components that you have injected through CDI. For any case where logic needs to be performed by the controller before the view is displayed, the `initialize()` method is preferable over an `@PostConstruct` method.

Note: Avoid using `initialize` as the method name for a method annotated with `@PostConstruct`. JavaFX will automatically try to call any `void returning` method of that name on a controller after it has been created. As the `@PostConstruct` method will already be called by CDI after construction, an `@PostConstruct` method named `initialize()` would be called twice.

Java 9 Modules

Java 9 introduced the concept of modules to the JVM. Modules are basically JAR files that contain a module descriptor. One of the biggest changes introduced with the module system is a much finer level of access control than was possible with the `public`, `private`, or `protected` keywords. Modules can restrict access to packages to be allowed from either only the same module, only a predefined set of modules, or any other module. This allows a module to hide its implementation details from being part of the exported API of the module. The module system also introduces stricter rules for reflective access. Without the module system, access restrictions on code can be easily bypassed using reflection. However, for code that is located in a module, attempting to bypass the access restrictions will throw an exception.

Hiding the internals of a CDI library can be very useful. Consider a library that provides two public classes that are in different packages. Both of these classes rely on a third internal class for their implementation. If both the public classes were in the same package, it would be enough to put the internal class in that package as well and declare it package-friendly. CDI would still be able to access and inject the internal class into the public classes but at the same time prevent easy access to the internal class from outside the package. However, as both classes that depend on the internal class are located in different packages, the internal class must be made public. This could allow users of the library to use (accidentally) what is meant to be solely an internal class. The module system fixes this by only allowing access to APIs that are declared as exported to other modules.

However, the CDI specification has currently not yet been updated for the module system. The stricter checks on reflective access can also have a big impact on CDI containers, as they rely heavily on reflection. One example of this is to inject dependencies into private fields; without reflective access, this would not be possible. A CDI container would also, by default, not be able to access any class that has not been made part of the exported API of a module. As a result, it is recommended that you avoid using the module system in a CDI application, at least until the specification is updated to explicitly address the module system.

If there is a strong need to modularize an application, there are a few options that can get CDI working with the JDK module system. The first is to avoid injection into private fields and use constructor injection. However, this only overcomes the problem with the new restrictions on reflection for the case of dependency injection. It doesn't solve the problem of decorating nonpublic classes with interceptors. If a bean depends on a large number of other dependencies, the constructor can also become fairly large.

A slightly better alternative is to declare a module fully open for reflection. Declaring the module itself open for reflection means that all packages it contains will become public and open to reflective access. Let's assume you have a model called `com.foo`. To declare the module fully open for reflection, the following module descriptor can be used. This module has a package named `com.foo.a` containing a class named `PublicA`, a package `com.foo.b` containing a class named `PublicB`, and a package com.foo.c containing a class named InternalC. Both PublicA and PublicB are part of the official API of the module; these are classes that users of the module can freely use. The class InternalC is an internal class of the module that is used by both PublicA and PublicB. InternalC should be used only within the module itself and never by users of the module.

Here is a module descriptor opening a module for reflection:

```
open module com.foo {
}
```

This approach allows CDI to access any private fields or classes through reflection, but it also makes every public class in the module part of the exported API of the module. Let's say that the module contains three bean classes: two classes that should be part of the public API named com.foo.a.PublicA and com.foo.b.PublicB and an internal class for a bean that is injected into both PublicA and PublicB that is named com.foo.c.InternalC. As PublicA and PublicB are in separate packages, InternalC must be public. Declaring the module fully open, however, means that any public class becomes part of the public API of the module. In this case, InternalC has inadvertently become part of the public API of the com.foo module.

An alternative approach is to explicitly declare the com.foo.a and com.foo.b packages as part of the exported API of the module. For CDI to be able to access and inject the InternalC class, the com.foo.c package must be explicitly declared as open to reflection. To inject InteralC into a nonpublic field of the PublicA and PublicB classes, their packages must also be explicitly declared as being open for reflective access; declaring these packages as part of the public API is not enough. The module descriptor would look something like the following:

```
module com.foo {
    exports com.foo.a;
    exports com.foo.b;
    opens com.foo.a;
    opens com.foo.b;
    opens com.foo.c;
}
```

This is a lot more verbose, but does it achieve what you want? The InternalC class is hidden from the exported API at compile time, while it is still accessible to the CDI container at runtime through reflection. The CDI container is also able to access any private fields in the PublicA and PublicB classes when performing dependency injection. However, the InternalC class is not just available to the CDI container through reflection; it is available to any code through reflection. A sneaky user of the module who is aware of the existence of the InternalC class could still access it if they wanted.

At some point in the future, the CDI specification may be updated to support the module system as well. Part of this support would cover providing an API module. Currently, there already is an official API JAR that is used by some containers, but an API module would allow for some extra benefits within the module system. API modules can delegate their access permissions to any module that provides an implementation for the API. As modules can export or open packages only to specific modules, this means that once the CDI specification defines an API module, it will be possible to grant reflective access to any CDI container without having to know which container will be used at compile time. Let's assume that the CDI defines an API module named cdi.api; the module-info for your module would then look something like the following:

```
module com.foo {
    exports com.foo.a;
    exports com.foo.b;
    opens com.foo.a to cdi.api;
    opens com.foo.b to cdi.api;
    opens com.foo.c to cdi.api;
}
```

In theory, it's already possible to do this with CDI 2.0 containers. The module system generates a module name for any nonmodular JAR file found on the module path. The generated module name is based on the file name. For example, a JAR file called cdi-api.jar would receive the module name cdi.api. It's also possible to use this module name to restrict the reflective access to a module. However, doing so would not be advisable. Different CDI containers may use different file names for the API JAR, leading to incompatible module names. Switching between CDI containers would necessitate replacing any references to the API module of the old container with a reference to the

API module of the new container. This may be fine for an application that will always be run in the same container, but it isn't great for a library that needs to be able to run on multiple different containers. Even worse, different versions of the same container may use different file names, leading to different versions of the same container being incompatible with each other. On top of that, if the CDI specification is updated to specify a module name for the API JAR file, this is most likely going to be a different name from the generated module names.

At the moment, it's still not clear how widely the module system will be adopted outside the JDK itself or if CDI will start supporting the module system. Even though the previous proves that CDI and the module system can work together currently, the earlier advice to adopt a wait-and-see approach still stands.

Index

J. Beernink and A. Tijms, *Pro CDI 2 in Java EE 8*, https://doi.org/10.1007/978-1-4842-4363-3

C

J

K

L

M

N

O

P

Q

R

S

T

U

V, W, X, Y, Z

Printed in the United States
By Bookmasters